The Dedalus Book of Literary Suicides

Dead Letters

Gary Lachman

Dedalus

Published in the UK by Dedalus Ltd,
24–26, St Judith's Lane, Sawtry, Cambs, PE28 5XE
email: info@dedalusbooks.com
www: dedalusbooks.com

ISBN 978 1 903517 66 6

Dedalus is distributed in the United States by SCB Distributors,
15608 South New Century Drive, Gardena, California 90248
email: info@scbdistributors.com   web site: www.scbdistributors.com

Dedalus is distributed in Australia & New Zealand by Peribo Pty Ltd,
58 Beaumont Road, Mount Kuring-gai N.S.W. 2080
email: peribo@bigpond.com

Dedalus is distributed in Canada by Marginal Distribution,
695 Westney Road South, Suite 14 Ajax, Ontario, LI6 6M9
email: marginal@marginalbook.com   web site: www.marginalbook.com

First published by Dedalus in 2008
The Dedaulus Book of Literary Suicides: Dead Letters copyright © Gary Lachman 2007

Typeset by RefineCatch, Bungay, Suffolk
Printed in Finland by WS Bookwell

THE AUTHOR

Gary Lachman was a founding member of the rock group Blondie and wrote some of the band's early hits. Before moving to London in 1996 and becoming a full time writer, Gary studied philosophy, taught English literature, was a science writer for a major American university, and managed a metaphysical bookstore.

His books include *The Dedalus Book of the Occult: A Dark Muse* and *The Dedalus Book of the 1960s: Turn Off Your Mind*. He is also the editor *of The Dedalus Occult Reader: The Garden of Hermetic Dreams*.

ACKNOWLEDGEMENTS

Many people have helped in the making of this book. I would like to thank Phil Baker for suggesting I take up my publisher's offer to do it, and for his insights into the curse of literature; Mike Jay and the inestimable Louise for a welcome break from its labours in the restorative quiet of Cornwall; Nicholas Christian of the Institut Français for information on the suicide of Henry de Montherlant; James Hamilton for needed material on Sylvia Plath and Albert Camus; Eric Lane, for his appreciation of the writer's life; and other friends, too numerous to mention, for allowing me to ramble on about the dark thoughts and sad lives that occupied me while writing it. I would also like to thank Colin Wilson for allowing me to quote from his book *Religion and the Rebel*, sadly out of print; Penguin Books for allowing me to quote from R.J. Hollingdale's brilliant translation of Nietzsche's *Twilight of the Idols*; and John Calder, for allowing me to quote from Tom Osborn's superb rendition of Frank Wedekind's *Spring Awakening*. I have endeavoured to locate the copyright source of quotations used in the book; if any have been overlooked, I offer my apologies and will happily redress any infringements. As always, my sons, Joshua and Maximilian, have been an inexhaustible well of inspiration; yet I would like to thank them specifically in this context, for providing two very good reasons for not following in the footsteps of the many tragic characters who fill these pages.

DISCLAIMER

Despite the best endeavours of the editors, it has not been possible to contact the rights holder of the front cover picture of Yukio Mishima. The editors would be grateful, therefore, if the rights holder could contact Dedalus.

Table of Contents

Woolf and sexual abuse. Writing and self-esteem. Wyndham Lewis. "The calm that always comes to me with abuse." Writers' insecurity. Compulsive journal writing. "I begin to loathe my kind." The last days of Sylvia Plath. The coldest winter in 150 years. "I'm just having a marvellous dream." The perils of biography. The girl most likely to succeed. Otto Plath sets an example. "How could such a brilliant man be so stupid." Sylvia's suicidal tendencies. Beautiful Smith girl missing at Wellesley. Spoiled, babyish, frightened. Escape from personality. "Oh, mother, the world is so rotten." Ted Hughes. Christmas Eve 1962. Trevor Thomas. The Scarlet Woman. Anne Sexton meets Sylvia. "I might be good at being a prostitute." Unable to function as wife or mother. Nana and sexual abuse. "A mental disorder that eluded diagnosis or cure." A patient for life. Anne Sexton's inadequacy. Fear of killing the children. Desperate housewives. Poetry as therapy. Death and other obsessions. A world without numbness.

To remain cheerful when involved in a gloomy and exceedingly responsible business is no inconsiderable art . . .

Friedrich Nietzsche

Is life worth living? This a question for an embryo, not for a man.

Samuel Butler

Part 1

A Taxonomy of Suicide

A Taxonomy of Suicide

If there is a problem in writing a book about literary suicides, it certainly isn't dearth of material. There, are course, the familiar names: Sylvia Plath, Virginia Woolf, Hemingway, Chatterton. These, I found, readily came to mind when I mentioned to friends that I was planning a book on writers who had killed themselves, or had tried to, or had written about suicide at some length and depth. But once I began to research in earnest and had moved past these well known figures, the field opened up considerably, and I found myself echoing that line from Eliot's *The Waste Land*: "So many, I had not thought death had undone so many" – so many, that is, killed by their own hand.

At the risk of bludgeoning the reader into a stupor at the outset, let me support this remark with a list, not exhaustive, sadly, but certainly representative. So, in no particular order, and in addition to those mentioned above – who died by gas, drowning, gun shot and arsenic respectively – we have Gérard de Nerval (hanging), Cesare Pavese (barbiturates), Yukio Mishima (hari kari), Heinrich von Kleist (gun shot), Georg Trakl (cocaine overdose), L. H. Myers (barbiturates), Robert E. Howard (gun shot), Jan Potocki (gun shot), Paul Celan (drowning), Walter Benjamin (morphine overdose), Guy Debord (gun shot), Gilles Deleuze (fall), Otto Weininger (gun shot), Anne Sexton (carbon monoxide), Empedocles (volcano), James Webb (gun shot)[1], Romain Gary (gun shot), Jack London (morphine overdose), Arthur Koestler (barbiturates), Ross Lockridge, Jr. (carbon monoxide), John Kennedy Toole (carbon monoxide), Geza Csath (poison), Stefan Zweig (barbiturates), Klaus Mann (sleeping pills), Thomas Lovell Beddoes (poison), Hart Crane (drowning), Primo Levi (fall), Harry Crosby (gun shot), Richard Brautigan (gun shot), Sadegh Hedayat (gas), Vachel Lindsay (poison), Hunter S.

Thompson (gun shot), B.S. Johnson (slit wrists), Sarah Kane (hanging), Malcolm Lowry (sleeping pills), Eugene Marais (gun shot), Jerzy Kozinski (barbiturates and asphyxiation), Philipp Mainländer (hanging), Mário de Sá-Carneiro (strychnine), Egon Friedell (fall), Marina Tsvetaeva (hanging), Charlotte Perkins Gilman (chloroform), Eleanor Marx (prussic acid), Henry de Montherlant (cyanide and gun shot), Sara Teasdale (sleeping pills), Adalbert Stifter (slit throat), René Crevel (gas), William Seabrook (sleeping pills) – and I think with any luck you get the idea.

If we add to these the names of writers and thinkers who have either written extensively about suicide or in whose work or life suicide played a important role, the list swells to unwieldy proportions. Shakespeare, Goethe, Dostoyevsky, Tolstoy, Nietzsche, Schopenhauer, Camus, Hesse, Wittgenstein, Kafka, Montaigne, Flaubert, Villiers de l'Isle Adam, Mary Wollstonecraft, Jorge Luis Borges are only some of the names. Others come to mind too, and to be perfectly honest it's difficult to decide who to include and who to leave out. So, for instance, at the end of his novel *Auto-da-Fé*, Elias Canetti's protagonist, Peter Kien, sets his library aflame and burns himself to death. Clearly this is a literary suicide (a very *literal* literary one) and also a symbol of the western intellectual's self-destruction. And the eccentric hero of Knut Hamsun's novel *Mysteries*. He kills himself, this time by drowning. Include these or not?

Faced with this wealth of dark thoughts and saddening lives, I at first thought to compile an encyclopaedia, but I rejected this idea for two reasons. Encyclopaedia entries on most of these individuals exist already, and not only would I be repeating work already done, the structure of the book would require me to either standardize the space devoted to each case, and so lose a great deal of important material, or to have some very long entries and some very short ones. And this consideration led to my second reason. Some of the cases simply seemed more interesting than others. In some, as in the case of the Japanese novelist Yukio Mishima and the American poet manqué Harry Crosby, suicide, their self-destruction, seemed an inevitability, and not because of manic-depression or some other mental instability, but because of who they were, their self-image and their self-obsession. Death, for both Mishima and Crosby, was an idea not far from their minds, and it was something they *looked forward to*, but neither were particularly depressive characters, unlike, say, the poet Paul Celan or the novelist Richard Brautigan.

In other cases, more understandable and external reasons led to the individual taking his or her own life. Illness was the motive for the philosopher Gilles Deleuze and the short story writer Charlotte Perkins Gilman, incipient blindness for the novelist and dramatist Henry de Montherlant (who, incidentally, once considered writing a handbook on suicide), and escaping old age for the gonzo journalist Hunter S. Thompson. All of these people are interesting because of their life and work, and that they committed suicide sets them apart from most other people. But their suicide itself isn't a focal point of their lives as it is, say, with the tragic French Romantic poet and writer Gérard de Nerval, who hung himself in a decrepit alley in Paris after battling years of madness and poverty, or the Austrian philosopher Otto Weininger, whose brilliant and extreme ideas about sex, race and genius led him to take his own life. In these and other cases, the suicide doesn't seem something 'tacked on' to their lives, something that, given other circumstances, may not have happened. With de Nerval, Weininger, Mishima, Crosby and others, their self-inflicted deaths have, as I've said, an aura of inevitability. And while I am aware how romantic such considerations seem, I nevertheless find them difficult to ignore.

If he hadn't shot himself, it's doubtful that Harry Crosby would be remembered today solely on the strength of his poetry, or as something more than a rich literati groupie, hovering in the vicinity of Hemingway and others in Paris in the 1920s. Perhaps more than anything else, this says something about the power of suicide as a publicity stunt, an idea not limited to moderns, as is evidenced by the case of the Greek Cynic philosopher Proteus Peregrinus, who capped off a turbulent career by publicly cremating himself in the Olympic flame in AD 165. Lucian's account of Peregrinus' self-immolation, "On the Death of Peregrinus," pictures him as an exhibitionist, eager for fame, and given that I am talking about him here, nearly two millennia later, he seems to have achieved some of it. But Crosby's death, narcissistic, juvenile and murderous as it was (he took a lover with him, unwillingly by some accounts), it nevertheless remains, for all its stupidity, something more than a headline grabber. Ironically, it was the meaning of his life.

So, for some, we can say suicide presented itself as a practical solution to a pressing problem. For others, however, it had a deeper, more vital meaning.

Suicide and Depression

That writers and poets seem to be prone to suicide has not gone unnoticed. More times than not, the connecting link most often suggested is some form of manic-depression – or, put less medically, melancholy. "Why is it," Aristotle asked, "that all men who are outstanding in philosophy, poetry or the arts are melancholic?" One answer to this question is "Are they?" One could, I think, produce a list of men (and women) outstanding in philosophy, poetry or the arts that are not melancholic, or at least no more melancholic than individuals less outstanding in these fields. One can be moved by *Weltschmerz* without being overwhelmed by it, and the list of writers and poets (and artists and composers) who *didn't* kill themselves is longer than the one above. Yet, it is clear that in some way Aristotle is right. Painters and composers are also melancholic, and they kill themselves too, but the numbers of suicides in their group seem smaller than those among writers.

"That such a final, tragic, and awful thing as suicide," writes Kay Redfield Jamison in *Touched by Fire: Manic-Depressive Illness and the Artistic Temperament*, "can exist in the midst of remarkable beauty is one of the vastly contradictory and paradoxical aspects of life and art."[2] Yet although, as she states, "recent research strongly suggests that, compared with the general population, writers and artists show a vastly disproportionate rate of manic-depressive illness,"[3] one of the arguments of this book is that, as in the case of Mishima, Crosby and others, not all literary suicides are the product of depression. Or, to put it another way, to equate all thoughts of suicide (and the act itself) with symptoms of manic-depression (or some other pathological condition) strikes me as overly reductive.

It may be unfashionable to think so, but *angst*, it seems to me, is something more than a chemical imbalance. The poet Robert Lowell once remarked about his own recurring manic attacks, "It's terrible [. . .] to think that all I've suffered, and all the suffering I've caused, might have arisen from the lack of a little salt in my brain."[4] Lowell's suffering was real, and I would not deny him his salt, but I want to argue that existential concerns about the value of life, and what we might call 'aesthetic' concerns about the freedom to leave it under one's own steam, are not necessarily manifestations of a pathology. Indeed, the whole shift in thinking about our inner states from a philosophical or metaphysical point of view to a medical one (melancholy as a state of mind, as opposed to manic-depression as a pathological *condition*) is something I find troubling. Clearly, I'm not suggesting that people who benefit from anti-depressant drugs should cancel their prescriptions. Nor that in many, probably most cases of suicide, depression is the root cause. I am saying that the reflections on suicide of writers and thinkers like Camus, Hermann Hesse, Dostoyevsky and others, which we will discuss further on, are something more than the morbid thoughts produced by a pathological condition. When breaking off a course in psychotherapy, the poet Rilke, no stranger to thoughts about death, famously remarked that "if my devils leave me, my angels will too." Rilke continued to be troubled by his devils, and he continued to write some of the most powerful poetry of the twentieth century. If I am here subscribing to the 'tortured genius' school of romanticism, I make no excuse for it.

As some have suggested, it may be irresponsible to think that the confusion, loneliness, despair and isolation experienced by many individuals of the 'artistic temperament' should *not* be lessened by the insights of psychopharmacology. The general feeling seems to be that if these can be eased, they should be. But consider this passage from Shaw's *John Bull's Other Island*, when the 'melancholic' priest Keegan, who sees the world as a "place of torment and penance" where we are sent to "expiate crimes committed in a former existence," confronts the businessman Broadbent, who finds the world "rather a jolly place."

KEEGAN. "You are satisfied?"
BROADBENT. As a reasonable man, yes. I see no evils in the world — except, of course natural ones — that cannot be remedied by freedom, self-government, and English institutions. I think so, not because I am an Englishman, but as a matter of common sense.
KEEGAN. You feel at home in the world, then?
BROADBENT. Of course. Don't you?
KEEGAN. [*from the very depth of his nature*] No.
BROADBENT. [*breezily*] Try phosphorous pills. I always take them when my brain is overworked.[5]

It's no coincidence that Colin Wilson, who himself came close to suicide in his teens, used this passage as the frontispiece to *The Outsider*, his study of alienation, extreme mental states and the crisis of meaning in modern man. The Outsider, Wilson tells us, sees "too deep" and "too much" to feel "at home in the world," and many of the writers and artists he discusses considered suicide as a real response to their alienation. The idea that their troubling reflections on life's meaning could be excised through a pill seems a clear negation of those reflections' value. Although it may be the case that his relations with people might have improved if he had, I somehow can't regret that Kafka, who often thought about suicide, didn't have the advantage of taking Prozac.

Yet, understandably, most attempts to grasp this link between writers and, as the philosopher William James, who entertained suicidal thoughts, phrased it, "the pistol, the dagger, and the bowl,"[6] have centred on depression. A. Alvarez titled his study of suicide – to which this book is indebted – *The Savage God*, and speaks of the urge as manifested in Sylvia Plath as "not a swoon into death, an attempt to 'cease upon the midnight with no pain' " but "something to be felt in the nerve-ends and fought against."[7] Alvarez writes of the "shabby, confused, agonized crisis which is the common reality of suicide,"[8] and of course he is right. In the majority of cases, which are not literary, suicide is a dark cul-de-sac in a trapped, despairing life. But when considering literary suicides, depression, as common and as devastating as it is, does not, it seems to me, cover all the bases.

A Taxonomy of Suicide

With this in mind, and thinking of how to structure this book, it struck me that I would have to do a 'taxonomy' or 'phenomenology' of suicide. Rather than look for some root cause, linking the different cases I had collected, I thought it better to simply describe and categorize them. There may not be an 'essence' shared by all the suicides in this book. There may not even be something like the notion of a 'family resemblance' *a la* Wittgenstein – who, incidentally, endured many a suicidal thought. But they do seem to fall into certain 'types'. There is the Existential Suicide. There is also the Romantic Suicide. There is the Aesthetic Suicide, and, as I've been discussing, the Manic-Depressive or Melancholy Suicide. There is also the Political Suicide and the Surreal Suicide. Each of these will be looked at in some detail as we go on. There are also some sub-categories, like the Fame Suicide, mentioned above, and the strange category of Imitative Suicides. One striking example of this type is the case of Eleanor Marx, youngest daughter of Karl Marx, and translator of Flaubert's *Madame Bovary*, which famously ends with the suicide of its heroine. Jilted by her socialist lover Edward Aveling, Eleanor was so impressed by Emma Bovary's death that she ended her own life in the same way, by taking poison. The imitation was not exact, however. Emma ate arsenic, but in Eleanor's case it was prussic acid.

Some cases are perhaps unique, and it might be a good idea to begin our survey by touching briefly on some of the different types of literary suicide that fall outside of the main categories mentioned above.

One such I might call the Fan Suicide. One disciple of Rousseau was so enamoured of his master that he blew his brains out at his grave; he is honoured with a tomb at Ermenonville, near Rousseau's own.[9] There is the philosophical suicide. The German Romantic playwright and short-story writer Heinrich von Kleist, who we will discuss in detail further on, may be the one case of a suicide over epistemological reasons; reading the philosopher Kant – not an enticing prospect for most of us – Kleist was led to blow his brains out. There is even a case of a suicide in the cause of literature. In Berlin in 1834, Charlotte Stieglitz stabbed herself to death, trusting her death would inspire her husband, the poet Heinrich Stieglitz, to greatness. Sadly, Heinrich remained a mediocre poet, and her sacrifice was in vain. Another example of the imitative type involves the Conan Doyle and Sherlock Holmes scholar Richard Lanceyln Green. There is the suspicion that he arranged his suicide to appear as a murder, in effect mimicking the plot of one of Doyle's last Holmes stories, "The Problem of Thor Bridge."

Methods of Suicide

Writers' methods of ending their life can also be unique and deserve some classification. The eighteenth century Polish traveller, ethnologist and fabulist Jan Potocki, author of the strange work *The Manuscript Found at Saragossa*, was a student of the occult, a Freemason and a possible member of the secret society the Illuminati. In his last days, suffering from ill-health, family troubles and disillusionment with the outcome of the French Revolution, Potocki had come under the belief that he had become a werewolf, and he took steps to remedy this. Taking the silver knob of a sugar bowl, he filed this into a silver bullet, had this blessed by a priest, and then blew his brains out with it by shooting himself in the mouth. The French romantic poet Gérard de Nerval, mentioned earlier, was, like Potocki, a student of the occult; he is also famous for walking a lobster on a leash through the Palais-Royal in Paris. After two stays in an insane asylum and several bouts of madness, he finally hung himself with a filthy apron string he had carried for years and which he assured friends was really the Queen of Sheba's garter.[10]

Other methods seem exceptional in their severity. The poet Vachel Lindsay killed himself by drinking Lysol, a powerful cleaning fluid. The playwright Sarah Kane, at twenty-eight enjoying success and a promising career, was found hanging in a bathroom in London's King's College Hospital. And after two unsuccessful attempts at taking his life, as well as enduring harrowing multiple courses of electro-convulsive therapy, which many believe only worsened his condition, Ernest Hemingway blew his brains out with a shotgun on the landing outside his wife's bedroom door; she had to step over his remains in order to get down the stairs.

Reasons for Suicide: Failure and Success
Of the many reasons for suicide, it seems obvious that failure would be a common cause among writers. In the case of John Kennedy Toole this is true. Toole's novel, *A Confederacy of Dunces*, was rejected by several publishers in the 1960s and this, combined with depression and possible confusion over his sexuality, led Toole to heavy drinking and eventually to gassing himself in his car. Toole's mother, a domineering woman, had absolute faith in her son's genius and after his death, she continued to hunt for a publisher for the book. Eventually, through the help of the novelist Walker Percy, Toole's novel was finally published, to great success. In 1981 he was posthumously awarded the Pulitzer Prize, and *A Confederacy of Dunces* has since achieved 'modern classic' status.

Yet, success, too, is no defence against the literary suicide. In 1948, *Raintree County* by Ross Lockridge, Jr., an epic of the US Civil War, was published to wide acclaim and massive sales, the sort of response every writer secretly (and not so secretly) desires. The manuscript, which Lockridge had been working on while ostensibly doing a dissertation on

Walt Whitman at Harvard University, weighed nearly twenty pounds, and was accepted by Houghton Mifflin almost on sight; he arrived at their offices carrying it in a battered suitcase. Prior to publication *Life* magazine ran an excerpt from it for a hefty sum. Lockridge also won an enormous prize offered by MGM Studios, as well as a movie contract (the film was eventually released in 1957 starring Elizabeth Taylor and Montgomery Clift, and seen as another *Gone With the Wind*) and it was the main selection of the Book-of-the-Month Club. Yet, two months after publication, and a day before *Raintree County* was announced as No.1 on the national bestseller list, Lockridge killed himself in the same way as John Kennedy Toole would twenty years later, by carbon monoxide poisoning. Lockridge too was suffering from severe depression, some of which was rooted in the anxiety such massive success often brings: the pressure of living up to the acclaim, the challenge, basically, of the second book.

The Unsuccessful Suicide
There are still other categories of literary suicide. One is the Ambiguous Suicide; another is the case of writers who attempted suicide, or were about to and, for one reason or another, were stopped, which I might call the Aborted Suicide. One of these, Mary Wollstonecraft, we will look at in some detail further on. Goethe, who is held responsible for a spate of copy-cat romantic suicides, and who will also be explored in detail further on, has the eponymous hero of his drama *Faust* stopped from killing himself by hearing the church bells on Easter Sunday.

One case in which a book, or at least a pamphlet, prevented a writer from killing himself is that of the Prague occultist and novelist Gustav Meyrink. Torn between the demands of his life as a sober financier, and the pleasures of being Prague's most extravagant dandy, Meyrink was at the brink of suicide when a pamphlet was pushed under his door. It was an advertisement for a book on occultism. Meyrink read the signs and decided not to end his life; when his Expressionist novel *The Golem* appeared some years later, it was a bestseller. The

French short story writer and novelist Guy de Maupassant seemed to presage his own suicide attempt in his story "The Horla," in which the hero's mind is increasingly dominated by a strange extra-dimensional creature, and he is eventually led to kill himself. Many see this eerie tale as a vision of Maupassant's own incipient madness, brought on by syphilis. His hero's suicide, however, was wish-fulfilment. Maupassant attempted to avoid the fate of his brother, who also went mad, by committing suicide, but was prevented by his servant.[11]

Another unsuccessful suicide was the Lithuanian poet, novelist, esoteric philosopher and diplomat O.V. de Lubicz Milosz, a writer little known in the English speaking world, although his reputation in his adopted country of France is secure. Milosz began his writing career as a symbolist and decadent, and at eighteen, was one of the habitués at the Kalissaya, the first American bar in Paris, where he was often in the group of would-be geniuses surrounding Oscar Wilde. Sitting at a table with George Moore, Ernest Lajeunesse and the poet Moréas, Wilde once remarked to a friend "This is Moréas, the poet." Seeing Milosz come in he continued "and that is Milosz – poetry itself." Milosz (who was the uncle of the Nobel Prize winner Czeslaw Milosz) was a devotee of Poe, Lamartine, Baudelaire, Novalis, Byron and Hölderlin, and he took part in café discussions at the Kalissaya and at another poetic watering hole, the Napolitaine. Yet, in spite of his decadent pose, Milosz was unhappy with notions of 'art for art's sake', and in a letter to his friend Christian Gauss, admitted to being "horribly sad . . . with a sadness that nothing can vanquish." "This life," he told Gauss, "is horribly empty with its anxious loneliness surrounded by the idiots of the Napolitaine and the Kalissaya . . ."[12] This loneliness increased and eventually led Milosz to a suicide attempt. As he told Gauss in another letter, on 1 January 1901, "towards eleven o'clock in the evening – with perfect calm, a cigarette at my lips – the human soul is, after all, a strange thing – I shot myself in the region of the heart with a revolver."[13] He botched the job, but his doctors didn't think he'd survive. Unexpectedly he did, and Milosz was sufficiently moved by the experience to cast off his aesthetic garb and turn himself into a philosophical poet of a highly metaphysical and spiritual character.

Another suicidal failure was the poet Charles Baudelaire, one of Milosz's heroes. In 1845, Baudelaire's extravagantly decadent tastes had depleted the inheritance he received from his father, who died when Baudelaire was six. His domineering mother and strict step-father took steps to curb the young aesthete's expenditure, effectively impounding the funds, and doling out to him a small allowance. This humiliation, combined with his masochistic dependency on the illiterate, coarse and frequently drunk mulatto woman Jeanne Duvall, led Baudelaire to despair, and he tried to escape his fate by stabbing himself. Like O.V. de Lubicz Milosz, he bungled the job, which we can assume only added to his humiliation. The crisis however had a beneficial result; out of it Baudelaire's first published writing, the *Salon* of 1845, was met with approval, and established him as a respected, if not well-paid, critic.[14]

Another failed suicide, a somewhat tragic–comic and colossal one, was William Cowper, whose account of his fruitless attempts to end his life are too long to quote here but can be found in the Suicidal Miscellany at the end of the book.

Suicide, or Not?
The writer Graham Greene presents us with a case that could be considered either a failed attempt or an ambiguous one, but in my opinion, and Greene's, doesn't qualify as a suicide attempt at all. In "The Revolver in the Corner Cupboard," Greene relates how he relieved his teenage boredom by playing Russian Roulette on Berkenstead Common. In his late teens Greene suffered from an acute case of ennui. He writes that "For years it seemed to me I could take no aesthetic interest in any visual thing at all: staring at a sight that others assured me was beautiful, I would feel nothing."[15] Here Greene echoes the ahedonia of an earlier, sometimes suicidal poet, Samuel Taylor Coleridge. In "Dejection: An Ode," Coleridge writes:

> Yon crescent Moon, as fixed as if it grew
> In its own cloudless, starless lake of blue;
> I see them all so excellently fair,
> I see, not feel, how beautiful they are!

Coleridge himself considered suicide in his early years, when, as his biographer Richard Holmes relates, he lived a kind of double-life at Cambridge, alternating "wild expenditure on books, drinking, violin lessons, theatre and whoring" with "fits of suicidal gloom and remorse." "He abandoned himself to a whirl of drunken socializing, alternating with grim solitary resolutions to shoot himself as the final solution to bad debts, unrequited love and academic disgrace."[16] Coleridge's older brother Francis had in fact committed suicide and the influence of Goethe's *The Sorrows of Young Werther*, which we will discuss further on, probably had something to do with these thoughts of self-annihilation.

Graham Greene, however, hit upon an effective means of dissipating his boredom. Discovering a revolver among his brother's things, Greene decided to try his hand at Russian Roulette, having read of Russian soldiers entertaining themselves in this way during long and dreary campaigns. Greene found some bullets and, loading one into a chamber, spun the revolver behind his back. Taking the pistol to the Common, he put the barrel to his temple and slowly pulled the trigger. He writes: "There was a minute click, and looking down at the chamber I could see that the charge had moved into place. I was out by one. I remember an extraordinary sense of jubilation. It was as if a light had been turned on . . . and I felt that life contained an infinite number of possibilities."[17] Greene continued the practice, finding a "craving" for its effects. Eventually, however, the kick of not blowing his brains out wore off, and he stopped.

Greene makes clear that his dangerous game, however, had nothing to do with suicide, although Kay Redfield Jamison counts him among her manic-depressives.[18] Greene writes, ". . . this was not suicide, whatever a coroner's jury might have said of it: it was a gamble with six chances to one against an inquest . . . The discovery that it was possible to enjoy again the visible world by *risking its total loss* (my italics) was one I was bound to make sooner or later." And to insure that his possible death would not be taken as intentional, Greene wrote a verse and left it on his desk, which included the line "I press the trigger of a revolver I already know to be empty."[19]

Ambiguous Suicides

Of other ambiguous or border-line suicides, the proto-surrealist Arthur Cravan is a good candidate. Cravan was a contemporary of Alfred Jarry, creator of the *Ubu* plays, and rivalled him in his eccentricities, combining a career in boxing – he once went six rounds with Jack Johnson – with aggressive, Dadaesque poetry. It is generally believed that Cravan committed suicide, throwing himself into the sea during a voyage from Mexico to Valparaiso to meet his wife, the poet Mina Loy; but an article by Charles Nicholl in the *London Review of Books* undermines this account, and suggests that he simply lost control of his less than seaworthy craft and sank; the voyage would in any case be demanding for even a highly competent sailor.[20] Like many surrealists, Cravan however had a predilection for suicide, and once filled a Parisian hall with his announcement that he would kill himself in public. But when the hall was full, he promptly accused his audience of crass voyeurism and treated them to a lecture on entropy instead. (One suspects many wished he would have stuck with the advertised entertainment.) Cravan's aesthetic 'terrorist' tactics would later be a major influence on the Situationist Guy Debord, who would commit suicide in 1994, shooting himself through the heart at his farm house in the Auvergne. Debord claimed that he wanted to see "whether one could live with the responsibility of committing an act of supreme transgression," and his biographer Andrew Hussey spoke of his "supreme and sovereign act of self-destruction."[21] This is a refrain that will accompany many who choose what we can call the Aesthetic suicide. The problem with this and with all notions of 'transgression', is that there are no acts of "supreme transgression." The other usual candidate for an act of "supreme transgression," murder, has its own drawbacks, but, as we shall see, in the case of some aesthetic suicides, like that of Jacques Vaché, these were apparently negligible.

Another ambiguous case is that of the novelist Malcolm Lowry, best known for his masterpiece *Under The Volcano*, an hallucinatory account of the last twelve hours in the life of Geoffrey Firmin, an alcoholic ex-British Consul, drinking himself to death in Mexico. The action of the novel takes place on the Day of the Dead, and the book is saturated in occult and mystical symbolism, much of it taken from the Tarot; one card with great meaning for Lowry was the Hanged Man. Firmin tempts certain death by frequenting a low tavern, the Farolito, and at the end of the novel is killed there by local fascists and Nazi supporters. Lowry's own life, filled with alcoholism, broken marriages, poverty and failure, seems a long, drawn out descent into a personal hell, and at the end of it, the official assessment was 'death by misadventure.' Yet there is some suspicion of suicide. The cause of death was asphyxiation – Lowry choked on his own vomit after a terrific binge. Yet a bottle that had contained twenty sodium amytal sleeping pills was found empty nearby. Lowry had been battling his addiction for years with little success and may have simply given up. But as his biographer Gordon Bowker suggests in *Pursued by Furies: A Life of Malcolm Lowry*, there is the possibility of foul play; it is possible that Lowry's second wife, Majorie Bonner, with whom he had quarrelled ferociously on the night of his death, had given Lowry the sleeping pills while he was in a drunken stupor.[22]

Another borderline case is the novelist Jack London. Associated with clean cut rugged boys' adventure tales like *The Call of the Wild* and *White Fang*, London had a dark side, an obsession with pushing himself to the limits, a kind of 'supersize' philosophy of life. His capacity for food and drink was enormous and would in the end kill him, although it is possible that the overdose of morphine which capped off his hedonistic career was intentional. Although London could say that, "After having come through all of the game of life, and of youth, at my present mature age of thirty-nine years I am firmly and solemnly convinced that the game is worth the candle . . ."[23] he would also keep a loaded revolver in his desk, ready to use against himself at any time.[24]

Addicted to morphine and opium, London was a phenomenal drinker and was one of the first major writers to publicly confess to his alcoholism; his "alcoholic memoir" *John Barleycorn* shocked the readers of his adventure tales and in puritanical America, turned many against him. In his passion for excess, it is easy to see a subliminal death-wish, a desire to pass beyond the limits of the self. London admitted to once almost drinking himself to death in a binge, and on another occasion, as he relates in *John Barleycorn*, he drunkenly stumbled into San Francisco Bay and "some maundering fancy of going out with the tide suddenly obsessed me." London drifted for hours with the intention of letting himself drown, but sobered up in the end and was saved by fishermen. The hero of his semi-autobiographical novel *Martin Eden* kills himself, and in *The Little Lady of the Big House* the heroine, suffering from a mortal and inoperable gunshot wound, is helped by her doctor to end the pain by taking her own life.

London may have killed himself or he may have died from the uremia that was killing him anyway (his kidneys were failing and filling his system with the waste product urea). Other suggested causes are a heart attack, a stroke, or an accidental overdose of morphine. Whatever may have killed him, like Ross Lockridge Jr. (and a cadre of rock stars), success, which he had a great deal of, was no fun for London. "Success – I despised it," he wrote, and one wonders if the collapse of ventures like the palatial Wolf House, his schooner the Snark, and his huge Beauty Ranch – all expensive enterprises that proved dismal failures – were brought about by an unconscious wish for annihilation. London's childhood with a depressive, unhinged mother – who lived with an astrologer and spiritualist after London's father deserted her – his early years working at a canning factory, and his frequent need to adapt to difficult environments made him in many ways a survivor. His own social views were very much in line with Social Darwinism. Yet, as one of his biographers suggests, they also came at a cost. "Jack never developed a robust sense of self, and he would enter adulthood with little self-esteem."[25] Although driven by an urge to better himself (he was a determined autodidact) and in every way a self-made man, London was plagued by what he called White Logic: "the messenger of truth beyond truth, the antithesis of life, cruel and bleak as interstellar space, pulseless and frozen as absolute zero, dazzling with the frost of irrefragable logic and unforgettable fact." For all his worldly success – he was, at one point, the highest paid writer in America – London never really felt good about himself. Possessed of a Nietzschean belief in the superman, he was also prone to a cosmic pessimism, a fatalism that prevented him from adjusting his behaviour when faced with the results of his superhuman excess. When the tide of drugs, alcohol, and a failing body started carrying him out to the cosmic sea, he may in the end have just let himself go.

The Slow Suicide
London's case raises the question of writers who may be seen as indulging in a slow drink or drug-filled suicide. That writers often have an unhealthy fondness for the bottle or drugs is well known. The Beat novelist Jack Kerouac is a case in point. After the initial success of books like *On The Road* and *The Dharma Bums*, Kerouac retreated into an increasingly esoteric prose style and an alcoholic solitude, effectively drinking himself to death while living with his mother; he died at forty-seven in 1969. Another is the decadent poet Ernst Dowson, a devotee of absinthe, opium, hashish, alcohol and other inebriants. Dowson, a friend of Arthur Symons, Yeats and others of the 'Tragic Generation', is described by one writer as "living almost hermit-like in a ramshackle house where he drank absinthe and took opiates in abundance."[26] He died at thirty-two of consumption, drink and overall self-abuse. Dowson's poetry is filled with images and metaphors of ennui, world-weariness, decline and early death; perhaps his best known poem is "They Are Not Long," with its cheery admonition that "They are not long/The days of wine and roses/ Out of a misty dream/Our path emerges for a

while then closes/" In another poem, "A Last Word," he wishes to go to "the Hollow Lands" where there is, "Freedom to all from love and fear and lust/Twine our torn hands/O pray the earth enfold/Our life-sick hearts and turn them into dust." Dowson may not have had the strength to commit suicide, and his world-weariness may have been something of a pose, one adopted by many of his peers, but he did nothing to halt his sure drift into non-existence. Yet if we allowed his case and that of Kerouac's (and sadly many others) to count as suicides, this book would grow unmanageable, and so I think we must leave them out.[27]

Fake Suicides

Some writers have a kind of 'double' relationship to suicide. The Portuguese poet Fernando Pessoa didn't commit suicide, but one of his 'heteronyms' did. Heteronym was the title Pessoa gave to the various literary alter-egos he created throughout his career; more than a pseudonym, Pessoa's heteronyms – he had dozens – were actual complete other identities, with histories, psychologies, and literary styles all their own. One of these, the Baron of Teive, author of a work entitled *The Education of A Stoic*, is led to suicide through strictly logical reasoning. Believing in the "impossibility of producing superior art," and deciding to kill himself after burning all of his works, the Baron works on one final piece of writing, a manuscript which will explain why it is impossible to capture in writing the literary works he imagines in his brain. As so often happens with Pessoa, this work, too, is only fragmentary, a literal testament to the impossibility of literature. The Baron has "reached the height of emptiness, the plenitude of nothing at all." What leads him to suicide is "the same kind of urge that makes one go to bed early."[28] As Heinrich von Kleist had discovered (as we shall see), Teive sees that "the rational conduct of life is impossible. Intelligence provides no guiding rule,"[29] and like Kleist, he concludes that there is only one option, suicide. "I feel I have attained the full use of my reason," Teive writes, and so "that's why I'm going to kill myself."[30] And after burning all of his previous fragments, he does.

Another of Pessoa's heteronyms, Bernardo Soares, the author of the best known (in the English speaking world) of Pessoa's works, *The Book of Disquietude* – although to call this enormous collection of fragments a 'work' is misleading – considers suicide as well. But, as is usual with Pessoa, his take on it is paradoxical. Pessoa/Soares writes: "The active life has always struck me as the least comfortable of suicides."[31] If that is the case, then Pessoa's own life, which, aside from his considerable literary activity was far from active, may be seen as a long avoidance of this particular method of doing yourself in: he spent nearly all of his life in Lisbon, practically in the same neighbourhood, had few friends and probably died a virgin. Yet anyone who reads *The Book of Disquietude* can't help but recognize its deep world rejection and unrelenting ennui, and, like myself, may feel that suicide was never far from Pessoa's mind. It's understandable then that he would find the idea of helping another poet fake his own suicide attractive. The poet in question, however, is more well known in his other guise as a magician, occultist and drug addict.

Pessoa came into contact with the notorious Aleister Crowley through their mutual interest in astrology, and on a visit to Lisbon, during which the Great Beast quarrelled with his current Scarlet Woman – his magical concubine – Crowley coaxed Pessoa into helping him with his prank.[32] Leaving a forlorn lover's note at a treacherous rock formation on the coast west of Lisbon, known as the Boca do Inferno – the Mouth of Hell – Crowley created the impression that he had ended it all by leaping into the sea. Pessoa explained to the Lisbon press the various occult symbols that accompanied the note and even offered the fact that he had seen Crowley's ghost the day after his disappearance. In reality, Crowley had left Portugal via Spain, and he enjoyed reading the reports of his death in the newspapers; among his other addictions, getting his name in the press was high on the list. Eventually, though, he tired of the ruse and 'miraculously' appeared at an exhibition of his paintings in Berlin, once again getting his name in print.[33] Pessoa, however, had a still more significant link to suicide. In 1916, his great friend and collaborator in

Lisbon on the avant-garde magazine *Orpheu*, the writer Mário de Sá Carneiro, author of the novel *Lucio's Confession*, committed suicide in Paris by swallowing five bottles of strychnine. He was only twenty-five, but like Dowson and others, was addicted to alcohol and opium.

Sá Carneiro's case suggests another category, which unfortunately I do not have the space to explore here: cities of suicide. Although all big cities have their share of suicides, there is something about Paris that gives the idea a romantic, poetic attraction. Along with Paul Celan, de Nerval, Gilles Deleuze, Sadegh Hedayat and others, Sá Carneiro seems to have taken seriously Rilke's remark about Paris, in *The Notebooks of Malte Laurids Brigge*: "So this is where people come to live; I would have thought it is a city to die in."

Agents of Suicide

Another category of suicides are writers who, while not committing suicide themselves, led others to it. The case of Goethe and *The Sorrows of Young Werther* will be considered at length further on, and in any case, in that instance, it was Goethe's work, not the man himself, who was responsible. Here I am talking about the writer himself. It may be stretching it to include Freud in this category, but it's not unusual today for Freud to be seen as more of a literary than a scientific or even a medical figure; and the fact that he was, say, compared to Jung, an exceptionally eloquent writer, helps.

As books like Paul Roazen's *Freud and his Followers* makes clear, the circle of Freud's disciples was like a secret society; Freud even handed out rings to his elect, a sign of the follower's acceptance into the esoteric clique. The flip side of this honour was Freud's wrath toward apostates. At the start of the courtship, the dogmatic and dictatorial Freud would allow new members a certain freedom of thought; but this was only, as one writer put it, "so that the ultimate triumph of the psychoanalytic doctrine would be the more complete." If it became clear to Freud that the newcomer had reservations, however slight and reasonable, about his theories – specifically the sexual basis of neuroses – then "there was a ritual of

excommunication," and the unbeliever was "solemnly anath-
ematised and placed on a list of 'prohibited persons'."[34] Jung
himself, who Freud considered the heir to his doctrine,
eventually broke with the master, and the experience was so
devastating for Jung that it led to something like a psychotic
episode. Jung survived and went on to start his own school of
analysis; others were not so strong. One of these was Victor
Tausk.

Tausk was a brilliant individual who basically accepted
Freud's vision; his problem was that he was *too* brilliant, and
his independence of mind, even when still working within
the Freudian framework, troubled Freud. Freud wanted followers, but he didn't want ones capable of thinking for themselves. Freud's ire turned toward Tausk when Tausk came to
the defence of the Viennese satirist Karl Kraus, who, wary of
Freud's ideas, made the perceptive remark that, "Psycho-
analysis is the disease for which it claims to be the cure."
Kraus also criticized Freud's attempt to reduce the genius of
men like Dostoyevsky and Leonardo to manifestations of
penis envy. Eventually the true believers fought back, claim-
ing that Kraus' own attacks on the tabloid press of the time
were an expression of *his* penis envy. Tausk would have none
of it and simply remarked that the shallow Viennese press was
worthy of Kraus' attack. This was enough for Freud, and
when Tausk, who was going through some difficult times,
asked Freud for help – specifically to psychoanalyse him – he
refused. Freud subjected Tausk to petty humiliations, suggesting that he submit to analysis with one of Freud's students
instead, and rebuffed any attempts to regain their former
intimacy. Tausk plummeted. Soon after the rejection, he
wrote a letter to Freud and one to his mistress, tied a curtain
cord around his neck, and shot himself in the head, strangling
himself as he fell back from the blast.

Another disciple to receive the Freud treatment was Herbert
Silberer "the most potentially brilliant and original of Freud's
followers."[35] Silberer made important observations about the
strange half-dream state called hypnagogia, and in his book
Problems of Mysticism and Its Symbols (1917), he explored the

relation between unconscious imagery and alchemy years before Jung did.[36] Although Silberer held Freud in high esteem, he also found much of value in Jung's work. Silberer politely questioned Freud's belief that the sexual theory offered a *complete* interpretation of alchemical symbolism, and suggested that this could also be seen 'anagogically', as an expression of a religious or mystical impulse, as 'instinctive' as the sexual one. He believed that his basic admiration for Freud would compensate for any differences of opinion. Freud disagreed, and cast the heretic into the outer darkness. When Silberer, increasingly puzzled by Freud's rejection, offered to call on him, Freud wrote back: "As the result of the observations and impressions of recent years I no longer desire personal contact with you." Silberer was shattered. A few years later, unable to throw off a sense of worthlessness, he hung himself from the window bars in his home. There must have been a touch of the morbid in Silberer. When he hung himself, he arranged a light so that when his wife came home the first thing she saw would be him.

Another writer surrounded by suicides is the Russian decadent Valery Briusov, author of the remarkable occult novel *The Fiery Angel*, the basis of Prokofiev's opera of the same name. Briusov was the magus of Russian Symbolism; as novelist, poet, editor and critic, in the early twentieth century, he was a supremely important figure in the literary cliques of St. Petersburg and Moscow. Like Paris and London, prerevolutionary Russia was caught up in a obsession with the occult. Satanism and diabolism in particular fascinated the Russian avant-garde, and one expression of this were the several 'suicide clubs' that sprang up among the intelligentsia. Briusov dominated the scene and gathered a coterie of followers. Highly disciplined and cautious, Briusov was attracted to wilder, more ecstatic types, one of whom, the precocious poet Alexander Dobrolyubov, was thrown out of high school at seventeen for preaching suicide to young female students, apparently with some success.

Another character who attracted Briusov was the novelist Andrei Bely, author of the modernist occult novel *Petersburg*.

Bely, a highly labile and poetic character, was an *infant terrible* of Russian Symbolism. At first attracted to each other, Briusov and Bely soon developed a feud. Bely believed Briusov was trying to hypnotize him, and an occult war sprang up between them. This became the basis of Briusov's *The Fiery Angel*. At the centre of the novel was the erotic triangle between Briusov, Bely, and the poetess Nina Petrovskaya.[37]

Nina loved Bely, but he spurned her for the wife of the poet Aleksandr Blok. She turned to Briusov for help; Briusov had a reputation as a magician and she hoped he could cast a spell to win Bely's affection. When this failed she became Briusov's lover, plunging into a seven year long sadomasochistic relationship, involving drugs, madness and suicide pacts. But after using Nina as a model for his novel, Briusov lost interest in her and dropped her. Crushed, she left Moscow and later committed suicide in Paris, joining the ranks of Sá Carneiro, Paul Celan and others. Another poet Briusov got involved with after Nina also committed suicide was Nadechda Lvova. According to the poet V.F. Khodasevic, Briusov encouraged Nadechda's suicidal feelings, and presented her with a pistol that Nina had once turned on Briusov himself. When Briusov ended their affair, she shot herself with it. Still another poet, the twenty-one year old Victor Gofman, was advised by Briusov to kill himself as well; he, too, apparently took the master up on this suggestion.

One last possible agent of suicide. At the time of writing, BBC 4 presented a remarkable documentary about the 'anthropologist' and drug-guru Carlos Castaneda. Much of it was familiar to me; having written about Castaneda in my *Turn Off Your Mind: The Mystic Sixties and the Dark Side of the Age of Aquarius*, I was aware that most likely Castaneda had pretty much invented the whole of his adventures with the Yaqui *brujo* Don Juan, depicted in a series of bestselling books. What I didn't know was that in the last years of his life, Castaneda had gathered a group of female followers with whom he apparently shared an esoteric teaching concerning a kind of cosmic resurrection after death, something along the lines of the Heaven's Gate cult.[38] Castaneda himself died of liver cancer in 1998, a shock to many of his followers who had accepted his own teaching that he would not die, but 'ascend' to some higher sphere. His death was kept secret for some time and was, as they say, shrouded in mystery. His body was cremated, and, according to Amy Wallace, author of a memoir of her time as one of Castaneda's disciples, lovers and wives (he had several simultaneously), burning was a means of releasing the spirit into a higher form.[39] Shortly after Castaneda's death, at least three of the women in his intimate group, known as 'the Witches', disappeared. Florinda Donner-Grau, author of bestselling books based on Castaneda's work, Taisha Abelar, and Patricia Partin, seemed to have simply vanished, and were never heard from again. In 2003, the wreck of a car was found in Death Valley, California, and had evidently been involved in a fire. DNA testing on human remains found in the wreck showed them to be those of Patricia Partin. Partin had a particular relation to Castaneda, as she was both his adopted daughter and his lover. To date the other women have yet to surface, and the assumption among some is that they may have taken the teachings of Don Carlos to a perhaps fatal extreme.

Against Suicide?

These, then, are some of the many types of literary suicide that deserve mention, but that fall outside of the main categories with which the rest of this book will be concerned. Needless to say, however, not all writers and poets are attracted to suicide. As several of the selections in the Suicidal Miscellany show, there were those who argued against it, those who made light of it, and those who, at first finding it attractive, were later purged of the idea. There is the question too of how sincere were the many writers who, writing darkly of the desirability of ending one's life, did not, in actual practice, end their own. In his novel *Manalive*, G.K. Chesterton, whose "Ballade of Suicide" starts off the Miscellany, offers a sure-fire (no pun intended) test to determine one's seriousness about the value of life. The only way to prove if someone who claims life isn't worth living is serious, Chesterton argues, is to point a loaded pistol at his head and propose to pull the trigger. If he remains unmoved, then his nihilism is sincere, and you would probably be doing him a favour if you carried on. If he flinches, then it's just a pose. Although poseurs are not hard to come by – and most of us have been one in our time – most of this book is concerned with those for whom, more or less, the question of suicide was deadly serious.

To end this introduction, let me add a personal note. In writing about suicide, more often than not, most writers devote some time to their own attitude toward it and describe, if such is the case, their own encounters with it. Like many people – writers or not – I have passed through difficult times, patches and even long stretches of my life when I was subject to much hardship and psychological and emotional suffering. But I have never attempted suicide, nor did I ever seriously consider it as an option, although the idea of ceasing the harangue of thoughts and anxieties that accompanies bad times at a single blow can be tempting. Why this is so probably depends on several factors, not the least of which is a recognition that, however bad my situation was, killing myself was certainly a shabby way of dealing with it. A sense of fastidiousness then, an awareness of the mess and complications and difficulties I would leave behind, ruled suicide out. I was also too aware of that piercing yet sadly useless consciousness, shared by Anna Karenina, Emma Bovary and others, that killing themselves was, in the end, a really bad idea and that in the face of that finality, life, as difficult as it is, is infinitely preferable. In more recent years, which have not been without their troubles, the fact that I am a father and that two young boys would, I think its safe to say, be severely upset at my absence, make it a definite non-issue. To avoid a long, slow, painful death through an incurable illness, to say farewell when it is still possible, before old age incapacitates one's lucidity and grasp on life: I can appreciate these circumstances and understand ending one's life in these cases, although how I will feel and react if I find myself in these situations remains to be seen. Everything else, however, strikes me as selfish and, realizing fully that most people bent on suicide will not be stayed by this, irresponsible, even egotistical. It is, I think, in some ways a kind of supreme egotism: the notion that my death will matter to the universe.

I will add one more thing. Reading these accounts of tragic and lost lives, it strikes me that it is never the major philosophical or religious arguments that convince people not to kill themselves – although in some cases, metaphysics does seem to have succeeded in prompting the opposite. What changes people's minds are the little things: Goethe's Easter bells, Chesterton's "little cloud all pink and grey," the glass of wine that Hesse's suicidal Steppenwolf drinks, avoiding the razor back at home. Like Graham Greene's experience of Russian Roulette, these things somehow trigger a sense of life's "infinite possibilities," the awareness of which makes suicide seem an absurd blunder. Why these everyday items, which we normally take for granted, can at times release a mystical sense of the absolute value of life, remains a mystery. Perhaps when we solve it, most reasons for suicide may become a thing of the past.

Notes

1 Unfortunately, space does not allow me to discuss the tragic deaths of all of these individuals. For more on the life and work of the occult historian James Webb, see my article "The Damned" at www.forteantimes.com/articles/150_webb.shtml

2 Kay Redfield Jamison, *Touched by Fire: Manic-Depressive Illness and the Artistic Temperament* (Free Press Paperbacks: New York, 1993) p. 46.

3 Ibid. p. 5.

4 Robert Lowell, quoted by Robert Giroux, Ibid. p. 250.

5 Bernard Shaw *John Bull's Other Island* in *The Complete Plays of Bernard Shaw* (Odhams Press Ltd: London, 1934) p. 441.

6 Quoted in Jacques Barzun *A Stroll with William James* (Harper&-Row: New York, 1983) p. 15.

7 A. Alvarez *The Savage God* (Bloomsbury: London, 2002) p. 34.

8 Ibid. p. 12.

9 Christopher Woodward *In Ruins* (Vintage: London, 2002) p. 152.

10 For more on Jan Potocki and Gérard de Nerval, see my *Dedalus Book of the Occult: A Dark Muse* (Dedalus: Sawtry, 2003).

11 For more of Gustav Meyrink and Guy de Maupassant, see my *Dedalus Book of the Occult: A Dark Muse*.

12 O.V. de L. Milosz *The Noble Traveller: The Life and Writings of O.V. de L. Milosz* ed. Christopher Bamford (Lindisfarne: West Stockport, MA, 1985) p. 438. See also *The Dedalus Book of the Occult: A Dark Muse*.

13 Ibid. p. 439.

14 For more on Baudelaire see *The Dedalus Book of the Occult: A Dark Muse*.

15 Graham Greene *The Lost Childhood and Other Essays* (Penguin: Harmondsworth, 1962) p. 202.

16 Richard Holmes *Coleridge: Early Visions* (Penguin: London, 1989) pp.49–52.

17 Graham Greene *The Lost Childhood and Other Essays* p. 204.

18 Kay Redfield Jamison *Touched With Fire* p. 43.

19 Graham Greene *The Lost Childhood and Other Essays* p. 205. Greene's attempts to shock himself out of a spiritual lethargy are an example of "living dangerously," an ideal which Colin Wilson associates with many of his Outsiders. Wilson argues that there is a kind of "indifference threshold" in human consciousness. "There is, "he writes, "a certain margin of boredom or indifference when the human mind ceases to be stimulated by pleasure, but can still be stimulated by pain or discomfort." (*Encyclopedia of Murder* with Pat Pitman [Arthur Baker: London, 1961] p.22) Greene (and Coleridge), who could *see* but not *feel* beauty, had reached this threshold, and the prospect of blowing his brains out, and then discovering he hadn't, for a brief time galvanised his consciousness. In her account of Greene's experience, however, Kay Redfield Jamison fails to mention that his motive in playing Russian Roulette was to achieve a feeling of greater life, not to end his own.

This is one of the problems with Jamison's book, which, as a study of manic-depression among writers and artists, is excellent, as far as it goes. But being a clinical psychologist, Jamison tends to see *everything* in terms of either mania or depression. One example she gives of 'manic' behaviour is Poe's short story "The Man of the Crowd." She quotes Poe's narrator remarking how, convalescing after months of illness, he finds himself in a London coffee house "in one of those happy moods which are so precisely the converse of *ennui* – moods of keenest appetency, when the film from the mental vision departs . . . and the intellect, electrified, surpasses . . . its everyday condition." For Jamison this is an expression or confession of Poe's manic states, but it is clear that Poe is simply speaking of the poetic condition itself, the kind of clarity and acute sensual and psychic appreciation which reveals to the poet the poetic object. Psychologically speaking, Poe's narrator is having what the psychologist Abraham Maslow called a 'peak experience'. This isn't 'manic' at all, and is something, Maslow argued, experienced by most healthy people. This kind of 'peak' is shared by many of the depressives Jamison writes about, people like Coleridge, William James and others. But she fails to recognize it as such, and erroneously speaks of it as an indication of a pathology.

20 Charles Nicholl "The Wind Comes Up Out of Nowhere," *London Review of Books* vol. 28 no. 59 March 2006.

21 Andrew Hussey *The Game of War: The Life and Death of Guy Debord* (Pimlico: London, 2002) p. 2.

22 Again, for more on Lowry, see *The Dedalus Book of the Occult: A Dark Muse*.

23 Quoted in Alex Kershaw *Jack London: A Life* (Flamingo: London, 1997) pp. 5–6.

24 Ibid. p. 153.

25 Ibid. p. 25.

26 Martin Booth *Cannabis* (Bantam Books: London, 2004) p. 155.

27 Another possible category is the strictly literary suicide. One candidate for this is the horror fiction writer H.P. Lovecraft, who two years before his death by cancer, had effectively given up writing. It is possible that Lovecraft's reluctance to 'sell' himself – he would rarely submit his work to another editor once it had been rejected – and general passivity to life, created the psychological conditions for his illness to establish itself.

28 Fernando Pessoa *The Selected Prose of Fernando Pessoa* ed. Richard Zenith (Grove Press: New York, 2001) p. 301.

29 Ibid. p. 304.

30 Ibid. p. 310.

31 Ibid. p. 287.

32 For more on Aleister Crowley, see *The Dedalus Book of the Occult: A Dark Muse*.

33 For more on Pessoa see *The Dedalus Book of the Occult: A Dark Muse*.

34 Colin Wilson *The Quest for Wilhelm Reich* (Doubleday: New York, 1981) p. 65

35 Ibid. p. 72.

36 For more on Silberer and hypnagogia, see my article "Waking Sleep" www.forteantimes.com/articles/163_hypnagogia.shtml

37 For more on Briusov and Bely and the Russian occult revival, see *The Dedalus Book of the Occult: A Dark Muse* and also my afterword, "Valery Briusov: Paradoxical Decadent," in *The Fiery Angel* (Dedalus: Sawtry, 2005).

38 In spring 1997 the comet Hale-Bopp became visible in our sky. Convinced a UFO accompanying the comet had come to take them away, thirty-nine members of the Heaven's Gate cult in Oregon committed suicide. In 1994, after their leader murdered a couple and their three-month-old baby (whom he believed to be the Antichrist), fifty-three members of the Order of the Solar Temple incinerated themselves in Quebec and Switzerland. And of course the Jonestown massacre in Guyana, 1978, in which almost 1000 people drank cyanide at the command of their leader Jim Jones remains one of the most gruesome group suicides on record.

39 Amy Wallace *The Sorcerer's Apprentice: My Life with Carlos Castaneda* (North Atlantic Books: 2004)

The Existential Suicide

Philosophers have thought about suicide – its implications and meaning, if not about engaging in the act itself – practically since philosophy began. Legend says that Empedocles, one of the earliest Greek philosophers, killed himself by secretly jumping into Mt. Etna in Sicily; his idea was that the volcano would destroy his corpse and people would think he had been transformed into an immortal god and had been raised to the heavens. This ruse was uncovered, however, when Etna, not agreeing with Empedocles' plans, threw up his golden sandal. Most historians discount the legend – there's good reason to think Empedocles died somewhere in Greece – but if it's true, then along with the less renowned Proteus Peregrinus, mentioned in the introduction, Empedocles belongs to the group of fame suicides, who used the act of taking their life as a means of promoting their celebrity. How successful Empedocles was at this can be judged by Matthew Arnold's account of his death, found in the Suicidal Miscellany.

Zeno, founder of the Stoics, who counselled suicide in some cases, is said to have hung himself at 98 when he stubbed his toe on a turtle. The Roman poet and philosopher Lucretius, author of *On The Nature of Things*, is said to have committed suicide after being driven mad by a love potion, but few historians give much credence to this idea today. Another ancient philosopher associated with suicide – although his death, I think, really doesn't count as one – is the one philosopher most people have heard of: Socrates. Rather than cease from pestering the Athenians with his incessant questioning, or go into self-exile, Socrates preferred to drink hemlock. Given that he could have avoided death by leaving Athens, which his followers suggested he do, and that Socrates would more than likely not have poisoned himself unless compelled to, I can't count his death as a true suicide. In this, Socrates is in some esteemed company. The other famous death upon which Western culture is based, that of Jesus, is, like Socrates, one that was consciously chosen; but although many would disagree, it was a death that could have been avoided. Judas Iscariot, the apostle who betrayed Christ and so was instrumental in his arrest and crucifixion, famously hung himself when he realized what he had done; yet there is some doubt about this as well, and in some apocryphal accounts, Judas doesn't kill himself, but is stoned to death by the other apostles.

Another example of self-killing from the classical period that, for me, falls outside of suicide is the writer and debauchee Petronius, whose *Satyricon* gives us the word satirist. During Nero's reign, Petronius, known for his profligate life, fell foul of Nero's minister and favourite Tigellinus, and was compelled to commit suicide. He did so by slitting his wrists and letting them bleed, then binding them, then opening them again, and so on. During this slow process of bleeding to death, he dined luxuriously and talked among his friends. Petronius enjoyed some poetic posthumous revenge when, under the reign of the emperor Otho, who found him despicable, Tigellinus was forced to cut his throat.

The Romans seem a people for whom suicide was something of a matter of course, and some of the greatest names in Roman letters, like Seneca, Cato, Lucan and Tacitus, either wrote of it or, in the case of Seneca and Cato, did actually kill themselves. Seneca, like Petronius, also got on Nero's bad side, and was ordered to take his life. He slit his wrists, but his arteries were clogged, and the blood came slowly and with much pain. He then procured some poison, but this didn't work either. Eventually, he took a hot bath, hoping the heat would thin his blood; in his *Annals of Imperial Rome*, Tacitus records that Seneca died of suffocation from the steam. Following the defeat of Metellus Scipio, with whom he sided against Caesar in the civil wars, Cato, refusing to live under the dictator, chose to kill himself with his sword. Plutarch recounts that because of an injured hand, Cato's attempt was unsuccessful. His servants found him, and called for a physician, who bandaged his wound. Cato waited until they left, tore open the bandage and apparently ripped out his intestines to finish the job.

Most early philosophical discussion of suicide centred around ideas of when it was justified; an example of this, from Epictetus, can be found in the Suicidal Miscellany. Later thought questioned the prevailing Christian idea that it was a sin; David Hume, for example, who can also be found in the Miscellany, argued against this. Some philosophers, like Arthur Schopenhauer (also in the Miscellany) argued, at different times, for and against suicide, and some, like the mathematician Alan Turing – considered the father of computer science – and the physicist Ludwig Boltzmann, best known for his work on the statistical interpretation of the second law of thermodynamics, did kill themselves. Depressed over his arrest and subsequent persecution for his homosexuality, in 1954, Turing is thought to have eaten an apple laced with cyanide. Boltzmann suffered from severe bouts of manic-depression, and, in low spirits over criticism of his theory of atomic structure, he hung himself while on holiday with his family in the Bay of Duino, near Trieste. Although the second law of thermodynamics may seem a rather specialized concern, Boltzmann's insights into the 'increase of entropy' (disorder) in a closed system, is linked to ideas about the eventual 'heat-death' of the universe that troubled Victorian thinkers like Arnold, Tennyson and Carlyle.

One philosopher who put the theory and practice of suicide together in a dramatic way was the little known German thinker, Philipp Mainländer, a disciple, like Boltzmann, of Schopenhauer. Schopenhauer's grim view of life, spelled out in detail in his single masterwork, *The World as Will and Representation*, can be summed up in this quotation. "We can regard our life," Schopenhauer tells us, "as a uselessly disturbing episode in the blissful repose of nothingness. Human existence must be a kind of error: it is bad today and everyday it will get worse, until the worst of all happens." That Boltzmann's calculations led to the conclusion that eventually, the organised energy in the universe – collected in planets, stars, galaxies and so on – would level out into a kind of lukewarm cosmic soup, suggest a kind of scientific proof of Schopenhauer's 'blissful repose of nothingness'. But although it's unclear how much, if at all, his philosophical beliefs motivated Boltzmann's suicide, Mainländer's was clearly prompted by a metaphysical pessimism that outdid even his master's.

Mainländer's central insight, which eventually led to his death, was that the universe itself is a result of God's suicide. As Jorge Luis Borges, in his essay *Bianthanatos*, which is a reading of Thomas De Quincey's abridgement of John Donne's treatise arguing that Christ's death was a suicide, remarks of Mainländer, "he imagined that we are fragments of a God who, at the beginning of time, destroyed himself, avid for non-being." "Universal history," Borges continues, "is the shadowy death throes of those fragments."[1] Borges rightly suggests that Mainländer's view is very reminiscent of that of the Gnostics, who believed this world was the creation of an evil demiurge, and that it was best to escape from it as soon as possible. This was a sentiment favoured by Aristotle as well; in his *Poetics* he suggests that it is best not to have been born, and second best to die young. Some later Gnostic sects, like the Cathars, sometimes helped the ill and aged among them to escape the demiurge by suffocating them. It is unclear what, if anything, Mainländer knew about the Gnostics, but he might have pointed out to them that, as he writes in his work *The Philosophy of Redemption*, "Our world is the means and the only means of achieving non-existence."[2]

Mainländer, whose real surname was Batz, was born in the small German town of Offenbach am Main in 1841. Although early on he showed an interest in literature and poetry, in order to please his father he studied commerce at Dresden. After a period in Italy, he returned to Germany, where he helped in his father's business. Then, in 1860, the single most important encounter of his life took place: he came across Schopenhauer's *The World as Will and Representation*; ironically, it was the year Schopenhauer died. The effect of Schopenhauer's work on Mainländer was similar to that on another one-time disciple, Nietzsche. Mainländer, as Nietzsche (and Boltzmann) would be later on, was stunned by Schopenhauer's pessimistic vision. Schopenhauer, whose thought is in many ways very similar to Buddhism, argued that the world was the result of a blind, compelling will, that forced human beings to live. All wills are in conflict and no sooner is a will satisfied than it is bored with its satisfaction and is once again driven by an unappeasable hunger. Like the Buddha, Schopenhauer argued that the higher life is achieved through cessation of the will and abstention from its desires, hence lessening suffering. Ironically, Schopenhauer, who preached a profound world-rejection, lived a rather comfortable life, and augmented his 'nay-saying' with many civilized pleasures; Nietzsche, his one-time disciple, who later created a 'pro-life' philosophy of 'yea-saying' (Mainländer in fact was one of his targets) had a miserable life, full of illness, loneliness and poverty.

Schopenhauer argued that by withdrawing from the will's compulsion one could attain a degree of freedom and a measure of 'blissful repose'. He also argued that life itself was a very big mistake, and that suicide was neither a crime nor a sin. But he didn't actively advocate killing oneself: suicide, he believed, was merely one more manifestation of the will, rather than a valid retreat from it. Mainländer, however, went further. Not only is suicide neither a crime nor a sin, it's the clearest act of devotion to God.

Mainländer argued that immortality – which Christians believe they will participate in after their death – is unbearable and agonizing, even for God. But being eternal by nature, God cannot avoid it. The only way for God to achieve the release – or 'redemption', as Mainländer puts it – of non-being, is by transforming himself into our world of time, space and matter, "which is constantly progressing from a transient existence into a permanent oblivion and death."[3] This, I may add, is precisely the condition that Boltzmann foresaw as the outcome of his 'increased entropy', a lecture about which, we remember, the pseudo-suicide Arthur Cravan treated his Parisian audience to, in lieu of killing himself.

As one commentator suggests, according to Mainländer's view, the Big Bang is basically the result of God blowing his brains out. "Everything in the universe," Mainländer tells us, "is directed toward non-existence." Mainländer argued that eventually, human beings will realize that non-existence is preferable to existence, and act accordingly. i.e. commit suicide, which, for him, is an "act of redemption."

Mainländer's own act of redemption took place in his thirty-fifth year. There may have been a suicidal strain in the family; three of his siblings would also kill themselves, although it is doubtful they were led to it via metaphysics. Mainländer had for some time deferred to his father's wishes and worked at a bank. He hoped to save enough of a nest egg so that he could devote himself to philosophy and poetry. The stock market crash of 1873, however, ruined him, and Mainländer was left adrift. He seemed to have a craving for 'submission and obedience' which led to him taking on menial work; it also led to him entering the military. But although he had signed up for a three year term, he was released early; it is unclear why. Prior to his service, Mainländer threw himself into writing *The Philosophy of Redemption*. When he finished, he gave the manuscript to his sister, charging her with the task of finding a publisher. His only request was that his surname, Batz, did not appear, and that he instead be known as Philipp Mainländer. His motivation for this seems to be a combination of love for his hometown, and a reluctance to "being exposed to the eyes of the world." Mainländer's mind then became unbalanced and he grew obsessed with his work, producing, in a short time, his memoirs, a novella, and a second volume of his magnum opus. He developed a kind of megalomania, declaring himself "the messiah of social democracy," and advocating celibacy as a means of avoiding the prolongation of life. The exact trigger of his suicide is unclear, but on 1 April 1876, the day after *The Philosophy of Redemption* was published, Mainländer redeemed himself by hanging himself, apparently by stepping off a stack of review copies of his work.

Although philosophers like Schopenhauer, and more extremely, Mainländer, gave reasons and arguments in favour of suicide, a later group of thinkers were focused on the question why, given the world was meaningless, more people *didn't* kill themselves. Inheriting a world that had already become inured to the idea of 'the death of God', the gradual rundown of the cosmos, and our own descent from the hairy ape, and to which the ideology of 'progress' no longer seemed to apply – a world in which human existence seemed pointless and accidental – beginning in the late nineteenth century, writers and thinkers began to chart the effect of this loss of belief on human consciousness. Nihilism, the belief, literally, in nothing, took hold of western consciousness and led those who were sensitive to it to an abyss. Unlike anarchists, with whom they are often confused, nihilists were not necessarily prompted to action by their belief. According to the historian Jacques Barzun, "The genuine kind believe in nothing and do nothing about it."[4] Although the pointlessness of life seemed apparent to them, most nihilists also recognized the pointlessness of killing themselves and avoided making the effort. Nietzsche, who considered himself an anti-nihilist, agreed with them that the universe is meaningless, but disagreed with them in believing that one's own life needn't be. Yet suicide was not far from his mind too. "The thought of suicide," he wrote in *Beyond Good and Evil*, "is a powerful solace: by means of it one gets through many a bad night."[5] And in *Thus Spake Zarathustra* he counsels us to, "Die at the right time."[6] Sadly, this is one counsel Nietzsche himself did not follow. Having gone insane in 1889, most probably from syphilis, he remained in a state of mental and physical paralysis until his death in 1900; during that time he was under the care of his anti-semitic, pro-nationalist sister Elizabeth, who forged his work, and often dressed him in a toga to impress important visitors.[7]

Nietzsche and another 19th century thinker, Søren Kierke-gaard, are credited with starting the school of philosophy known as existentialism, the most famous exponent of which was Jean Paul Sartre, whose *Being and Nothingness* is a massive elaboration on Hamlet's suicidal query "To be or not to be." Existentialism is concerned with questions about the meaning of life and the significance of one's actions, considerations that it believed had been lost in the abstract academic approach to philosophy, still dominant today. Kierkegaard thought that in the 'present age', life had become so abstract that even suicide was affected. "Not even a suicide does away with himself out of desperation," he wrote, "he considers the act so long and so deliberately, that he kills himself with thinking – one could barely call it suicide since it is thinking which takes his life. He does not kill himself with deliberation but rather kills himself because of deliberation."[8] But the existentialist writer and thinker with whom the philosophical question of suicide is most often associated is Albert Camus.

Camus is best known for his novels *The Stranger* and *The Plague*, but he first made a name for himself with his long philosophical essay, *The Myth of Sisyphus*, which asks the simple question, "Is life worth living?" "There is but one truly serious philosophical problem," Camus writes, "and that is suicide. Judging whether or not life is worth living amounts to answering the fundamental question of philosophy."[9] Camus himself didn't commit suicide, although his death in a road accident in 1960 at the age of forty-six seemed, as one writer thought, to make sense.[10] Another writer agreed. In his account of his own depression and near suicide, *Darkness Visible*, William Styron remarks apropos of Camus' death that "there was an element of recklessness in the accident that bore overtones of the near-suicidal, at least of death flirtation [. . .]"[11] Styron also remarks that his and Camus's friend, the novelist Romain Gary, who later committed suicide following the suicide of his ex-wife, the actress Jean Seberg, had told him that Camus had often spoken of suicide, if in a darkly comical way.[12] Styron, understandably focused on his own harrowing experience of depression, wonders if Camus' philosophical preoccupation with suicide "might have sprung at least as strongly from some persistent disturbance of mood as from his concerns with ethics and epistemology,"[13] an expression of the 'pathologizing' of metaphysics I talk about in the introduction.

The Myth of Sisyphus is concerned with why we should not kill ourselves, given we live pointless lives in a meaningless universe, a universe that Camus calls 'absurd'. In such a universe, there is no reason why we should do anything, including live. Earlier God had given a direction and meaning to existence, but since God's 'death' – not by his own hand *a la* Mainländer, but chiefly through the increase in scientific knowledge – that direction and meaning has vanished, and we are left facing a vast, empty space that is oblivious to our presence. As the existentialists pointed out in various ways, there is nothing *necessary* about us being here; there is, in fact, no reason why anything should exist at all. This, more or less, has been the dominant view ever since.[14]

Camus ranges through a gallery of existential thought, encountering and rejecting the work of figures like Karl Jaspers, Edmund Husserl, Lev Shestov and others, and the essay rambles on much more than I recall from my first reading as a teenager many years ago. Suicide is the hook on which Camus hangs his thought, but his central preoccupation is with delineating what he calls 'the absurd', a theme he shares with Sartre, who spoke of the experience of 'the absurd' as 'nausea'. In a oft-quoted passage, Camus writes of that "odd state of the soul in which the void becomes eloquent, in which the chain of daily gestures is broken, in which the heart vainly seeks the link that will connect it again," and in which he detects "the first sign of absurdity." "Rising, tram, four hours in the office or factory, meal, tram, four hours of work, meal, sleep and Monday, Tuesday, Wednesday, Thursday, Friday and Saturday, according to the same rhythm [. . .] But one day the 'why' arises and everything begins in that weariness tinged with amazement."[15] Faced with the inability to answer that 'why', we are, Camus tells us, confronted with the 'absurd', and with the inescapable meaninglessness of our lives. To be sure, we are fenced in by a variety of immediate 'meanings': we work in order to feed ourselves, to support our families, to go on living. "You continue making the gestures commanded by existence for many reasons, the first of which is habit."[16] But, he continues, sometimes the habit falls away and we are left asking *why* we go on living, and then we are adrift.

Another writer, one we wouldn't usually associate with Camus, asked a similar question some years earlier. In his *Experiment in Autobiography*, H.G. Wells hit the existential note a decade before Camus when he wrote that, "What was once the whole of life, has become to an increasing extent, merely the background of life. People can ask now what would have been an extraordinary question five hundred years ago. They can say, 'Yes, you earn a living, you support a family, you love and hate, but – *what do you do*?' "[17] Surprisingly, Wells, who had hitherto looked to science as the great emancipator and agent of human progress, took a darkly existential view in his last book, *Mind at the End of Its Tether*, in which he announced that "the end of everything we call life is close at hand" and that "everything was driving anyhow to anywhere at a steadily increasing velocity . . ."[18]

Camus calls on the figure of Sisyphus from Greek mythology to symbolize his answer to the question of suicide. Although Sisyphus is doomed to a pointless, repetitive act – rolling a boulder up a mountain, only to have it roll down again, "futile and hopeless labour," his own version of the workaday week – we must, Camus tells us, "imagine Sisyphus happy."[19] If anyone should have cause to embrace suicide as a means of escaping an 'absurd' existence, Sisyphus does. Yet he is "happy." We, then, Camus suggests, should be too. Yet how can Sisyphus be happy?

Although Camus rejects any religious or metaphysical ban on suicide and wants to live life "without appeal" to anything beyond it, and although he faces the 'absurd' squarely without flinching, he rejects suicide. For Camus, "killing yourself amounts to confessing." "It is confessing that life is too much for you or that you do not understand it . . . It is merely confessing that that 'is not worth the trouble'."[20] Yet it is not only this. "Dying voluntarily implies that you have recognized, even instinctively, the ridiculous character of that habit [life], the absence of any profound reason for living, the insane character of that daily agitation and the uselessness of suffering."[21] So in an absurd universe, suicide is an expression of man's freedom, perhaps his only one. We can, as Ivan

Karamazov would like to in Dostoyevsky's *The Brothers Karamazov*, return to God the entrance ticket to this absurd universe, and not subject ourselves to its cruelties and point-lessness. Yet, for Camus, this would somehow be beneath the dignity of the 'absurd hero'. "There is no fate," he tells us, "that cannot be surmounted by scorn,"[22] a sentiment remin-iscent of Ernest Hemingway's dictum that "a man can be destroyed but not defeated." Hemingway, too, was a writer with an interest in the question of suicide, a question which he eventually answered by blowing his brains out, although there is good reason to believe that the electro-shock therapy Hemingway received as treatment for his depression, and which left his memory and his ability to write in ruins, was what finally sent him over the edge.

Although the world is absurd, our lives contingent, and the future without reprieve, and although Sisyphus, "the proletar-ian of the gods [. . .] knows the whole extent of his wretched condition,"[23] yet he can rise above it, be greater than it by not giving in to the impulse to give back the entrance ticket and sink into non-existence. Existence, for all its absurdity, is preferable to its opposite. In the face of it, Camus tells us, "the absurd man says yes."

Dostoyevsky, who Camus refers to frequently, and whose novel, *The Possessed*, he adapted into a play, was another writer obsessed with questions of life or death. Camus and Sartre had both put their lives in danger while being members of the resistance during the Nazi occupation of France. But Dostoyevsky had a more intimate encounter with his possible immediate death. Arrested for subversive activities, Dos-toyevsky was facing a firing squad in the St. Petersburg's Semyonovsky Square when a last minute reprieve was issued; the experience was so shattering that one of his fellow prison-ers went insane. This near miss produced in Dostoyevsky a mystical appreciation of the absolute value of life, a vision of its "infinite possibilities" (Graham Greene) that returned in the visionary states preceding his epileptic attacks. Possibly the most concise expression of this insight occurs in *Crime and Punishment*, when Raskolnikov contemplates that:

. . . someone condemned to death says, or thinks an hour before his death, that if he had to live on a high rock, on such a narrow ledge that he'd only have room to stand, and the ocean, everlasting darkness, everlasting solitude, everlasting tempest around him, if he had to remain standing on a square yard of space all his life, a thousand years, eternity, it were better to live so than die at once.[24]

Dostoyevsky is full of these strange visions of meaning. In *The Brothers Karamazov* he tells the story of an atheist who disbelieved in life after death; when he dies, God, as a penance for his disbelief, sentences him to walk a million miles before he can enter heaven. The atheist refuses, and for a million years he doesn't take a step. More time passes and he still doesn't move. Finally, he gives in, and grudgingly does his penance. When he is allowed to enter heaven after walking his million miles, he immediately declares that a penance ten times as great would be nothing compared to five minutes in heaven. Yet there is also the counter image. Again in *Crime and Punishment* there is the criminal Svidrigalov, who sees eternity as the corner of a small dusty room, full of cobwebs and spiders. Like several of Dostoyevsky's characters, Svidrigalov kills himself.

The novel that more or less has suicide as the main theme is *The Possessed*; in it two of the central characters kill themselves, and there are also some murders. Dostoyevsky wrote for a popular audience, and books like *Crime and Punishment, The Possessed* and *The Brothers Karamazov* are in many ways 'thrillers'. (We can say this of practically all the fiction written by existentialists; given that they deal with 'life at the edge', they tend to evoke a 'noir' atmosphere; the anti-hero of Camus' *The Stranger*, for example, is arrested for shooting an Arab.) Yet in focusing on crime, murder, suicide, and other dark aspects of human existence like incest, paedophilia, and madness, Dostoyevsky can throw a spotlight on the extremities of human life, and through this arrive at a deeper insight into its meaning.

The plot of the novel centres around the activities of the radical Pyotr Verkovensky, who is based on the real-life anarchist Sergei Netchaev. A ruthless fanatic, who combined political idealism with the mind of a thug, Netchaev is believed to have been involved in the plot to assassinate Alexander II while imprisoned in the Peter and Paul fortress; when asked by his followers whether they should rescue him or focus on killing the Tsar, he replied unhesitatingly that they should kill the Tsar. Alexander II was removed, and Netchaev remained in prison, where he died of scurvy. The plot of *The Possessed* is based on an incident in Netchaev's career. Posing as a representative of the 'European Revolutionary Alliance', Netchaev brought together small groups of student radicals into what he called "revolutionary committees", which he planned to use to unleash a wave of killings. When one student thought better of this, the others suspected that he would betray them. Netchaev arranged for him to be murdered. One of his followers had conveniently planned to commit suicide, and Netchaev intended to have him write a suicide note, confessing to the killing and to various other crimes committed by the 'revolutionary committees'. In the novel, this student is the 'suicide maniac' Kirilov. But while Netchaev/Verkovensky provides the action – there are several murders and a town is set on fire – the real heart of *The Possessed* is the existential drama of Kirilov, and his fellow suicide, Stavrogin.

Although Kirilov and Stavrogin both commit suicide, they do so for very different reasons. As Camus suggests, suicide can be seen as an act of human freedom. This is how Kirilov sees it. And in a godless world, such an act is the paramount expression of the fact that Kirilov *himself* is God – or at least that there is no will greater than his own. Kirilov cannot believe in the Old Testament God, because he cannot conceive of anything more *real* than his own inner world, his subjectivity, his will. And to prove this, he decides to kill himself. Suicide is the one, ultimate irreversible act by which he can assert his absolute freedom. The logic isn't easy to follow, and as one of the few likable characters in Dostoyevsky (most often they're rather unpleasant individuals, like the anti-hero of *Notes From Underground*), one wants him to find some other way to show his freedom. But this willingness to give up his life at any time in order to express his freedom, creates in Kirilov a profound detachment from life's pettiness and point-lessness. Like Graham Greene, he is aware of life's "infinite possibilities;" and like Greene, by "risking the total loss" of the world, Kirilov becomes almost painfully aware of its beauty. He speaks of seeing a leaf, and its sheer 'is-ness' pro-duces in him the recognition that "all is good." (Again, this is another example of Dostoyevsky's 'visions of meaning', and the reader is referred to the selection from *The Possessed* in the Suicidal Miscellany.) As he is about to be shot, Graham Greene's 'whisky priest' in *The Power and the Glory* under-stands that it would be "easy to be a saint." Kirilov knows this too. Verkovensky and his plans are irrelevant. Kirilov's display of will is essential, and one has the impression that if Kirilov doesn't kill himself now, the idea will haunt him, and that eventually, he will do it.

But if Kirilov kills himself in order to express his freedom, Stavrogin does so because of *too much* freedom. Again, like the teenaged Graham Greene, Stavrogin has reached a state of spiritual emptiness, the *accidie* that attacked many Christian mystics, "a paralysis of the will, a failure of the appetite, a condition of generalized boredom, total disenchantment."[25] Like Hamlet, for Stavrogin, the world has become "weary, stale, flat and unprofitable." But if for Hamlet, the Everlasting has "fix'd his canon against self-slaughter," Stavrogin knows no such hesitation. He will kill himself, eventually. But to get to that point, he will have to make a few detours.

Throughout the novel, Stavrogin engages in what appear to be rather strange, pointless acts, as if he had been possessed by Poe's 'imp of the perverse'. At a very proper social event, he kisses someone else's wife. He pulls a retired general's nose, bites the ear of an old man, and lets himself be slapped in the face without hitting back. He's involved in a duel and lets his opponent fire first; when its his turn he merely shoots in the air. He admits that an imbecilic peasant woman is his wife, when practically every desirable woman in the book would

55

be happy to sleep with him. Yet this is only the surface of his unaccountable behaviour, and in the 'confession' that was left out of early editions of the book, he relates a series of acts that the writer Merezhkovsky regarded as "the concentrated essence of horror." "Stavrogin's Confession" (originaly published by Virginia Woolf's Hogarth Press; Woolf, of course, was another suicide) recounts how Stavrogin shifts from these odd but harmless gestures, to acts of sheer evil. He steals money he doesn't need from a poor family, when he knows they will be devastated. He lets the young daughter of his landlady be punished for stealing his penknife, when he knows it has only been misplaced. He later rapes the girl and, although he could stop her, allows her to kill herself when she realizes what has happened. Through all this, Stavrogin remains impassive; he *feels nothing*, and his whole array of crimes is an attempt to shock himself into some sense of reality. They fail. His 'freedom' offers no resistance, he encounters no barriers, and he may just as well do good as do evil: the result is the same. Where Kirilov embraces suicide as an act of freedom in a world brimming with 'meaning' ("Everything's good"), Stavrogin finally kills himself because he is weary of *not existing*.

One writer who seems to have combined Kirilov and Stavrogin in one character is the German novelist and Nobel Prize winner Hermann Hesse. Harry Haller, the middle-aged existential hero of Hesse's *Steppenwolf*, is another suicide. At the beginning of Harry's journal, which makes up the bulk of the novel, Haller reflects that his life has become full of "the moderately pleasant, the wholly bearable and tolerable, lukewarm days of a discontented middle-aged man; days without special pains, without special cares, without particular worry, without despair; days on which the question whether the time has not come to follow the example of Adalbert Stifter and have a fatal accident while shaving should be considered [. . .]"[26] (Adalbert Stifter was a 19th century German writer who slit his throat with a razor.) Although Haller admits "there is much to be said for contentment," after a short time it fills him with "irrepressible loathing and nausea"[27] and he finds he must throw himself on the road to pleasure, or if that fails, to pain. "A wild longing for strong emotions and sensations seethes in me, a rage against this toneless, flat, normal and sterile life. I have a mad impulse to smash something, a warehouse perhaps, or a cathedral, or myself, to commit outrages, to pull off the wigs of a few revered idols [. . .]" even, as Stavrogin did, "to seduce a little girl."[28]

Like Stavrogin, Haller too suffers from a sense of unreality which he cannot bear, and which he tries to relieve by drastic measures (although he is too decent to commit the crimes Stavrogin does) and he decides that on his fiftieth birthday, which is approaching, he will allow himself to give back the entrance ticket, and commit suicide. Yet, like Kirilov, Haller too has his moments when "Everything is good." Sitting in a tavern, resting from an evening walk in which he bemoaned the cheapness and emptiness of the modern age ("I cannot understand what pleasures and joys they are that drive people to the overcrowded railways and hotels, into the packed cafés with the suffocating and obtrusive music . . ."[29]), Haller sips a glass of wine. Suddenly, his despair vanishes. He is no longer the "beast astray, who finds neither home, nor joy, nor nourishment in a world that is strange and incomprehensible to him."[30] No. "The golden trail was blazed and I was reminded of the eternal, of Mozart, and the stars."[31] Harry is always having these flashes of poetry and the sublime, which blow away his dark mood and remind him that he is not a wretched "wolf of the steppes", a lonely, solitary, unhappy man (a 'lone nutter', as we would say today), but something akin to the gods. Yet these moods pass, and he finds himself once again back in his discontent, considering the example of Adalbert Stifter.

That Harry's initials and those of his creator are the same suggests that Hesse is writing about himself. And it is true that Hesse went through a spiritual crisis in middle age, a plunge into debauchery peppered with thoughts of suicide – including his fiftieth birthday as the day to end it all – which is depicted in the novel and in a series of poems entitled *Crisis*, written at the same time. Hesse had earlier brushes with suicide as well. A 'problem child' who rejected the authoritarian educational system of his day, in his teens Hesse ran away from the seminary at Maulbronn (later used as the setting for his novel *Narcissus and Goldmund*) where he was groomed for a career in the clergy; when found he was sent to a institution for the mentally retarded. Soon after he made his first suicide attempt, after being rejected by a girl seven years his elder. He made another attempt not long after, and throughout his life, which was filled with personal, marital, health and professional problems, Hesse's mind always turned toward suicide as a possible means of escape. It was also a theme in much of his fiction, practically all of which is a thinly disguised account of Hesse's own life and struggles. The eponymous hero of the early novel *Hermann Lauscher* kills himself. So does the schoolboy Hans Giebenrath in *Beneath the Wheel* (also published as *The Prodigy*). Heinrich Muoth in *Gertrude* takes his life, as does Klein in the novella *Klein and Wagner*. Emil Sinclair in *Demian*, written after Hesse's psychoanalytic sessions with the Jungian Josef Lang, counsels another lost youth against killing himself. Hesse's Indian alter ego, Siddhartha, in the novel of that name, makes an unsuccessful suicide attempt. And although it is not an outright attempt at suicide, Joseph Knecht, the hero of Hesse's last and monumental novel *The Glass Bead Game*, spurred by thoughts of youth and the encouragement of his young student, yet knowing the danger, plunges into an ice cold lake and is overcome and drowns.

Steppenwolf however is the novel with suicide at its centre. Hesse's theme in all of his work is the reconciliation of opposites; he most often depicts this through the device of two characters, who embody the conflicting poles of this struggle, which was Hesse's own. In *Beneath the Wheel*, for example, Hans Giebenrath, the gifted schoolboy crushed by the system, is the Hesse who was led to attempt suicide by the unfeeling teachers and ignorant philistines who disparaged his sensitivity and yearning to be a poet; Hermann Heilner is Hesse's idealized self-image, the young rebel who runs away from home and school and successfully becomes a poet.[32] Probably the most well known of these dual personalities are the world-rejecting monk Narcissus and the life-affirming artist Goldmund. Whether Hesse ever successfully reconciled the conflicts in his psyche is debatable; in *Steppenwolf*, however, he discarded the motif of embodying them in two characters, and placed them, Faust-like, in one.

Because of its drug references, ample sex and psychedelic setting – Harry tries opium and cocaine, enjoys a threesome and experiments with homosexuality and most of the action takes place in the surreal Magic Theatre, reserved "For Madmen Only" – *Steppenwolf* was understandably a hit with readers in the 1960s.[33] But the book's essence, which most readers missed, can be found in the remarkable "Treatise on the Steppenwolf," that Harry purchases from a mysterious man wearing a sandwich board advertising "anarchist entertainment." What the treatise turns out to be, is actually an essay on the metaphysics of suicide.

After delineating Harry's own crisis in remarkable detail, and arguing that, far from being miserable parasites on society, Steppenwolves like himself are actually the "vital force of the bourgeoisie," enabling it to prosper and grow, admittedly at the expense of their own happiness[34], the Treatise focuses on the central issue of Harry's and Hesse's own lives. Its analysis arrives at some surprising insights. "To call suicides only those who actually destroy themselves," it tells us, "is false." There are many "who in a sense are suicides only by accident and in whose being suicide has no necessary place." There are many "of little personality and stamped with no deep impress of fate, who find their end in suicide without belonging on that account to the type of the suicide by inclination; while on the other hand, of those who are to be counted as suicides by the very nature of their being are many, perhaps a majority, who never in fact lay hands on themselves." The peculiarity of the suicide is that "his ego . . . is felt to be an extremely dangerous, dubious, and doomed germ of nature; that he is always in his own eyes exposed to an extraordinary risk, as though he stood with the slightest foothold on the peak of a crag whence a slight push from without or an instant's weakness from within suffices to precipitate him into the void."

These individuals believe that suicide "is their most probable manner of death," and while one might suspect that such characters are inherently weak, the opposite is actually true: "among the suicides are to be found unusually tenacious and eager and also courageous natures." But these souls "develop at the least shock the notion of suicide." They "present themselves as those who are overtaken by the sense of guilt inherent in individuals," who find the aim of life "not in the perfecting and moulding of the self, but in liberating themselves by going back to the mother, back to God, back to the All." Yet although "many of these are wholly incapable of ever having recourse to real suicide," conscious of it being a sin, they nevertheless are suicides, for they see "death and not life as the releaser."

They also know that suicide, "though a way out, is rather a mean and shabby one, and that it is far nobler and finer to be felled by life than by one's own hand." Knowing this, they are left to a "protracted struggle against their temptation," as a kleptomaniac struggles against his.[35]

As Hesse did himself, Harry Haller struggles against his temptation, and by the end of novel, among other things, he experiences a night at the Magic Theatre, which includes masochistic submission, group sex, terrorism, murder and even a "delightful suicide: you laugh yourself to bits." He realizes the truth the treatise has made known to him. Although his ego yearns to be dissolved and his self obliterated in the embrace of the Mother, he rejects this path. "The way to innocence, to the uncreated and to God leads on, not back, . . . but ever further into sin, ever deeper into human life. Suicide, even, unhappy Steppenwolf, will not seriously serve your turn. You will find yourself embarked on the longer and wearier and harder road to human life." He recognized the truth discovered in the Magic Theatre, that "the conquest of time and the escape from reality, or however else it may be that you choose to describe your longing, means simply the wish to be relieved of your so-called personality. That is the prison where you lie."[36] He was, he knew, "determined to begin the game afresh." "I would sample its tortures once more and shudder again at its senselessness. I would traverse not once more, but often, the hell of my inner being." And one day he would be "a better hand at the game."[37]

Notes

1 Jorge Luis Borges *The Total Library* (Allen Lane: London, 2000) p. 336.

2 There is little on Mainländer available in English, and for interested readers I suggest an article I came across on the net, and to which this section of this book is indebted. See *www.thebigview.com/discussion/index.php* Oddly, Mainländer turns up on quite a few Islamic websites, mostly in a note about the death of God and the virtues of suicide.

3 Ibid.

4 Jacques Barzun *From Dawn to Decadence* (Harper Collins: New York, 2000) p. 630.

5 Friedrich Nietzsche *Beyond Good and Evil* (translator R.J. Hollingdale) (Penguin Books: Harmondsworth, 1977) p. 85.

6 Friedrich Nietzsche, *Thus Spake Zarathustra* (Penguin Books: Harmondsworth, 1969) p. 99.

7 Elisabeth's husband, Bernard Förster, however did commit suicide.

8 Kierkegaard seemed to see the humorous side of suicide. In one of his books he tells the story of a man who walked around contemplating suicide. From out of nowhere a huge stone falls on him, and his last thought is, "Thank the Lord!" He also speaks of a horsefly which lands on a man's nose just as he is about to throw himself into the Thames.

9 Albert Camus *The Myth of Sisyphus* (translator Justin O'Brien) (Penguin Books: London, 2000) p. 11.

10 Colin Wilson "An Essay on Albert Camus" in *Anti-Sartre* (Borgo Press: San Bernardino, 1981).

11 William Styron *Darkness Visible* (Picador: London, 1991) p. 22

12 Jean Seberg, perhaps best known for her part in Jean Luc Godard's *A Bout de Souffle*, killed herself in 1979 with an overdose of sleeping pills. She was found several days later in her car in a cul-de-sac in Paris. She had previously tried to throw herself in front of train. A year later, her ex-husband, Romain Gary, author of *The Roots of Heaven* and other successful novels, shot himself in his flat in the rue du Bac. Gary is unique in being the only author to win the Prix Goncourt twice: once under his

real name, and a second time under the pseudonym Émile Ajar. He also wrote books under the names Fosco Sinabaldi and Shatan Fotog. He was a film director, a diplomat, and in WWII a pilot with the Free French forces. Other suicides that Styron discusses are that of the political activist Abbie Hoffman, the poet Randall Jarrell, and the writer Primo Levi. Although many who knew Hoffman deny that his death was self-induced, they are unable to account for the fact that he had somehow swallowed 150 Phenobarbital pills. Although the official ruling in Jarrell's death was 'accidental', he had been struck by a car while walking on a stretch of highway near Chapel Hill, North Carolina. His presence on the road at night is unaccountable, and *Newsweek* reported the death as a suicide. Jarrell, too, suffered from depression, and had slashed his wrists while in hospital. At sixty-seven, Primo Levi, a survivor of Auswitch, threw himself down a stairwell in Turin.

13 *Darkness Visible* p. 24

14 It is a view not limited to the humanities. The physicist and Nobel Laureate Steven Weinberg famously remarked that, "The more the universe seems comprehensible, the more it also seems pointless." In Weinberg's view the universe, and everything in it, including ourselves, was created 15 billion years ago, when less than nothing exploded for no reason (the Big Bang). One almost prefers Philipp Mainländer's idea of creation via cosmic suicide. Such pronouncements as Weinberg's troubled thinkers like Camus, but our own *post*-post-modern sensibility, nursed on nihilism as on mother's milk, accepts them as given and leaves it at that.

15 *The Myth of Sisyphus* p. 19.

16 Ibid. p. 13.

17 H.G. Wells *Experiment in Autobiography* (Gollanz: London, 1934) p. 16.

18 H.G. Wells *Mind at the End of Its Tether* (Heinemann: London, 1945) pp. 1, 4.

19 *The Myth of Sisyphus* pp. 107, 111. The Greeks had a genius for images of futility. Think of Midas, Tantalus, even Penelope's weaving in the *Odyssey*. It suggests that 'the absurd' is perhaps not as modern a discovery as the existentialists thought.

20 Ibid. p. 13.

21 Ibid.

22 Ibid. p. 109.

23 Ibid.

24 Fyodor Dostoyevsky *Crime and Punishment* (translator Constance Garnett) (Heinemann: London, 1945) p. 142.

25 Robert S. DeRopp *The Master Game* (Picador: London, 1974) p. 11.

26 Hermann Hesse *Steppenwolf* (Penguin: Harmonddsworth, 1983) p. 33

27 Ibid. pp. 34–35.

28 Ibid. p. 35.

29 Ibid. p. 39.

30 Ibid.

31 Ibid. p. 45.

32 Hermann Heilner, like Harry Haller, and the unnamed H.H. of Hesse's esoteric fantasy *The Journey to the East*, are clear indications that like Goethe's, Hesse's writings form "the fragments of a great confession."

33 For more on Hesse and the sixties, see my *Turn Off Your Mind: The Mystic Sixties and the Dark Side of the Age of Aquarius* (Disinformation Company: New York, 2003).

34 A theme taken up in Colin Wilson's *The Outsider*.

35 *Steppenwolf* pp. 58–61.

36 Ibid. p.206.

37 Ibid. pp. 252–253.

The Romantic Suicide

Steppenwolf is an anomaly among Hesse's novels. It's the only one that takes place entirely within a city, albeit a city more aligned with Hesse's psyche than with the Zurich and Basel upon which it's based. Unlike the urban milieu of much existential writing, Hesse's other fictions inhabit more exotic locales: an idealized Medieval Age, a mystic orient, a future utopia, or, in the tradition of German Romanticism, against the backdrop of a beautiful, idyllic nature. And while the existential suicide is led to self-destruction either as a gesture of his sovereign freedom, or, with Stavrogin, as an escape from a deadening half-life, like Harry Haller, the romantic suicide has a more emotional, even erotic, relationship with death. The romantic suicide has moments when, like Kirilov, he experiences a kind of ecstasy, an overwhelming feeling that, "Everything is good." Yet, it's precisely this ecstasy that undermines him. After his flights of deep feeling (which, more times than not, are triggered by the opposite sex), the return to the mundane world is a shock. Stolid, implacable reality remains, and the world, life, and self-consciousness become unbearable. Death, the great unknown, with its apparent promise of release from the cares of a troublesome existence, takes on an alluring appeal. As the lyrics of a sentimental pop song of the 1970s, about another suicide, Vincent Van Gogh, have it, many romantics came to believe that "this world was never meant for one as beautiful as you," the "you" more often than not being themselves.

Death has seemed the way out of inescapable situations for many tragic couples. Cleopatra followed Mark Anthony in suicide. The story of Tristan and Isolde inspired Richard Wagner to compose probably the most seductive piece of music in the repertoire, the *Liebestod*, "love death." Romeo, mistaking a sleeping Juliet for a dead one, kills himself; and

Juliet, when she awakes and finds Romeo dead, follows suit. The equation love = death seems somehow imprinted in the western psyche; certainly this seems the case at least since the late eighteenth century and the rise of the Romantic movement. Death and sex are so entwined in our cultural consciousness, that the sexual orgasm has even earned the sobriquet of *la petite mort*, 'the little death'. The ecstasy of orgasm obliterates our rational consciousness, and, with any luck, for a brief while we enter a kind of trance, in which we are 'dead to the world'. Obliteration of their rational consciousness is something many romantics sought, and the most obliterating experience of all seemed to be death. With this in mind, it's strange to think that a session of mutually satisfying sex is something like a suicide pact.

Perhaps the most extreme example of this erotic yearning for nothingness is found in Villiers de l'Isle Adam's influential Symbolist play *Axel*. Although little read and even less performed today, Villiers' play had a profound effect on the literary elite of the time, especially W. B. Yeats, who was among the audience at the play's first performance in Paris in 1894. The plot of *Axel* is somewhat convoluted, involving mystical societies and hidden treasures, but the central characters are the ennui-ridden Rosicrucian aesthete Axel d'Auërsperg and the ex-nun Sara Emmanuèle de Maupers. Axel spends his days studying occult texts and mystical philosophy in his castle, cut off from crude reality. When his philistine cousin Kaspar d'Auërsperg suggests that Axel enjoy himself by making use of the treasure his father has hidden in the castle, Axel runs him through. And when Axel discovers Sara, the renegade nun, who has come looking for the treasure, they battle, only to discover that they are soul mates. Yet Axel's romantic world rejection is so deep that, after announcing their love to each other, he convinces Sara that their passion can only be consummated in a higher sphere, i.e. death, and suggests a dual suicide. Sara, more red blooded than the dreamy Axel, suggests at least one night of a more earthly passion, before they quit their mortal coils. Yet Axel rejects the idea with contempt. "O Sara," he cries. "Tomorrow I would be prisoner of your splendid body. Its delights would have fettered the chaste energy impelling me at this instant. But . . . suppose our transports should die away, suppose some accursed hour would strike when our love, paling, would be consumed by its own flames . . . Oh! Let's not wait for that sad hour . . ."

Still not convinced that suicide is their best choice – after all, they are young, beautiful, rich, and have an entire castle at their disposal – Sara makes one last attempt to draw Axel back into the world. Compressing her argument into a single plea, she throws herself at Axel and commands him to, "Come, live!"

> "Life?" asks Axel. "No – Our existence is already full and its cup runneth over! What hourglass could measure the hours of this night? The future? . . . we have exhausted it. . . . As for living? Our servants will do that for us."

This haughty, "As for living? Our servants will do that for us," became the motto of scores of delicate, world weary aesthetes that followed Axel in his world rejection. Although most associated with the *fin-de-siècle*, it's a sensibility common to youth, whose idealism, as yet not chastened by the rough surface of life, finds the contrast between the world as it is and the world as it *should* be unacceptable. Unwilling to give up the ideal, they hold reality in contempt, and, in different ways, seek an escape from it. Most often the means of escape are drugs, but in some extreme cases, the preferred method is death.

One romantic who sought in death release from an impossible situation, and whose actions are said to have triggered a spate of copycat suicides, was the unfortunate hero of Goethe's early novel *The Sorrows of Young Werther*. Goethe's novel of unrequited love, social barriers, romantic extremes and suicide, kick-started the period of *Sturm und Drang*, 'storm and stress', that blazed across Europe in the late eighteenth century, before blossoming into full-blown Romanticism. Yet Goethe himself soon outgrew this sensibility and remarked that by the time he had completed *Werther*, he experienced a sense of freedom and deliverance which allowed him, more or less, to grow up. Goethe wasn't lacking unsuccessful love affairs, but in writing *Werther* he recognized that, unpleasant and disappointing as they were, they weren't as devastating as many believed. In later years, commenting on the fate of his hero, Goethe remarked: "I was never such a fool as Werther." Women are delightful and love rapturous, but neither, Goethe implies, are worth killing yourself over.

The novel, which has come to be seen as the first great example of 'confessional' literature, is based on two real life incidents: Goethe's own brief unrequited loved for Charlotte Buff, who was already engaged to another man; and the actual suicide of Karl Wilhelm Jerusalem, an acquaintance of Goethe's who killed himself over his love for a married woman.

In 1772, Goethe, who had already earned some notoriety as the author of the drama *Götz von Berlichingen*, arrived in the small town of Wetzlar, near Frankfurt, sent there by his father to make contacts and find a career for himself. The twenty-three year old poet and playwright preferred spending his days reading Homer or Pindar and following his interests wherever they may lead. One place they led to was a ball held at Volpertshausen, a small village not far from Wetzlar. There he met and promptly became enchanted with Charlotte Buff. Nineteen, lively and "physically attractive in a rather conventional style,"[1] Charlotte captivated Goethe and the next day he called on her family home. Charlotte's father was the administrator for a wealthy aristocratic society called the Order of the Teutonic Nights; the social connections, grand farmhouse, and mixture of sophisticated and rural character appealed to Goethe, and this made the already alluring Charlotte even more desirable. Yet Goethe soon discovered another had got there first. Charlotte was engaged to Johann Christian Kestner, a serious minded thirty-one year old who, like Goethe, was attached to the Imperial Court. Unlike Goethe, Kestner pursued his career options with greater purpose; hence it was that after spending many hours drafting legal papers, he would show up at Charlotte's home and discover that Goethe had already spent much of the afternoon with her.

Kestner, who was as amused as he was annoyed at Goethe's puppy love, knew the poet was no real threat. Charlotte was a sensible young woman who realized that Goethe could spend time with her being charming because he had little else to do; she also recognized that Kestner's absence was the cause of providing the two of them with the wherewithal to get married and have a life together. Kestner, in fact, displayed the virtues of maturity, tolerance and patience that Goethe himself would extol in later years. Unlike many jealous lovers, Kestner could speak highly of Goethe. Writing to a friend, Kestner spoke of Goethe as "a man of many talents . . . a true genius and a man of character." Although Kestner recognized that Goethe was "altogether a man of violent emotions," he also saw that he exhibited "considerable self-control," a virtue Goethe later found lacking in the Romantics that followed him. Goethe took to Kestner as well, commenting on his "calm and even behaviour, clarity of opinions, and firmness in action and speech."[2]

The three became good friends, not quite forming a *Jules et Jim* ménage, but establishing for a time something of a unit. Nevertheless, knowing well that she was already engaged, Goethe fell in love with Charlotte. His devotion and ubiquity at times irritated Kestner, whose work often drew him away. Writing in his diary, Kestner complained of Goethe that "however much of a philosopher he is, and however well-disposed he may be towards me, he does not care to see me coming to pass my time in pleasures with my girl." Understandably, although he was "well-disposed towards him," Kestner admitted that he did "not like to find him alone with my girl, entertaining her."[3] Yet for the most part Kestner tolerated Goethe's attentions, and Charlotte herself never encouraged Goethe to believe they could be anything more than friends.

Looking at the affair now, it seems clear that Goethe was

probably more in love with being in love than he was with Charlotte. In any case, she was too sensible a woman to make him happy. The practical, orderly virtues he admired in her wouldn't have mixed well with his poetic temperament, and she herself wanted a dependable mate, a 'good earner', which at that point Goethe wasn't. What Goethe really wanted was for the situation to continue indefinitely. Consummating his desire in some act of betrayal would only make things sordid. Goethe was no seducer, at least not in this instance; the idea of the beloved, and the enchanting glow contemplating her gave to the world, was what he wanted. More than likely he already knew the truth of what his friend Johann Heinrich Merck told him: that if Charlotte broke off her engagement to Kestner in order to marry him, Goethe would head for the hills, a scenario he had already acted out on more than one occasion. Like the Romantics that followed him, the young Goethe "sought to make permanent the fleeting experience of falling in love."[4] The practical realities of human relationships would only be a bother.

Such ecstasy, however, is by definition short-lived, and Charlotte finally brought an end to the daydream. She gently but categorically let Goethe know that anything deeper than friendship was impossible between them. After four months of worshipping her, Goethe finally got the message, and left. Charlotte cried when she read his farewell note, yet he and Kestner were soon corresponding. In Koblenz, Goethe met up with Merck, and was introduced to Maximiliane von La Roche, the sixteen-year-old daughter of the authoress Sophie von La Roche. Not surprisingly, he promptly became enchanted with her too. In *Dichtung und Warheit* ("Poetry and Truth") Goethe remarks that, "It is very pleasant if a new passion awakens within us before the old one has quite faded away." Fickle, perhaps, but his interest in Maximiliane weaned him off his dreams of Charlotte. Maximiliane, too, disappointed him; she married a merchant instead. But by then unrequited love was only one more of life's continuous lessons.

Karl Wilhelm Jerusalem, an acquaintance of Goethe, Kestner and Charlotte, was a less robust soul than Goethe, and

when it became clear that his passion for the married Elizabeth Herd would go unfulfilled, he chose a more drastic
option. On the night of 29 October 1772, little more than a
month after Goethe had left Wetzlar, Jerusalem shot himself
with a pistol he had borrowed from Kestner. It's a truism that
life imitates art, but in Jerusalem's case the parallel is striking.

Jerusalem was among a group of people that Goethe knew
in Wetzlar, but although they had studied law in Leipzig at the
same time, they were never close. Jerusalem had a reputation
as an agreeable and dependable character; the famous writer
Gottfried Lessing knew him and thought highly of him,
and while not engaged as a secretary to the ambassador of
Braunschweig, Jerusalem occupied himself with philosophy,
poetry and painting. Unlike Kestner, Jerusalem had a low
opinion of Goethe, calling him a "fop" and a "scribbler". In
Dichtung und Warheit, Goethe describes Jerusalem as polite and
gentle, and pointed out his appearance, remarking on his blue
frock-coat, buff leather waistcoat, and breeches — attire that
would become very popular in years to come.

Jerusalem had a reputation for being eccentric. Kestner
speaks of his habit of long walks in the moonlight, his taste for
solitude and tendency to brood, and the social snub these
character traits had cost him. He had a penchant for drawings
of deserted landscapes and had written an essay defending
suicide, but the most memorable feature about Jerusalem was
his doomed love for the married Elizabeth Herd. Apparently
Herd did little to encourage Jerusalem's affections, and when
he announced his love to her, she begged her husband to
forbid Jerusalem entry to their home. Soon after Jerusalem
wrote to Kestner, saying he was about to take a long journey,
and asking for the loan of Kestner's pistols, a not unusual
precaution at the time. Kestner wasn't suspicious and didn't
guess the use his loan would be put to. After setting his papers
in order and making arrangements, Jerusalem spent the evening at his home, in front of a fire and a jug of wine, having told
his servant to be prepared for an early departure. Then, some
time between midnight and one am, Jerusalem shot himself
with Kestner's pistol, sitting in his chair, dressed in his buff

waistcoat, boots, and blue frock-coat. When his servant found him the next morning, he was still alive. A great deal of blood stained the floor; Jerusalem had apparently dragged himself across the room to the window. A doctor was called but it was no use. When Kestner heard the news he rushed to Jerusalem's rooms, realizing the real reason for the loan of the pistols. By noon Jerusalem was dead and he was buried that night. Goethe heard the story from Kestner and wrote back, telling of his meeting Jerusalem once in the moonlight and remarking on the young man's loneliness. Taking his own experience with Charlotte, and Jerusalem's sad death, Goethe brought the two together and created a classic of tragic Romanticism.

When Goethe's *Die Leiden des jungen Werther* appeared in 1774, two years after Jerusalem's suicide, it was an immediate success. It told the tale of a passionate, poetic, idealistic young man, his ill-fated love for a woman betrothed to another, and his tragic suicide when that love was unrequited. It was clear the story was based partly on Goethe's own love for Charlotte Buff, and partly on Jerusalem's sad end. The fact that Werther's suicide was only one among several indications – albeit the most drastic – that his idealistic temperament was ill-suited for coming to grips with life, went practically unnoticed. Understandably, the fact that it was based on a real life suicide overshadowed everything else. Kestner and Charlotte were not entirely pleased about their inclusion in the book, and the notoriety they earned from it annoyed them. The character 'Albert' (based on Kestner) became synonymous with a philistine sensibility, and to be called 'an Albert' was considered an insult. 'Lotte' (Charlotte) was suspected of being Goethe's mistress, which she never was, and was the subject of abuse when her virtue became known. In a letter to a friend, Kestner pointed out that in the first half of the book, Werther is Goethe; in the second half, he is Jerusalem. Kestner made clear that although some of the incidents had a basis in their relationship with Goethe, many were pure invention. But to the general reading public, none of this mattered. What struck their imaginations was that the suicide was based on a 'real' character, and the strange triple entity of Werther – Jerusalem – Goethe became an overnight sensation. The fact that practically all of the novel's readers misunderstood Goethe's intent was ignored.

Within a few months of the novel's publication, Europe was in the grip of Werthermania, and Goethe became the most famous German writer in the world. As often happens with this kind of early success, Goethe spent much of his subsequent career trying to show he was more than 'the author of *Werther*'; even his masterpiece *Faust*, which is a classic on a par with Shakespeare and Dante, was less known in his lifetime. The 'Werther costume' – blue coat, buff waistcoat, breeches and riding boots – became de rigueur among the young set. There was a Werther tea, a Werther cologne, young people took to taking long walks in the woods, reciting Homer and Ossian (one of Werther's favourite poets), and torchlight processions made their way to Jerusalem's grave. Pilgrims from all over Europe flocked to the place, and the site was included in the travel guides of the time. Werther style poems, plays and novels were bought and read as fast as they could be published, most of an inferior literary quality which, as can be imagined, hardly mattered. There were Werther fireworks, Werther wax figures, Werther songs, Werther porcelain, and Werther jewellery. Questions posed by the novel were hotly debated: should Lotte have continued to see Werther after she and Albert were married? Romantic displays of solidarity with Werther were common. A group of Englishmen toasted Werther over Jerusalem's grave, drew their daggers, and made speeches, but evidence for the many Werther copy-cat suicides that remain part of the novel's myth is scant. As Michael Hulse remarks, although there are a few deaths linked to the book (and these in fact were women), reports of a 'suicide epidemic' are exaggerated and "the young men of Europe contented themselves with dressing in blue frock-coats and buff waistcoats, and sensibly preferred not to pull the trigger."[5] But if *Werther* didn't send a generation to an early grave, as has been reported, it's popularity was dangerous in another, less drastic way. It was less as an endorsement of suicide, than in the way its many readers misunderstood Goethe's message, that the book was a danger. That the book was nevertheless banned in Leipzig, and that a Danish translation was aborted did little to stop the spread of the Romantic sensibility that Goethe had purged himself of by writing the book.

From his creator's point of view, that Werther was a fool to commit suicide over a woman is clear, but that is not the extent of his foolishness. Goethe's younger contemporary Heinrich Heine pointed out that the social issues raised in the novel were as important as the romantic ones, and that if the book had been published in the 1800s, this would have been recognized. Werther's problem – which we can assume was Jerusalem's as well, and indeed Goethe's at one point – was that he did not 'fit' into society. He is intelligent, idealistic, poetic: valuable traits all, but not ones that guaranteed that he would be judged as an equal by his social betters. Lotte's rejection of his love is mirrored by the rejection he receives by the aristocratic society he encounters during his tenure as secretary to an ambassador, a position taken so that he could master his feelings toward Lotte. The ambassador himself he finds difficult to take. Werther finds him "extremely trying," "the most punctilious oaf imaginable, doing everything step by step, meticulous as a maiden aunt."[6] Werther can't understand why he must "despair of my own powers, my own gifts, when others with paltry abilities and talents go showing off, smugly self-satisfied."[7] "What people these are, whose entire souls are occupied with protocol and ceremony, who devote their devious creative energies, for years on end, to moving one place higher up at table!"[8] Werther's own intelligence and energy is often too vital to suppress, and he frequently contradicts or corrects his employer, behaviour that earns him rebuke and the admonition to control his "hypersensitivity", and the advice that he must learn to "moderate it and divert it into areas where it can be put to proper use and produce its rightful powerful effect."[9]

Werther tries to abide by these counsels, but something happens that makes him throw his position over. A count who appreciates his talents and is fond of him invites him to dine on the same evening that he held a regular soirée with his fellow nobles. Werther did not know that he, as a subordinate, should not be present, and so he lingered, although the turned up noses of the aristocrats were enough to make him flee. Then a young woman, Miss B., whom he had got to know and whom he felt had "retained a very natural manner amidst this inflexible life" and who accepted his request to call on her, arrived. Although his "heart always feels freer" the moment he sees her, he soon realizes that she was not as 'natural' with him then as she had been. "Can she too be like the rest of them?" he asks. Gradually the room fills and his presence becomes an issue. Eventually and apologetically, because he does truly like him, the count has to ask him to leave. Werther makes his exit, and drives to a hill to "watch the sun set and read that magnificent book in Homer where Odysseus enjoys the hospitality of the excellent swineherd."[10] Later he discovers that his faux pas is the talk of the town, and he hears from Miss B. that she had been warned against keeping up an acquaintance with him. The idea that he is being talked about enrages him. "I wish someone would have the courage to mock me to my face, so that I might thrust my sword through his body . . ." But thoughts of suicide are not far behind either. "I have snatched up a knife a hundred times, meaning to relieve my sorely beset heart . . ." Like the "noble breed of horses that instinctively bite open a vein when they are exhausted and feverish," Werther too is "tempted to open a vein and so find eternal freedom."[11]

But this humiliation is only the last in a series of unendurable conditions for Werther. "There is not a single instant when the heart is full," he cries, "not one single hour of bliss!" In the evenings he resolves "to enjoy the next day's sunrise, but I cannot quit my bed;" during the day "I look forward to the delights of moonlight, and then I stay in my room. I do not quite know why I rise or why I go to bed."[12]

Werther's problem, however, is not that of social snobbery, or of the impossibility of having Lotte. It is more than this. As John Armstrong points out in his book *Love, Life, Goethe*,

Werther's experience with Lotte, and with Miss B and the count, "seems to suggest something terrible about life." Werther "regards love as sacred – as the most important emotion. However, there is no guarantee that love, however, ardent, will be returned: that the world will meet it and reward it. He feels as if the most valuable thing that he has is useless in the world as it is. Existence is perverse."[13]

That "the race is not given to the swift, nor the battle to the strong, neither yet bread to the wise, nor yet riches to men of understanding, nor yet favour to men of skill; but time and chance happen to them all," as Ecclesiastes pointed out long ago, remarking on a clear design fault in life, is something Werther has difficulty accepting.

Lotte's attempt to convince Werther that she is not the only woman in the world, that his talents, abilities and capacity for love will certainly find a place for him, are fruitless. Werther, Armstrong tells us, is on the road to ruin "not because of the faults of the world, but because of some flaw in his inner condition."[14] Werther is discovering the truth of Schopenhauer's belief: that existence is an absurd game, and that desire only breeds unhappiness. Werther's problem is that, as far as he can see, his deep feelings and longings can *never* be fulfilled in the world as it is. Goethe, who was no stranger to deep feelings and yearnings – indeed, in many ways he taught Europe how to have these – realised that such unappeasable desires can only weaken one for life, unless one develops the discipline to face life on its own terms. Like most of us, Goethe faced disappointment and humiliation, but he was strong enough to grow beyond the childish desire to knock over the chess board if the game wasn't going his way. Werther is unable to do this. He refuses to grow up. Goethe is *not* saying we should jettison our feelings, our idealism and dreams and find a good job in order to get on in the world. But he is saying that our dreams and idealism are useless unless we can learn how to fulfil them *in* the world. Having written *Werther*, Goethe left the kind of rash immaturity that leads to romantic suicide behind, and went on to become one of the greatest creative geniuses in history, turning his mind and vitality to a dozen things, from science to statesmanship. He turned his dreams into reality, rather than letting reality be destroyed by his dreams.

Unfortunately, the damage was done, and Europe (and somewhat later, America) witnessed a rash of romantic death worship. That poets seemed not made for this world was evidenced by the early deaths of Keats, Shelley, Byron, Poe, Baudelaire and dozens of other 19th century figures. Probably the most iconic 'real life' Romantic suicide – although, as we shall see, there is some doubt it was a suicide at all – was the death at seventeen of the boy poet Thomas Chatterton. That life seemed a "dim vast vale of tears," and the poet destined to "cease upon the midnight with no pain" – or at least to want to – became part of the Romantic's job description. Thomas Lovell Beddoes' near-pathological death obsession – which we will look at in more detail further on – is perhaps the most unrelenting expression of a theme that dominated the cultural consciousness in the west for decades, reaching into the twentieth century, and late Romantics like the composer Gustav Mahler, whose *Das Lied von der Erde* is a sumptuous, seductive farewell to life, and the poet Rilke, whose *Duino Elegies* celebrates death not as a end, but as the 'other side' of being. The poet manqué Harry Crosby carried this idea to kitschy extremes, but for the most part the twentieth and twenty-first centuries have seen death on such massive scales – wars, genocides, natural disasters – that aside from adolescent excursions in the garb of 'goth' or 'death' rock, the idea of 'worshipping' it no longer strikes the imagination. Yet after the last gasp of tragic Romanticism in the decay of the *fin-de-siècle*, the literary suicide took on a possibly even darker character, as an expression of a grimly sardonic, stridently nihilistic 'black' humour, a macabre comedy most characteristically associated with surrealism.

Notes

1 John Armstrong *Love, Life, Goethe* (Penguin Books: London, 2006) p. 54.
2 Introduction to Johann Wolfgang von Goethe *The Sorrows of Young Werther* (Penguin Books: London, 1989) translated and introduction by Michael Hulse, p. 6.
3 Ibid. p. 7.
4 *Love, Life, Goethe* p. 57.
5 Michael Hulse, Introduction to *The Sorrows of Young Werther*, p. 12.
6 Johann Wolfgang von Goethe *The Sorrows of Young Werther* p. 74.
7 Ibid. p. 73.
8 Ibid. p. 77.
9 Ibid. p. 79.
10 Ibid. p. 82.
11 Ibid. p. 83.
12 Ibid. pp. 77–78.
13 *Love, Life, Goethe* p. 61
14 Ibid. p. 62.

The Surreal Suicide

Literary suicides seem to span all genres, including pulp, as the
suicide at age thirty of Robert E. Howard, the creator of
Conan, King Kull and other brawny sword and sorcery heroes
argues. (See the Suicidal Miscellany for Howard's poem
"Lines Written in the Realization that I Must Die"). But
one literary movement, Surrealism, even more than existentialism, seems to have attracted an inordinate number of
writers obsessed with self-destruction, individuals who either
wrote about suicide extensively, play-acted it, or, in more than
one example, went through with it. It can even be argued that
Surrealism itself was founded on a suicide, although once
again, there is some debate over whether the death in question
was really a suicide or not.

The term 'Surrealism' became part of our cultural vocabu-
lary in 1917, coined in Paris by the poet Guillaume Apollinaire
in the programme notes for Erik Satie's ballet *Parade*, which
featured choreography by Massine, a backdrop by Picasso, a
scenario by Jean Cocteau, and a performance by Serge
Diaghilev's Ballets Russes. The 'new alliance of the arts' that
Apollinaire celebrated in the notes was really not that new –
the idea of the *Gesamtkunstwerk*, or 'total art work', had been a
staple of Symbolist aesthetics decades before – but Satie's
score for typewriter, propellers, sirens, Morse code and other
forms of *musique concrete* prompted Apollinaire to call *Parade* a
work of 'Surrealism'.[1] What exactly he meant by this is
unclear; the general idea, however, is that in *Parade* art had
done life, or reality, one better ('sur' refers to a kind of addition, as in 'surplus' or 'surcharge'). Apollinaire had at first
considered adopting 'Supernaturalism' for this new trend in
art, but this term was already in use and had already acquired a
clutch of literary and philosophical interpretations which
would only have confused matters. Apollinaire's own stab at

defining the new term, Surrealism, is suggestive, but is hardly the stuff from which revolutions are made. "When man tried to imitate walking," he wrote, "he created the wheel, which does not resemble a leg. He thus performed an act of Surrealism without realizing it." New, creative and unusual at the time, 'surreal' has by now become a clichéd term used to indicate anything 'strange' or 'weird' and has really lost most of its true meaning, as is also the case with 'existential' and 'romantic'. Its once shocking images and unlikely juxtapositions are run of the mill, adorning everything from T-shirts to shopping bags, enjoying a ubiquity the Surrealists themselves once sought, without, however, triggering the profound transformation of life they hoped to achieve.

The name most associated with Surrealism, however, is not that of Apollinaire, but of his one-time protégé, the poet André Breton. Appropriating the term from his master, who seemed not to appreciate the marketing value of a good 'brand', Breton became its spokesman, promulgator, ideological leader and notorious 'Black Pope', ruthlessly excommunicating those who fell foul of his stringent aesthetic and political criteria. Yet although Breton became the name associated worldwide with Surrealism, the 'living face of Surrealism', at least for Breton himself, was that of a character who could barely be called a literary figure at all. In the *Second Manifesto of Surrealism*, Breton made a pronouncement that, for good or bad, has become one of the most quoted examples of what something 'surreal' would be like. "The simplest Surrealist act," Breton declared, "consists of dashing down into the street, pistol in hand, and firing blindly, as fast as you can pull the trigger, into the crowd"[2] – and with this in mind, one wonders if the proliferation of terrorism and 'motiveless murders' in the twenty-first century indicates the victory of Surrealism after all . . . For all his bellicose pamphleteering, however, Breton does not come across as a violent man, yet the trope of guns and suicide is something more than posture and rhetoric; at one Surrealist shindig, Breton wore a pair of pistols strapped to his head, and at the Dada festival of 1918, realizing they needed a real show-stopper to end their sketch

S'il Vous Plait, Breton and the poet Philippe Soupault (with whom Breton collaborated on the first work of 'automatic writing', *The Magnetic Fields*) decided to put their names in a hat, and which of the two was picked would close the show by blowing his brains out, a nod, perhaps, to Arthur Cravan's aborted public suicide a few years earlier.

Breton's fascination with guns and suicide can be traced to another early surrealist event, again involving Apollinaire. A few weeks after the success of *Parade*, Apollinaire's play *Les Mamelles de Tirésias* (The Tits of Tiresias) was performed at the Conservatoire Renée-Maubel, a tiny theatre on the Rue de l'Orient in Montmartre. The audience had to wait for hours for the play to begin, and were hardly in the best of moods, and once it had started their frustration only increased at what they saw on stage. Soon into it, a riot broke out, and the crowd, which included Matisse, George Braque, Modigliani, Ferdinand Leger, Cocteau, Breton and others of the Parisian avant-garde, were, as one witness put it, "howling wildly." During the intermission the ruckus became even worse, and Apollinaire himself mounted the stage to call for order. At this point Breton noticed a military officer in the front row, standing up and waving a pistol, evidently about to open fire on the mob. Realizing who the 'officer' was, Breton rushed to him, and prevented him from firing the gun; he even managed to calm him enough to sit down and watch the rest of the show, which, they later both admitted, was something of a disappointment. Tiresias' tits were not a big hit, but the evening was nevertheless crucial for Breton. "Never before, as I did on that evening," he later said in an interview, "had I measured the depth of the gap that would separate the new generation from the one preceding it . . ."[3] The figure that Breton had just prevented from carrying out an act of aesthetic homicide was very familiar to him. It was indeed his friend, Jacques Vaché, whom he had only recently met, yet who had, and would continue to have, an enormous influence on Breton and, through him, on twentieth century art and culture. "If ever someone's influence touched me to the core," Breton said of Vaché, "it was his."[4]

For us, inured to theatrical violence through years of performance art, the idea of someone pulling a gun on an audience is no longer shocking. Yet what is really strange – I was about to say 'surreal' – about the event is that no one else in the theatre that night seemed to have witnessed it. None of the dozens of reviews of the play made a mention of it. Vaché himself, who, it is true, was not a prolific writer – if a writer at all – never remarked on it in his letters to Breton. Two of Breton's biographers both suggest that the incident may have been invented, or at least that its importance may have been exaggerated by Breton.[5] Then again, perhaps, as Breton himself would argue, such an event needed the illuminating eye of a poet, for its true significance to come to light.

Breton and Vaché met in Nantes, Vaché's hometown, in February 1916, in the middle of World War I. Breton, who was twenty, was there serving as a medical auxiliary in the neurological centre; Vaché, twenty-one, was hospitalised with a wound to his calf. Breton was struck by Vaché's appearance, and in subsequent writings, described him in terms that, to today's sensibilities, suggest at least a touch of homoeroticism, although Breton's antipathy to homosexuality would later become legendary. Breton spoke of Vaché as "an elegant young soldier with flaming red hair," and admits that he was immediately captivated by his "studied arrogance and otherworldly detachment."[6] As Ruth Brandon points out, Vaché was everything Breton wasn't and yet yearned to be: "confident, cynical, stylish, where Breton was awkward, earnest, enthusiastic."[7] Enthusiasm in particular was something for which Vaché had nothing but disdain, and this pose of nihilistic dandyism fascinated Breton.

Vaché impressed Breton with his total indifference to practically everything, and his preoccupation with seemingly insignificant matters. Breton remarks on how Vaché, who was supposed to be an art student, would spend a morning while convalescing arranging objects on a small table, devoting considerable attention to the correct placement of photographs, flowers, paint pots and other items, in a kind of exercise in *feng shui*. Breton, who was devoted to poetry, spoke with Vaché of his interests and heroes, yet Vaché dismissed nearly all of them, except for the work of Alfred Jarry, the creator of *Ubu Roi* and other black comedies, with whom he shared some things in common.[8] Like Jarry, Vaché adopted the demeanour of the then stereotypical Englishman, perfectly dressed, sporting a cane and monocle, unruffled by anything; he even spoke with an English accent and claimed English descent (he did actually have Irish ancestry).[9] Also like Jarry, he had a penchant for adopting disguises and striking disconcerting poses. Vaché would sign himself Harry James or Jean-Michael Strogoff, a character from Jules Verne. He would dress as an airman, a hussar, or a doctor and walk down a crowded street. If he saw you, he wouldn't always acknowledge you, and might simply walk by, as if you were a stranger; when he was with you he would often leave abruptly, without a word: he never said hello or goodbye. He told Breton that he wanted to create a military uniform that would be mistaken by either side as one of their own. He would introduce Breton to others as the famous poet André Salmon, or by some other name, and once told Breton that his ambition was to "wear a red shirt, a red cravat and high boots – and to belong to a pointless Chinese secret society in Australia." Breton also noticed that this "bitterly light-hearted poseur,"[10] spent a great deal of time drawing sketches that looked like men's fashion illustrations.

Vaché's attitude toward women was equally bizarre. He professed no interest in them at all, except, perhaps, for "some mysterious, inscrutable little girls" who would nevertheless need to be killed off before they lost their charm. Vaché did live with a woman, Louise, and even shared a bed with her. But the relationship was platonic; Breton also noticed that when he visited Vaché, Louise was made to sit quietly, in a corner. The only attention Vaché showed her was to kiss her hand after she had made them tea. Vaché was apparently fond of Baudelaire's remark apropos women: "Woman is natural, in other words abominable." It doesn't take much to find in this at least a suspicion of homosexuality. Breton's own attitude toward women was as different as possible, nearly puritanical, seeing in them the embodiment of the poetic muse.

All this may sound like fairly tame material, familiar to fans of Monty Python and other forms of 'absurd' theatre. But for Breton it was a revelation. "The time I spent with him at Nantes in 1916," Breton wrote of Vaché, "seemed almost enchanted. I shall never forget it, and although I still meet people I am drawn to, I know I shall never abandon myself to anyone in quite that way again." Remarks like these suggest that Breton was simply in love with Vaché, whether they were actual lovers or not, which seems doubtful. Vaché seems to have had on Breton the effect that Neal Cassady had on Jack Kerouac, as documented in *On The Road*: both seemed to be characters that embodied the ideas and attitude toward life that both writers embraced. In Breton's case, his attraction to Vaché is reminiscent of Valery Briusov's predilection for 'ecstatic types' (see Agents of Suicide in A Taxonomy of Suicide), individuals of a freer, less inhibited character; like Briusov, Breton had a stern temperament, and was known for his 'totalitarian' personality. Opposites attract, and while for Breton Vaché's good fortune was to have produced nothing, the disciplined and determined Breton went on to erect a formidable apparatus of philosophical, literary and political ideas that influenced French culture for forty years.

Aside from Vaché's behaviour – which we could call 'subversive' or 'transgressive' or simply annoying – what impressed Breton most about him was his idea of 'umour', a notion of what Breton later called 'black humour' and which certainly has its roots in Jarry's *Ubu* plays, and which Breton gleaned through the letters he received from Vaché while they were separated during the war. The essence of 'umour', as Mark Polizzotti puts it, is in its "dismissive whatever"[11], an attitude today enjoyed by readers of Michel Houellebecq. Vaché's own attempt at a definition, while less succinct than Polizzotti's, is equally deadpan: umour for Vaché meant a recognition of "the theatrical (and joyless) futility of everything." At twenty-one, Vaché had seen through it all, and, like the Dadaists Breton was soon to encounter, he was prepared to accept nothing, trust no one, and ridicule everything. In this he was truly ahead of his time, and what was for Breton a manifestation of "joyful terrorism" (and not 'joyless', as Vaché characterized it) is today pretty much taken as read.

Yet even more than his umour or diverting antics, it was Vaché's death that had the most profound impact on Breton.

On 7 January 1919, *Le Télégramme des Provinces de l'Ouest* ran a headline that read "Two Youths Dabble with Drugs," and went on to report a "regrettable incident that brings tragedy to two of the most respected families in Nantes . . ."[12] One of those families was Vaché's, and the regrettable incident was the death of Jacques Vaché and a "Paul B." from an apparent overdose of opium.

At around 6:00 p.m., the article continued, an American soldier named Woynow had rushed from a second floor room at the Hotel de France in Nantes, demanding to see the manager. Two young men, his friends, he said, had died in the room. A physician was called and on entering the room he found two men lying stretched out on the bed, "undressed for sleep," which, later reports explained, meant naked. One of the bodies was cold – this was Paul Bonnet – the other, that of Vaché, was still warm. The doctor diagnosed an opium overdose and turned his attentions to the warm body, which he was nevertheless unable to revive. He then treated Woynow, who had by this time become ill with the drug as well. The police later found a small container filled with the narcotic, a knife bearing remnants of it, an opium pipe, and "innumerable Egyptian cigarette butts" near the bed. The report continued that Vaché and Paul Bonnet – as well as Woynow, we assume – belonged to a group of "French and American 'thrill-seekers' " who "frequented places of amusement," and had apparently killed themselves in pursuit of "the high that this terrible drug brings." A follow-up article asked, "Can't these hare-brained youths understand that, in their quest for certain unhealthy sensations, they shouldn't carelessly play around with a drug that stupefies even when it doesn't kill?" It also suggested that the facts surrounding the case indicate that they "could not have been experienced smokers."[13]

Vaché's death may very well have been the most profound emotional event to happen to Breton. He told the poet Jean Paulhan that it was "the most painful event of my life," and that ever after he had to wear a "suit of armour" against emotion.[14] To another friend he wrote, "I cannot express here the pain that the news of his death caused me, or the trouble I had getting over it."[15] All this is understandable, but what Breton made of the death became something of an obsession. Although on the face of it, Vaché and his friend had succumbed to an unfortunate but not uncommon misuse of the drug, Breton became convinced that the deaths were intentional, that Vaché planned his suicide – and also the apparent murder of one, and attempted murder of another, of his companions. It was, Breton maintained, the crowning display of umour.

Breton's 'evidence' for this reading of Vaché's death is indeed suggestive. He quotes a remark Vaché was said to have made only hours before his overdose: "I will die when I want to die . . . But I'll die with someone else. Dying alone is too boring. Preferably with one of my very best friends . . ."[16] If that was the case, then Vaché wasn't reluctant to engage in murder in the cause of umour, and he then joins the ranks of Harry Crosby, Heinrich von Kleist and Arthur Koestler, as a suicide who took others with him. In a letter to Breton's friend, Theodore Fraenkel, Vaché wrote of "some funny murders" he wanted to tell him about, and of his dream of performing "some good well-felt Eccentricities, or some amusing deception that would result in lots of deaths," although it has to be admitted that he thought of performing these "while wearing a very light athletic-style form-fitting costume . . . with wonderful open-topped canvas shoes."[17] (Then again, no clothes at all is pretty close to a "very light form-fitting costume" . . .) Vaché's penchant for the absurd non sequitur makes judging the cogency of these remarks difficult; yet his letters leading up to the time of his death do display a sense of crisis. While the war was on, Vaché could indulge his nihilism with some justification; now that it had ended (he died shortly after the armistice) he seemed to succumb to a sense of aimlessness: "You see, I don't know where I am any longer,"[18] he wrote to Breton from Brussels. Mention of suicide is made in the later letters, and there is a shrill anxiety in passages like "ART IS STUPIDITY – Almost nothing is stupid – art must be funny and a little tiresome . . . Everything is so funny, very funny, it's a fact – Everything is so funny! (and if we killed ourselves also, instead of merely going away?")[19] He was at the end of his rope, but he still looked forward to "the rather amusing things to do once I'm unchained and at liberty."[20] He had also told Breton that he didn't want to die in wartime – meaning that he didn't want his death to be as banal and uniform as those of thousands of other soldiers. He had to, as Nietzsche advised, "die at the right time," and although Vaché had little use for Apollinaire, the old master, he said, was at least "wise to stop in time," remarking on Apollinaire's death only a month earlier. Perhaps coming so soon after Apollinaire's death (two months separated them), Vaché's death *had* to be special for Breton – a conceit shared by many literary suicides. Yet, whether Vaché had achieved this or not, Breton was in no doubt; he was determined that the death of the man most important to him, whom he once described as "more beautiful than a reed pipe," *would* be special. His death was "admirable," Breton declared in one of the four essays he wrote introducing Vaché's letters, "in that it could pass for accidental."[21] And his unfortunate friends' ignorance of the power of the drug, allowed Vaché the opportunity to commit "one last 'humorous deception' at their expense." Again, if this was the case, then Breton is close to applauding his friend for committing murder.

Yet the evidence for an accidental overdose is just as suggestive. To begin with, as Mark Polizzotti points out, there were originally four men in the room with Vaché, not two, and at least one of them was homosexual (the two others left early, one not interested in drugs, the other because he felt ill after taking the opium; he later had his stomach pumped: along with smoking opium, they also ate it.) The newspaper article which reported that Vaché and Paul Bonnet were "undressed for sleep" cushions the fact that they were simply naked, early in the day, in an unheated room in January. When we remember Vaché's curious relationship with Louise, and the fact that he found only "young girls" – who often have boyish figures – attractive, we can be excused for wondering if sleep was the only thing on Vaché and Bonnet's mind – at the same time recognizing that opium is one of the least aphrodisiacal of drugs. And for all his dandified nihilism, there is scant evidence that Vaché was a particularly experienced opium user, as Breton had suggested. As for his intention to kill himself and a few close friends, Woynow, one of the elect group, denied that there was anything in Vaché's behaviour that day to indicate this, although of course Vaché was adept at concealing his intentions, if he had any, under one of his adopted personae. But if Vaché planned to take a close friend with him, did he really want to take four of them?

Most likely these questions will never be answered, although Breton's notorious intolerance of homosexuality, coupled with his clear love of Vaché, suggest that he suspected something more than umour went on in that cold hotel room in Nantes that fateful January day. Perhaps in reaction to this, Breton created the myth of Vaché as an *überdandy* to counteract what could only strike him as sordid banality.[22] That Vaché himself was uncomfortable with the significance Breton placed on him can perhaps be felt in his last letter, when Vaché, "What do you want of me – my dear friend? – UMOUR – my dear friend, André . . . this is no trivial matter," and when he seems to pass on the burden of drawing out whatever importance this might have to his "dear friend": "I'm depending on you to prepare the way for this deceptive God, sneering slightly and terrible in any case – You see, how funny it'll be if this NEW SPIRIT breaks loose."[23]

*

The new spirit did indeed break loose and, as may be expected, suicide was one of its concerns. In December 1924 the first issue of *La Révolution surréaliste* appeared, a journal edited by Pierre Naville and Benjamin Péret. Towards the beginning of the journal the editors had placed an announcement with an unusual intent.

Inquest

You live, you die. What has free will got to do with it? It seems you kill yourself in the same way as you dream. This is no moral problem we are posing.

IS SUICIDE A SOLUTION?

The editors invited their readers to respond, and may have expected some remarkable replies, in keeping with the character of the inquiry – although no one, it seems, asked the obvious question: a solution to what? But what they received was something else. The Symbolist poet Francis Jammes answered with a perhaps surprising indignation: "Only a wretch would ask such a question, and if some poor child were to kill him or herself, you would be the murderer." And, being a Catholic, Jammes added: "The only resource open to you, should you have the slightest conscience left, is to throw yourselves into a confessional." Breton's publisher, Léon Pierre-Quint, fared little better: "I can't think of a more absurd question." And Breton himself avoided any unequivocal response by citing the philosopher Théodore Jouffroy, who wrote that, "Suicide is a poor word; the one who kills is not identical to the one who is killed"[24] The one clearly positive reply came from a relatively recent addition to the surrealist ranks, René Crevel. "A solution?" Crevel asked. "Yes," he answered.

"It is said," Crevel continued, "that one commits suicide from love, fear or venereal disease. Not so. Everyone is in love, or thinks they are. Suicide is a matter of conscious choice. Those who commit suicide are the ones who are not imbued with the quasi-universal cowardice of fighting against a certain feeling in the soul which is of such intensity that it has to be taken, until it is proved otherwise, for the truth. This is the only sensation that allows a person to embrace a solution that is clearly the fairest and most definitive solution of all, suicide. There is no love or hate which is simply fair or definitive. But the respect – in spite of myself and notwithstanding a tyrannical moral or religious upbringing – which I am bound to show to anyone who does not timorously withhold or restrain that impulse, that moral impulse, leads me to envy more and more each of those persons whose anguish is so intense that they can no longer accept life's little games."

That Crevel believed, "Suicide is a matter of conscious choice" must have enamoured him to Breton, and throughout their relationship, which was full of contradictions and crises, and which ended with Crevel's own suicide at the age of thirty-five in 1935, Breton was something of a father figure for Crevel (who was only four years younger than Breton). That Crevel sought such figures and that the question of suicide was associated with them, is rooted in the gruesome circumstance of his own father's suicide, when Crevel was fourteen. His father, a music-publisher, hanged himself, and René's mother, an apparent sadist, intent on teaching the boy some lesson, forced him to look at the dangling body while she cursed it.[25] Understandably, Crevel loathed his mother thereafter. The rest of his life was punctuated by episodes of a similar traumatic character. In answer to a similar questionnaire posed by another avant-garde journal, *Le Disque vert* (edited by Henri Michaux and Franz Hellens), Crevel had written, "Is not the fear of suicide the best remedy against suicide?" Perhaps Crevel didn't fear it enough, or perhaps this is simply not true. Or perhaps Crevel was simply trying to bolster his own defences against something that he may have felt was inevitable, just as it is possible that his remark about suicides being free of the "quasi-universal cowardice" mistakenly associated with the taboo was a way of refuting the hysterical abuse his mother threw at the defenceless corpse of his father.

Crevel came to Breton's attention when it became known that he was an adept at the 'sleeping fits' that were for a time the centre of Surrealist attraction. With the poet Robert Desnos – with whom he vied for Breton's attentions – Crevel developed a strange facility for passing into a trance and producing the kind of 'stream of unconsciousness' verbiage that fascinated Breton, and which was the subject of his and Philippe Soupault's collaboration *The Magnetic Fields*. Crevel discovered his talent for producing the 'psychic automatisms' by which Breton later defined Surrealism while attending a séance. Sitting around the table holding hands, Crevel almost immediately nodded off and, as reported by the others, produced some remarkable statements, of which he later had no memory. When Crevel heard that Breton was exploring dreams and other altered states of consciousness, he told him of his experience. Breton was intrigued, and for a time Crevel and Desnos ran a sort of contest to see who could fall into trance quickest and produce the most fascinating material.

But poetic 'channelling' wasn't the only attraction Crevel had for Breton. Like Jacques Vaché, Crevel was handsome, a beautiful boy with an angelic face ringed with golden curls; Dali, with whom he also had a close relationship, described Crevel's looks as "the sullen, deaf, Beethovenesque, bad-angel face of a fern shoot."[26] Also like Vaché, and perhaps less attractive, Crevel was a drug user, more or less an addict, and bouts of heavy opium and cocaine use would alternate with periods of detoxification, a routine that hardly helped the tuberculosis he suffered from and which, just prior to his suicide, was diagnosed as incurable. Another trait he may have shared with Vaché was his homosexuality, which Breton could not have been ignorant of, but which Crevel, because of his devotion to Breton, was forced to hide as a kind of open secret. Crevel may really have been bisexual, as he did have relationships with women, but it's clear that, for the sake of his relationship with Breton, he *pretended* not to like men.

Crevel's sexual preference was enough to create inner conflict, given that his surrogate father abhorred it. But there were other contradictions. Crevel was a fervent Marxist and a believer in the proletarian revolution – as many middle-class people were – yet, like Jean Cocteau (another opium user), he was a darling of high society, and enjoyed rubbing elbows with the rich and famous. He was also the author of novels, a literary form that Breton in particular loathed. His political beliefs finally led him to reject the Surrealists, but his devotion to Breton, and his attempts to reconcile it with his commitment to the revolution, was in the end what killed him.

Although Breton had embraced the revolution and, like other avant-garde poets – Mayakovsky, for example, about whom we will have more to say later on – he had seen his work as a means of effecting political change, he grew disenchanted with the communists and by the early Thirties, was an outspoken critic of Stalin and the show trials. Crevel had joined the French Communist Party in 1927, but, as with the rest of his life, his relations with it fluctuated. In 1933 he, along with Breton and the other Surrealists, was expelled from the party and from the Association of Revolutionary Writers and Artists, a group that participated in agit-prop activities more or less sanctioned by the communists. For all their dedication to 'the revolution', most of the politicos exhibited rather bourgeois tastes and found Surrealism too strange and subversive for their liking. Crevel had also published a novel, *Les Pieds dans le plat* ("Putting My Foot In It"), in which he made blatant reference to his, and others, homosexuality, a candour unwelcome among the Stalinists, who were as bourgeois in their ideas about sex as they were in those about art. Breton remained adamantly beyond the pale, but Crevel managed to get readmitted to the party the next year.

Although emotionally loyal to Breton, Crevel disagreed with him politically; he had also disagreed with the tribunal Breton subjected Dali to over his unseemly glorification of Hitler, whom, Dali insisted, should be considered surrealistically, and whom he referred to as the "edible-paranoid great man," whose "soft eyes" and "curvaceous fanny" were "possessed of an irresistible poetic charm."[27] (Dali's politics, at the best of times madcap, did turn toward fascism and he ended up a devout Francoist.) By this time Crevel had also realized that, given the increasing fascist threat, his most immediate loyalty must be to the communists, who seemed to form the only real opposition to Hitler, Dali's appreciation of him notwithstanding. Yet although he withdrew from most Surrealist activities, he was loathe to let Breton go – if only to avoid suffering the fate of those who had gotten into the Black

Pope's bad books – and he lobbied hard for Breton to take part in the Congress of Writers in Defence of Culture organized by the party, to be held in Paris in June 1935. Crevel seemed to be making some headway, but, ironically, because of a chance event – something Breton prized highly – Crevel's efforts in the end were practically useless.

Shortly before the Congress, Breton, his second wife Jacqueline Lamba, Benjamin Péret and some members of the Czech Surrealist group were out one evening, when one of the Czechs saw the Soviet critic Ilya Ehrenburg leaving a café. Breton had never met Ehrenburg, although he was well known in Paris, but a year before Breton was enraged by a pamphlet Ehrenburg had written, denouncing Surrealism and the Surrealists as 'pederasts' and 'dreamers' among other things and singling out Breton in particular. The Czechs pointed Ehrenburg out, and Breton went up to him and introduced himself by announcing that he had a bone to pick with him. Ehrenburg feigned not to know the name 'André Breton', and, to refresh his memory, Breton slapped him in the face, each time repeating one of the epithets from his pamphlet: "André Breton the pederast" (slap) "André Breton the dreamer" (slap), and so on. Then it was Péret's turn. Ehrenburg merely covered his face with his hands and said, "You'll be sorry for that." He then promptly reported the incident to his superiors and the idea of a Surrealist speaking at the Congress – which would include major players like Gide, Thomas Mann, Robert Musil, Malraux, E. M. Forster, Brecht, Aldous Huxley among others – became a non-issue.

Crevel was not ready to give up and he spent the forty-eight hours before the Congress trying to get the party to change its mind, and trying to get Breton to make a conciliatory gesture. Neither injured party was ready to budge, and in a last chance effort, Crevel addressed a committee meeting. Ehrenburg merely remarked that Breton had "acted like a cop," and that seemed enough: none of the Parisians wished to alienate the Russians, and were Breton allowed to speak, Ehrenburg assured them the Soviets would boycott the Congress, which was unthinkable.[28] Crevel was humiliated. He then went home, swallowed a massive dose of sedatives, turned on the stove and gassed himself.

In looking for a trigger for Crevel's suicide, we have several candidates: his failure to dissuade the communists to relent or to persuade Breton to apologize; his inability to reconcile his love for the Black Pope with his rejection of his politics; his repeated drug addictions; his homosexuality; the fact that on the day he committed suicide he had discovered that his tuberculosis, which he believed had been cured, had in actuality gotten worse and was spreading; his recent pitiful performance lecturing to workers who he realized saw him as "just a rich kid with problems, slumming;"[29] or, underlining all the rest, what must have been the gruesomely traumatic memory of his father's death. Dali, who was a close friend, hearing about the Congress debacle, realized Crevel needed some support, and telephoned him, only to receive what must have seemed like a particularly surreal answer: an unfamiliar voice advised him to get a taxi and come at once, as Crevel was dying. When Dali arrived, he found a fire engine parked in front of Crevel's building, and firemen in his flat. "With the gluttony of a nursing baby," Dali wrote, "René was sucking oxygen. I never saw anyone cling so desperately to life."[30] His attachment to it, sadly, was brief; he died in hospital that evening. Crevel's note, tied to his wrist, speaks of his self-hatred. It read, "René Crevel. Please cremate me. Disgust."[31]

Although Crevel had called suicide a matter of "conscious choice," it isn't difficult to see that his was the product of an inordinate number of personal crises, compounded by desperation and a sense of personal failure. Even Breton, who had been accused in print of practically murdering Crevel by one of René's Catholic friends, understood this, and in his defence spelled out the probable reasons, listed above, for Crevel's death. Six years earlier, however, another young Surrealist who had taken his own life seemed to meet the Vaché standard with greater accuracy. According to Tristan Tzara, Jacques Rigaut committed suicide "after having exhausted all the reasons for living a man can offer himself."[32] For Breton, Rigaut had "sentenced himself to death at about the age of twenty and waited impatiently for ten years, ticking off the hours, for exactly the right moment to put an end to his existence. It was, in any case, a fascinating human experience, to which he knew just how to give that peculiar tragic–comic twist which was unique to himself."[33] One doesn't want to deny Breton his insight into his friends' lives and deaths, but it is interesting how often they seem to coincide with his own personal mythology.

Jacques Rigaut resembles Vaché in another way: his literary remains are very slim, and what there are of them display an obsessive preoccupation with suicide. This was something that was more or less applauded by those of his friends who enjoyed a greater literary girth. For Paul Eluard, "The weapon aimed at life by the suicide is always right. No rubble nor ruins shall be left standing after the will which burns and destroys everything has passed by. But such an act leaves the strength of whoever has committed it intact. The regret at having been born and the need to die vanish with the world they have killed." For Breton, "Jacques Rigaut . . . slips a revolver under his pillow every evening. Such is his way of expressing agreement with the generally held opinion that the night will give you council, and of hoping to dispose of the malefactors within, in other words all conventional means of adaptation." Yet for the successful portrait painter Jacques-Emile Blanche, for whom Rigaut worked as a secretary, and who seemed to understand him better than his younger friends, "Theoretic suicide, which was already all the fashion, and which was to become one of the *leitmotifs* of Surrealism, had left its funeral mark on him, even to his affectation of 'accepting' a life of the most conventional and futile sort."[34] He was also for Blanche, "one of those wayward sons for whom a mother, a father, his sisters are everyday led to fear the worst."[35]

Like Vaché, Rigaut's contribution to Dada, and later to Surrealism, was his "total world weariness and cynical humour,"[36] a qualification that, however, could be applied to practically all of his compatriots. He once told Jacques-Émile Blanche that during the war he had "no feeling whatsoever as he saw his dearest comrade drop at his side," displaying a predilection for 'umour that no doubt would have met with Vaché's approval. But to the more perceptive, Rigaut's "haughty attitude," which was "quite in fashion at the time in Dada circles," was merely "the absurd braggadocio of a mild and timid being."[37] Yet this mild and timid being was obsessed with his own death.

Although at times Rigaut's take on suicide was equivocal – "There are no reasons for living, but there are also no reasons for dying either," he wrote, "Life is not worth the trouble of departing from it"[38] – these hesitations are perhaps the somewhat mandatory expressions of a truly total world-weariness, weary even of itself. But on the whole, suicide was something he identified with deeply. "As long as I cannot overcome my taste for pleasure, I well know that I shall be susceptible to the intoxication of suicide."[39] "Try, if you can, to arrest a man who travels with suicide in his buttonhole."[40] "Suicide should be a vocation."[41] In a sketch published many years after his death, "The General Suicide Agency," Rigaut is "pleased to announce to its clients that it can now GUARANTEE THEM AN INSTANTANEOUS DEATH," a claim that promises to be attractive to those who put off killing themselves "for fear of making a mess,"[42] and an idea that Robert Louis Stevenson employed some years earlier (see "The Suicide Club" in A Suicidal Miscellany). In an untitled piece, Rigaut informs us that "The first time I killed myself it was to annoy my mistress." The second time, he tells us, it was from laziness. And third time,

I had just gone to bed after an evening on which my boredom had been no more overwhelming than any other night. I took the decision and, at the same time, I clearly remember that I articulated the sole reason. Then, drat! I got up to go and look for the only weapon in the house, a little revolver that one of my grandfathers had bought and which was loaded with bullets from the same epoch . . . Lying down naked on my bed, I was naked in the room. It was cold. [Shades of Vaché!] I hurriedly buried myself under the blankets. I cocked the hammer,

I could feel the cold of the steel in my mouth. At that moment I could probably feel my heart beating, just as I could feel it beating as I listened to the whistle of a shell before it exploded, as if in the presence of something irrevocable but still unconsummated. I pressed the trigger, the hammer clicked, but the shot didn't fire. I then laid the weapon on a small table . . . Ten minutes later I was asleep . . . It goes without saying that I did not for an instant consider firing a second shot.[43]

Rigaut concludes by saying that, "The important thing was not whether I died or not but that I had taken the decision to die." It was a decision the fulfilment of which came a decade later, although one wonders if at this point he had already begun the habit of making his decisions based on a throw of dice, a motif that would later be put to successful use by Luke Rhinehart, in his novel *The Dice Man*. In the meantime, Rigaut engaged in what was increasingly the surreal norm. After WWI, he worked, as mentioned, as a secretary for Jacques-Émile Blanche. Then in 1924 he met a rich American divorcee – like Crevel, he had an entrée into the world of money – and when she returned to New York, he followed her. They married, but it was not a success, and a year later they separated. Rigaut remained in New York where he lived in poverty and became addicted to alcohol and drugs, mostly heroin, again like Crevel. In 1928 he returned to France, where he admitted himself to several detoxification clinics, hoping to kick his habit, but with little luck. We don't know whether he threw his dice or not, but on November 5, 1929, he finally came around to firing that second shot, that he put on hold ten years earlier. In a clinic at Châtenay-Malabry, "after paying minute attention to his toilette, and carrying out all the necessary external adjustments demanded of such a departure"[44] (again the similarity to Vaché is striking), Rigaut placed a rubber sheet under his body, lined up the trajectory of the bullet with a ruler, and, using a pillow to muffle the sound, shot himself through the heart.

Rigaut's "affectation" of a "most conventional life," which

included doing his best not to leave a mess or to disturb his fellow patients, must rank as one of the most considerate suicides on record, perhaps topped only by the German-Jewish writer Egon Friedell who, facing arrest and deportation to a death camp, chose instead to throw himself out of a window, calling to the people below to "watch out." Friedell belongs to the Political Suicides. They may or may not have been a polite bunch, but as we will see in the next section, he was sadly not alone.

Notes

1 Satie's score, considered revolutionary at the time, owes much to an earlier and sadly little-known pioneer in the art of 'noise composition', the Symbolist and Futurist painter and 'noisician' Luigi Russolo. See my article "Ready to Rumble: Luigi Russolo and The Art of Noise" in the December 2003 issue of *Wire*.

2 André Breton *Manifestoes of Surrealism* (University of Michigan Press: Ann Arbor, 1974) p.125. Breton was, to be sure, not the only surrealist who indulged in visions of violence. Salvador Dali once remarked, apropos of an anarchist bomb planted in a first class carriage of a train, that planting it in a third class one would have made a greater scandal. He went on to declare that, aside from its political and surreal value, blowing up the poor was a form of sexual perversion for him, providing "erection, irresistible masturbatory desires, [and] splendid wet dreams." Quoted in Ruth Brandon *Surreal Live: The Surrealists* (Macmillan: London, 1999) p. 395.

3 André Breton *Conversations: The Autobiography of Surrealism* (Paragon House: New York, 1993) p. 19.

4 Ibid. p. 17.

5 Mark Polizzotti *Revolution of The Mind: The Life of André Breton* (Bloomsbury: London, 1995) p. 61; Ruth Braddon *Surreal Lives: The Surrealists* (Macmillan: London, 1999) p. 11.

6 Mark Polizzotti, p. 38.

7 Ruth Brandon, p. 28.

8 The other literary figure that Vaché had something good to say about was, oddly enough, André Gide, whose *Les Caves du Vatican* was a favourite among the proto-surrealists. Gide's hero, Lafcadio, is given to what Gide calls 'gratuitous acts,' such as murdering a stranger on a train for no apparent reason, what we today would

call a 'motiveless' killing. Lafcadio's 'gratuitous acts' share much with the behaviour of Dostoyevsky's Stavrogin, whose penchant for performing 'unnecessary' acts of evil included rape and near murder. Although Gide maintained that Lafcadio was pure invention, Jean Cocteau claimed that the character was based on the boxing Dadaist Arthur Cravan. Vaché, Cravan and Stavrogin are, of course, all examples of the literary suicide. For an interesting treatment of the 'gratuitous act' and its relation to the 'motiveless crime', see "The Passive Fallacy" in Colin Wilson *Order of Assassins* (Panther: St. Albans, 1975).

9 The attraction that the image of the perfectly dressed, restrained Englishman had on the early avant-garde warrants a study; along with Vaché and Jarry, the Portuguese poet Fernando Pessoa also sported a bowler and other 'perfectly English' attire.

10 Ruth Brandon, p. 27.

11 Mark Polizzotti, introduction to André Breton *Anthology of Black Humour* (City Lights: San Francisco, 1999). p.v.

12 Jacques Vaché and André Breton *War Letters* (Atlas Press: London, 1993) p. 56.

13 Ibid. pp. 57–58.

14 Quoted in Polizzotti p. 87.

15 Ibid.

16 Breton, *Anthology of Black Humour* p. 294.

17 Vaché *War Letters* p. 50.

18 Ibid. p. 54.

19 Ibid. pp. 48–49

20 Ibid. p. 53.

21 Ibid. p. 20.

22 At one of the many and interminable meetings of the Surrealist group chaired by Breton, in which sex was the topic of discussion, he once threatened to walk out if Man Ray, Louis Aragon and Raymond Queneau persisted in their "promotion of homosexuality. "I am absolutely opposed to continuing the discussion of this subject . . ." Quoted in José Pierre ed. *Investigating Sex: Surrealist Discussions* (Verso: London, 1992).

23 Vaché *War Letters* p. 54.

24 *4 Dada Suicides* (Atlas Press: London, 1995) p. 7; Mark Polizzotti *Revolution of the Mind* p. 227. Jouffroy, incidentally, is associated with the philosopher William James' own retreat from suicide and his recovery from what we are forced to call 'depression'. During a period of deep existential despair – brought on by

his acknowledgement of the ostensible scientific 'fact' of determinism – in which James likened himself to a catatonic patient he treated in a mental asylum, he pulled himself back from the brink of suicide through reading Jouffroy, whose 'proof' of free will – the fact that he could think of one thing rather than another – was sufficient encouragement for James to fight back. "My first act of free will," James declared, "would be to believe in free will."

25 There is some suspicion that the suicide was prompted by his involvement in "some homosexual scandal." See Edouard Roditi's introduction to Crevel's novel *Putting My Foot in It* (Dalkey Archive Press: Illinois, 1992.) p. xx.

26 Salvador Dali, preface to René Crevel *Difficult Death* (North Point Press: San Francisco, 1986). P. ix.

27 Ibid. p. xii.

28 In the end Paul Eluard was allowed to read Breton's address, but after midnight, after practically all the attendees had left, and in the dark.

29 Ibid. p.xxv.

30 Ibid. p. xiii.

31 Even in death, Crevel sparked a Surrealist event. Word had got around that, against his wishes, his parents were to ensure that he received a proper Catholic burial. Breton and Co. gathered at the cemetery, intent on disrupting the proceedings. But in the end their vigil was unnecessary, as the parish priest made clear that the church does not bury suicides.

32 Quoted in Terry Hale, introduction to Jacques Rigaut *Lord Patchogue & Other Texts* (Atlas Press: London, 1993) p. 7.

33 Ibid. p. 8.

34 Ibid. p. 6.

35 From Jacques-Émile Blanche *A Young Man of the Century* quoted in *4 Dada Suicides* p. 124.

36 Ibid. p. 8.

37 *4 Dada Suicides* p. 124–126

38 Ibid. p. 120.

39 Ibid. p. 122.

40 *Lord Patchogue & Other Texts* p. 51.

41 Ibid. p. 58.

42 *4 Dada Suicides* p. 97.

43 Ibid. pp. 122–123.

44 André Breton *Anthology of Black Humour* p. 310.

The Political Suicide

"In a situation with no escape, I have no other choice but to finish it all. It is in a tiny village in the Pyrenees, where no one knows me, that my life must come to its end. I would ask you to pass on my thoughts to my friend Adorno and to explain to him the situation in which I have found myself. I no longer have enough time to write all those letters I would dearly have written."[1]

Such are the last words reportedly written by the German-Jewish literary critic and philosopher of culture Walter Benjamin. Benjamin had penned them in Port Bou, Spain, on the evening of 25 September 1940, presumably after he had swallowed the overdose of morphine that, by the next day, would kill him. The note was intended for Henny Gurland, later the second wife of the psychologist Erich Fromm; with her son Joseph, Benjamin, and a guide, Gurland was trying to escape the Nazis by fleeing France, crossing the Pyrenees into Spain, and reaching Lisbon, where they could board a ship for the United States.[2] The "friend Adorno" is the neo–Marxist philosopher Theodore Adorno who, with hindsight, had the good sense to escape Europe before the tide of barbarism provided by Hitler and his henchmen made that impossible. Benjamin too, had many chances to escape before fate led him to the small Catalan village on the Mediterranean coast, just south of the French-Spanish border, where he took his life. Yet, although friends and associates urged him to leave, Benjamin maintained his position as "the last European," assuring them that he was, "Like one who keeps afloat on a shipwreck by climbing to the top of a mast that is already crumbling. But from there he has a chance to give a signal leading to his rescue."[3]

The recipient of this remark, the Kabbalist scholar Gershom Scholem, Benjamin's friend since 1915, had taken leave of what would become a very dark continent years before, and he repeatedly urged Benjamin to join him in Palestine. But Benjamin was never one to decide things quickly – he would, Scholem said, take forever to make a move in chess, exhibiting a "reckless indecision rooted in chronic depression"[4] – and one wonders if sheer vacillation was as much an influence on his reluctance to leave as was his determination to see things out to the end. Another possibility, one rarely voiced (as, since his 'discovery' in the 1960s, Benjamin has become a major intellectual cult figure for the Left), is that his personality had a very strong self-destructive streak, as well as more than a touch of narcissism. While the Europe around him sank into cruelty and madness, Benjamin may have enjoyed his status as a last, lingering agent of reason and humanity.

There was, too, in Benjamin an appreciation of the apocalyptic. Although cloaked in Marxist rhetoric, Benjamin's philosophy was essentially religious, as Scholem would ceaselessly argue *contra* Adorno and Brecht (another of Benjamin's friends), and his vision of history was messianic; he seemed to be awaiting some final, conclusive event, whether revolutionary or theological, which would restore the fallen world to paradise. In an essay on "The Destructive Character," which, for all his obsessive mandarin courtesy and tact[5], can apply to Benjamin himself, he says that such a temperament "knows only one watchword: make room; only one activity: clearing away."[6] Benjamin was a reader of the anarchist philosopher George Sorrell and, like the Surrealists, had a penchant for violence. In torturously reasoned essays like "Critique of Violence" and his "Theologico-Political Fragment," Benjamin leads the reader to see the need for the "violence of divine intervention" and the necessity for "sudden eschatological change."[7] Eruptions, cataclysms, disasters fascinated Benjamin, and he liked to imagine himself as a sole surveyor, walking amidst their ruins; "solitude," he once said, "appeared to me as the only fit state of man."

In one of his most frequently quoted essays, "Theses on the Philosophy of History," Benjamin describes history not as "a chain of events," but as "a single catastrophe which keeps piling wreckage upon wreckage."[8] Looking at Benjamin's life, it's tempting to turn the metaphor on its author, and to see his choice of suicide as a final surrender to his inherent millenarian personality. As his biographer Momme Brodersen remarked, "The temptation to 'solve' all his existential problems in one go by suicide had followed Benjamin throughout his life."[9] How such a melancholy temperament, "born under the sign of Saturn, the star of slowest revolution, the planet of detours and delays . . ." could align itself, however equivocally, with as superficial and shallowly optimistic a creed as Marxism, is only one of the many ironies in his short life.

Benjamin's flight from the Nazis, his doomed last days and suicide, have by now passed into the realm of myth. In 1968, during the brief explosion of the student revolutions, the Institute for German Studies in Frankfurt was renamed temporarily the Walter Benjamin Institute, in honour of the posthumous hero of the New Left. In 1994, the Israeli artist Dani Karavans unveiled his memorial to Benjamin, "Passages," an eerie flight of steps leading nowhere, cut into the stone of the cliff overlooking the Mediterranean near the cemetery where Benjamin is believed to be buried, although exactly where his grave is remains unknown.[10] More recently, Benjamin's last days have been fictionalised in Jay Parini's moving novel *Benjamin's Crossing*, in which the author takes poetic liberty and suggests that it was not the threat of arrest and the dead end of a concentration camp that killed Benjamin; rather, "It was the world itself. He could no longer attach himself willingly to its bleak trajectory."[11]

Although during his lifetime Benjamin published few books and was virtually unknown – the bulk of his work appearing in newspapers and journals – and his great opus the 'Arcades Project' remained unfinished, perhaps unfinishable, today practically everything he wrote has been preserved between two covers, and most of this has been translated into other languages. A virtual 'Benjamin industry' has grown up around his writings, producing hundreds of texts, most of them as obscure and esoteric as the original. Even the image of

Benjamin – metal rim glasses, tousled hair, bushy moustache, hand at pensive chin sporting a cigarette – has appeared on T-shirts and other popular paraphernalia. (The fact that, among other things, he wrote about hashish and popular culture has helped spread his reputation to readers not usually given to messianic neo-Marxist critiques of late-capitalism.) Yet, while much of Benjamin's work still remains somewhat impenetrable for the general reader, many of his more immediately available pronouncements on culture and society have not fared well against the facts. In perhaps his most well known essay, "The Work of Art in the Age of Mechanical Reproduction," Benjamin argued that technology – in his day the cinema and radio – would be put to use in the service of the 'revolution', dissipating the elitist 'aura' surrounding works of art, and allowing the masses a hitherto denied access to culture. Admittedly it was an idea shared by other radical thinkers of the time, but one wonders how Benjamin would view the ubiquitous I-pod or tally up the revolutionary potential of *Big Brother*? Aldous Huxley, whom Benjamin quotes in the notes to his essay as an example of a 'non-progressive' attitude toward the technological advances in popular culture, seems, in *Brave New World* and elsewhere, to have hit the nail on the head, perhaps heavy-handedly but certainly more accurately than Benjamin and the other 'radicals' who envisioned the 'masses' 'liberated' by 'mechanical reproduction'. As mentioned in the preceding chapter, the 'revolutionary' power of Surrealism added up to a glut of by now barely noticeable images crowding postcard racks and poster shops, and the only liberation enjoyed by the masses seems to be the freedom to purchase them.[12]

It is perhaps a churlish thought, but one further wonders how pervasive 'Benjaminmania' would be if its subject had taken the repeated advice of friends and left his "crumbling mast" while he still had a chance and not continued on to an end that those closest to him, like Scholem, believed he was heading toward well in advance of Port Bou? I have read and continue to read Benjamin with much profit and sympathise with his plight, but there is something annoying about a man who refuses to leave a burning building, and at each suggestion to do so replies, "Yes, in a few minutes, after I finish this paragraph . . ."[13] Whatever the intrinsic value of his work, and of course this is substantial, the cachet of being a martyr to the cause of radical politics, critical thinking, modernity and 'otherness' – the sacrificial victim of an unequivocal fascism – cannot have hurt the cult that has mushroomed around Benjamin since his death. As Peter Demetz ironically remarks, "for the last seven years of his life, Walter Benjamin was condemned to a way of life closely resembling that of the émigré extras in Rick's Café in *Casablanca* . . ."[14] Romantic to us, perhaps, but it must have been hell for Benjamin.

Although Benjamin was not the only German writer to be led to suicide by the triumph of Nazism – Stefan Zweig and Klaus Mann are among some of the others – his death has become something of an archetype of the political literary suicide. The facts of his death seem to be the following. When it became clear even to Benjamin that he could no longer remain in France – having exiled himself there from Germany when the Nazis came to power – he decided to try to reach Lisbon where he would be able to use exit visas for the United States provided by Max Horkheimer, Adorno's colleague at the Institute for Social Research, which had relocated from Frankfurt to New York, and from whom Benjamin had been receiving a barely liveable monthly stipend. Benjamin had already endured being corralled with other German refugees at the Stade Colombe in Paris in September 1939, when Germany invaded Poland, and England and France declared war on the Third Reich. Although like most other refugees Benjamin was unambiguously anti-Nazi, the French authorities made no such distinctions, and announced that all Germans, Austrians, Czechs, Slovaks and Hungarians between the ages of 17 and 50 were to be interned as potential 'enemies of France'[15].

Along with the thousands of others who crowded into the football stadium, Benjamin lived for ten days in appalling conditions, sleeping on straw without blankets, eating nothing but cheap liver paté, with no facilities for washing or bathing.

He was then sent to an internment camp at Nevers, a small town on the route between Paris and Lyon. The French, who were themselves taken by surprise by the sudden turn of events, made little or no provisions for their prisoners, and Benjamin, who was inordinately impractical (he blamed his mother for his "inability even today to make a cup of coffee")[16] had to fend for himself. He had the rare good fortune, however, of meeting a young man who was a reader of his work, and who gladly took on the task of taking care of the older writer (although only 47, Benjamin had the appearance and deportment of someone much older) and becoming, more or less, his servant (even in prison, Benjamin retained the habits of his upper middle-class background). He was finally released from the camp after more than a month through the efforts of the French PEN Club.

Back in Paris, the reality of the situation finally hit Benjamin; yet he tried to continue work on his interminable 'Arcades Project', a practically indefinable study of the philosophical, social and historical significance of the Paris arcades (a similar work today might have the shopping mall as its focus). Although there is some controversy about this, it's believed that the bulky suitcase Benjamin lugged with him from Paris to the Pyrenées contained a manuscript of his gigantic fragment, and he's said to have told his companions that it was more important that the suitcase got to America than that he did.[17] After Benjamin's death, the suitcase was confiscated by the police; its contents were later scattered or destroyed. What exactly the manuscript he carried in it was, remains unknown.

When Hitler's army crossed the border and headed toward Paris, the city emptied, its fleeing inhabitants adding to the millions who were already heading south from Belgium and northern France. Overweight, inept, exhausted, and unhealthy (he suffered from a heart complaint), Benjamin joined the mass exodus. Before marching south, Benjamin managed to put the bulk of his papers in safekeeping, giving a collection of notes for the 'Arcades Project' to the renegade Surrealist Georges Bataille, who hid them in the Bibliothèque Nationale, where he worked as a librarian. What he couldn't take with him was confiscated by the Gestapo when they raided his flat. At Lourdes he waited throughout the summer for the entry permit to the United States; then, in late August, he went to Marseilles to collect the emergency visa Horkheimer had arranged for him. Not surprisingly, Benjamin couldn't gather all the papers he needed to leave France legally, and he uncharacteristically quickly decided to cross the border into Spain without them. It was a wise decision: Pétain's government soon agreed to hand over all emigrants found in Vichy France to the Nazis as well.

At first light on 26 September 1940, Lisa Fittko, a guide not entirely familiar with the terrain, set out from Banylus-sur-Mer with Henny Gurland and her son, to cross the mountains into Spain. The previous day Benjamin had taken part in a hiking tour; when the rest of the group returned, he stayed behind, spending the night in the open air on the mountain. That morning the others collected him, and together they headed toward the village of Port Bou. Although Benjamin's health required frequent stops, the journey went smoothly, and the route the group took had recently been taken by Heinrich Mann, his wife, Alma Mahler and Franz Werfel. (One wonders if today it's marked as the 'escaping intellectuals' hiking trail?) By the afternoon they reached their goal, and from Port Bou they hoped to journey to Lisbon by train, and from there to New York.

But bad luck – something that Hannah Arendt claimed "was very prominent in Benjamin's life" [18] – was waiting for "the last European." On announcing themselves to the Spanish police, the group were told that the transit visas which until then were valid, were no longer so, having been made null and void overnight. All refugees from France, they were informed, were to be sent back. Benjamin knew what this meant and not surprisingly he decided to forego the pleasure. Benjamin had written that, "The destructive character lives from the feeling, not that life is worth living, but that suicide is not worth the trouble," [19] a sentiment echoed by many throughout this book. On that afternoon, after a long, exhausting and apparently fruitless journey to freedom, he seemed to decide it was worth the trouble after all. That night Benjamin is thought to have swallowed an overdose of morphine tablets, a supply of which he had carried with him for many years. He had in fact given Arthur Koestler, who himself was on the run, some of his stash when they met in Marseilles, just before Benjamin's last journey. (Koestler was Benjamin's neighbour in Paris, and the two were members of a weekly poker group – Benjamin had a weakness for gambling. Benjamin asked Koestler if he "had anything to take" in case "things went wrong;" when Koestler said he hadn't, Benjamin gave him half of his own supply; Koestler remarks that Benjamin did this reluctantly, unsure if what was left would do the trick.)[20]

It's unclear whether the morphine alone killed Benjamin, or whether his death was a result of the combination of exertion, the effects of the drugs, and his weak heart. Or again, whether he actually took the drug at all. Or, yet again, whether what he took was morphine or some generic sedative. The exact time, too, of his death is also uncertain. What is known is that the next day, when the police came to escort Benjamin and the others to the French border, they discovered that he was dead. In a cruel display of irony, the police then decided to forget the new regulations, and allowed Henny Gurland and her son to carry on with their journey. It may have been that their orders had again been changed, or perhaps they were mistaken about them in the first place. Again, as has been suggested, the shock of Benjamin's death may have moved the guards and they may have allowed his companions to go because of this. If this was the case, and if Benjamin did commit suicide, then his death is a rare example of something good emerging from someone's self-destruction.

That the myth that has grown up around Benjamin's death may be rooted in muddle and sheer bad luck is possible, as apparently a great deal in his life was. Yet Gershom Scholem had no doubts that his long time friend had taken his life. Suicide was not something foreign to him. At the outbreak of WWI, Benjamin's closest friend, the poet Fritz Heinle, and his fiancée Rika Seligson, gassed themselves. Fritz's brother, Wolf, decided to follow suit, and, as Momme Brodersen explains, neither Benjamin nor any of his friends felt compelled to prevent him. As with Jacques Vaché, the war had provoked a kind of violent nihilism in Benjamin's peers: "Those close to [Wolf] had adopted the same gesture, the same smile (of being over and above everything) and the same physical movements as he."[21] Scholem gives additional evidence that suicide was an option open to Benjamin, whether he was escaping from the Nazis or not. Diaries from 1931 show that Benjamin was not only a destructive, but a self-destructive character. Scholem speaks of Benjamin's "increasing readiness to take his own life." "This was probably due [. . .] to his 'general battle fatigue on the economic front' and his feeling that basically he had lived his life in the fulfilment of his greatest desires."[22] A later diary of the same year was dated "from the seventh of August nineteen hundred and thirty-one to the day of death," and began, "This diary does not promise to be long."[23]

Although both the general social and political situation, as well as Benjamin's own personal economic prospects, were bleak (throughout his career as a writer, Benjamin pretty much lived in poverty), another factor, not mentioned in other accounts, may have been in play. By this time Benjamin had read with great interest Hesse's *Steppenwolf* – indeed, his experiments with hashish were prompted by the drug experiences depicted in the book – and the idea of suicide, latent in Benjamin, may have been stimulated by the novel.[24] A year later, in 1932, in Nice, Benjamin again considered suicide, this time occasioned by his fortieth birthday; he made elaborate plans to carry it out, and wrote letters of farewell, but then suddenly abandoned the idea. On yet another occasion he wrote to Scholem, telling him of an evening he spent, drinking a glass of wine, waiting for a guest to join him. The 'guest', Scholem surmised, was death. Summing up Benjamin's situation, Scholem wrote: "After all I have told here it is evident that Walter repeatedly reckoned with the possibility of his suicide and prepared for it. He was convinced that another war would mean a gas war and bring with it the end of civilization. Thus what finally happened after he crossed the Spanish border was not a surprising irrational act but something he had prepared inwardly for. Despite all the astonishing patience he displayed in the years after 1933 [. . .] he was not tough enough for the events of 1940."[25]

★

Mention of Benjamin's fear of "gas war" which would "bring with it the end of civilization," reminds us of another literary suicide who "was not tough enough for the events of 1940," although his own death anticipated Benjamin's by a year. Stanisław Ignacy Witkiewicz – otherwise known as Witkacy, a name he took to distinguish himself from his father, a well known art critic, painter and author – was perhaps the most important figure of the Polish avant-garde in the early twentieth century, although at the time of his death on 18 September 1939 he was little known outside of a small circle of friends and other artists. As fearful of the spread of western capitalism as he was of the rise of communism – both ideologies, he believed, spelled doom for the individual – on hearing that the Russian army had crossed the border into Poland (a result of the infamous non-aggression pact between Hitler and Stalin), Witkacy took an overdose of veronal and slit his wrists. His mistress tried to accompany him in death by also taking an overdose, but she survived.

A polymath, Witkacy applied himself to a dizzying number of disciplines, producing influential work in painting, theatre, and the novel; he also wrote important theoretical essays on aesthetics, most of them focusing on the problem of "Pure Form." The novel, however, for Witkacy wasn't an art form; it was a "sack" into which the writer could throw whatever interested him, and probably his most famous work in the genre, *Insatiability*, is a good example of his theory put into practice. An account of a young Pole's adventures during the imminent breakdown of western civilization following an invasion by a Communist China (it was written in 1927, well in advance of Mao), it's been described by Czeslaw Milosz as being "a study of decay: mad, dissonant music; erotic perversion; widespread use of narcotics; dispossessed thinking;

false conversions to Catholicism; and complex psychopathic personalities."[26] For a reader used to the straightforward narrative of the realistic novel, Witkacy's own authorial self in *Insatiability* can at times fall under this last category.

Among many other things (Witkacy's novels tend to be rather large 'sacks') in *Insatiability*, Witkacy blended scenes of violent eroticism with critiques of Edmund Husserl, Rudolph Carnap and other contemporary philosophers. Husserl and Carnap were targets for Witkacy because he was a philosopher himself, one obsessed with "the mystery of existence;" his main work in this area is *Concepts and Theorems Implied by the Concept of Being*. He dedicated his life to confronting the primal questions: "Why am I this and not any other being? In this place of infinite space and at this moment of infinite time? In this group of beings, on this planet? Why indeed do I exist? I could have not existed at all;" queries that place him firmly in the existentialist camp, although Witkacy was plumbing these uncomfortable depths years before they became fashionable on the Left Bank. Along with these main lines of work, Witkacy threw himself into several other areas of exploration. He experimented with and wrote about a variety of drugs: peyote, morphine, cocaine, ether, nicotine and alcohol; in the 1920s, there were scandalous reports of drug and alcohol ridden 'orgies' taking place among his associates. After the suicide of his fiancée in 1914, just after his twenty-ninth birthday, in an attempt to get over his depression, he accompanied the anthropologist Bronislaw Malinowski on his first scientific expedition to Australia and the South Seas. As a young man he cultivated the friendship of fellow artists like Karol Szymanowski,[27] Arthur Rubenstein, and Sholem Asch; later his circle included Bruno Schulz, Witold Gombrowicz and Tadeus Miciński.

Yet although Witkacy shares being a political suicide with Benjamin, their characters are as unlike each other as can be imagined. Where Benjamin lacked spontaneity, even, perhaps, a personality – Adorno said of him that "there was something almost incorporeal about him . . . he seemed alienated from his own *physis* . . . he seems hardly to have been a person at all . . ."[28] – Witkacy was a 'multiple personality', an instinctive and incessant self-dramatist who disconcertingly adopted numerous poses, guises and costumes in order to shock his acquaintances into a more vivid appreciation of life's 'strangeness'. Although Witkacy's role-playing has echoes of Jacques Vaché, and his need to adopt different identities – based on a fundamentally weak self image – can remind us of Fernando Pessoa's numerous 'heteronyms', there was something more serious behind these tactics, a concern with human psychology that suggests more a parallel with the psycho-drama of the enigmatic Armenian esoteric teacher G.I. Gurdjieff, than with the narcissistic self-absorption of Vaché.[29]

Witkacy would ring a doorbell, then crouch down on all fours before it opened, in order to see the reaction to this. He wore cowboy hats and phosphorescent ties. While in conversation, he would suddenly turn away for a moment; when he turned back, his eyes would be covered with two halved ping-pong balls, their centres pierced so he could see through them. He had a talent for mimicry and would impersonate his acquaintances, often acting out elaborate scenes between them. He would gather a crowd of 'odd' visitors and then turn up with them at a stranger's door. On one occasion he cajoled the poet Aleksander Wat into pretending to be an Italian aristocrat; during the course of the evening, Wat drank so much that he eventually became convinced that he *was* Italian, ran amok, and had to be restrained. At social gatherings Witkacy would give his friends various roles they were to perform, and he would scold them vigorously if they failed to take them seriously. He would see visitors in bed, in his night clothes, but on occasion naked. During a conversation he would suddenly adopt the role of a drunk, or a policeman. At a restaurant he would order a cutlet and when it arrived slip it into his wallet. He also had a touch of obsessive-compulsive disorder, and would wash his hands several times a day, a ritual probably prompted by a fear of venereal disease which began after a visit to a prostitute in his youth. Yet, along with displaying Witkacy's knack for absurdist comedy and existential psycho-drama, these antics indicated something else as well.

"From periodical, most acute, ghastly fits of spleen" one friend remembered, "Witkacy switched to violent outbursts of biological robustness."[30]

It wouldn't be surprising if Witkacy's penchant for constant novelty grew out of a need to fend off some deeper sense of emptiness. The philosopher Roman Ingarden said of him: "He was a man full of shyness and anxiety as to the essential value of his own artistic and scholarly achievements. He also frequently occupied beforehand and totally unnecessarily an aggressive-defensive position . . . In company he often behaved in an extravagant way in order to cover up for his discomfort and to overcome shyness . . . He could sense in himself some deficiency, some distressing void in the final core of his person-ality . . ."[31] And not everyone was amused by his behaviour. The novelist Witold Gombrowicz, who said of *Insatiability* that it had demolished the genre of the novel itself "in a manner far exceeding the ruthlessness of a Virginia Woolf, James Joyce or Franz Kafka," found Witkacy's 'theatre' annoying. "From the first moment, Witkacy tired and bored me – he could never relax, was always tense, badgering himself and others with his constant theatricals, the urge to make an impres-sion and focus everyone's attention on himself, always toying with people cruelly and painfully."[32] Gombrowicz recognized that there was something "truly dramatic" to Witkacy's 'games'. Yet "one got the impression that something remark-able was becoming distorted and pushed to the bottom of painful tomfoolery." Gombrowicz came to the conclusion that in Poland "superiority and inferiority are incapable of co-existing and instead plunge one another into farce."[33]

Gombrowicz's recognition of "the urge to make an impres-sion" seems accurate, and can be seen in Witkacy's fascination with being photographed, a trait he shared with the Japanese novelist – and fellow literary suicide – Yukio Mishima. Yet in practically every photograph I've seen of Witkacy, he is in costume, or in a 'role' and in some way 'acting out', and the effect, after a time, is wearying. A well known photograph of Witkacy, *Multiplied Self-portrait reflected in Mirrors*, has him in his army uniform – he was in the Russian army during

WWI – facing a corner where two large mirrors connect. The viewer then sees four images of Witkacy – two profiles and two full faces – but, with his back to the viewer, Witkacy's own face is hidden. His painting is also full of many self-portraits, most of them with 'piercing' eyes. Where is Witkacy? It seems clear that he himself didn't know.[34] Linked to this compulsion – the term doesn't seem an exaggeration – is Witkacy's professed need for other people, that is, an audience. In his drama *The Mother* he writes, "I am like some highly charged missile that is laying calmly in a meadow. But so far there has been no cannon and no one to launch me. And I cannot do it by myself – I have to have people."[35]

Such self-obsession born of a tenuous ego not uncommonly prompts an attraction to suicide. At an early age, Witkacy developed a strange, near schizophrenic detachment from himself. He saw his own life and existence as an object of study. As a student at the Academy of Fine Arts in Cracow, he told his friends that he "would like to take a look at myself during my death, when full freedom is reached for interpretation of pure aesthetic experiences dissolved into one! I imagine the loss of the proportions of my body and the growing devastation of my consciousness. It must be very exciting. Perhaps someday I shall be able, at least for a minute, to imitate the work of death."[36] Unlike Thomas Lovell Beddoes – see 'Ten Suicides' – who developed a fascination with the dead *body*, Witkacy's obsession seemed to be with the actual process of dying. This kind of self-obsession can also prompt profound feelings of dissociation. In 1913, while his father, with whom he had a long and difficult relationship, was ill, Witkacy lived with his mother at the boarding house she ran to supplement her income from music lessons. Witkacy felt a deep self-contempt, considering himself a parasite – he was twenty-eight and not earning any money; during most of his life he was dependent on his family – which resulted in a kind of 'other self' or *Doppelgänger* taking over his identity. He suffered hallucinations and hysterical fits and sought treatment from the first Polish Freudian psychiatrist. This crisis came to a head in early 1914, when, as mentioned, his fiancée killed herself, presumably over an affair with the composer Szymanowski. Madness, death and suicide not surprisingly became central themes in Witkacy's work.

The trigger for Witkacy's actual suicide, however, was something other than his long fascination with death. As mentioned, *Insatiability* depicts the imminent breakdown of western civilization; as such, it's been described as "a metaphor of total suicide."[37] Predating Huxley and Orwell and written in the same year that Yevgeny Zamyatin's *We* was first published in its original Russian,[38] *Insatiability* gives a demonic form to Witkacy's long felt apprehension about a coming European catastrophe, a socio-political cataclysm that would result in "the ultimate metamorphosis of mankind into a collectivised, technologized, and asexual beehive."[39] Witkacy had long feared that modern man was moving toward a technologically propelled totalitarian society, in which the individual – specifically, individuals like himself, artistic, philosophical, and out of the ordinary – would become obsolete. As war clouds gathered once again over Europe, and the rise of both Fascism and Communism seemed to insure the collapse of western democracy (about which Witkacy held no illusions), Witkacy's own personal depression and sense of failure combined to create an atmosphere of imminent doom. He had no money, his work had received repeated critical rejection, and his relationships with women were less than successful. By the late thirties, Witkacy had stopped writing plays and had practically given up painting, and had devoted himself almost solely to philosophy, beginning a long correspondence with the philosopher Hans Cornelius. Friends detected in him a growing gloom, and a return of his fascination with suicide. He spoke of it as a "necessity." "There is much I could endure," he told a friend, "but I could never stand to be tortured . . . What awaits us in the near future is one enormous concentration camp."[40]

To another friend he declared, shortly before committing suicide:

You have no idea what a hell awaits this world . . . a hell

114

very few will survive . . . Not a single stone will be left standing of our generation or our age. . . . We are the new Atlantis which is being inundated by a ferocious flood, along with all our theories with which we tried unsuccessfully to subdue life and to plumb its mysterious mechanism; with our hysterical catastrophism, as refined and heady as that whole decadent epoch of ours searching in vain for its compass, a cursed epoch . . . I feel as if I, too, am nearing the end, along with that epoch – I, who was always obsessed by a frantic desire to suck all the magic out of life and to discover its mystery, to transcend its laws and penetrate its most essential meaning.[41]

To another friend, Witkacy wrote: "I often think about suicide – that it's going to be necessary to bring my life to an end a bit earlier that way, out of a sense of honour, so as not to live to see my own total comedown."[42]

His "total comedown" was avoided by the outbreak of WWII. Witkacy was in Warsaw on 1 September 1939 when Germany invaded Poland. He had volunteered for military service, but was rejected because of his age (fifty-four) and deteriorating health (like Benjamin, his heart was bad; he was also going deaf). So, like thousands of others, he joined the refugees fleeing to the eastern provinces, where it was hoped that a second front could be established. When the Germans bombed Brześć, Witkacy and his lover Czesława Korzeniowska set out on foot into the Polish countryside, carrying knapsacks packed with food and clothing. Again like Benjamin, Witkacy was not really up to the journey; his legs were bad, and the couple had to make frequent stops. In the village of Jeziory he reached the end of his road. With the Nazis approaching from the west, Witkacy heard the news that on 17 September, the Russians had invaded from the east, intent on regaining land lost under the Tsar. Witkacy must have wished his prophetic powers were less acute.

Realizing there was nowhere to turn, Witkacy decided to end his life. Czesława's diary recounts that they went to the woods, and sat down under an oak. Witkacy then began to take ephedrine tablets, his experience with drugs being put to a grisly use. He intended to slash his wrist, and the ephedrine would help his blood flow faster. Czesława was determined to join him, and the two drank a mixture of luminal and cybalgine, then said goodbye. Witkacy slit his wrist but, like Seneca's, the blood didn't flow. He then tried a varicose vein in his leg, but this also didn't work. As Czesława began to drift off, Witkacy told her to wake up, and to not leave him alone. He then thought better of it and said, "Once you fall asleep, I'll cut my throat." He told her the name of the vein he intended to cut, and that if "you knew how to do it right, everything would go smoothly" – which suggests that he had done some research on the matter. When Czesława woke the next morning, Witkacy's body was lying next to her; she said his face had a look of relief, "a relaxing after a great fatigue." Ironically, she was seeing double and once again Witkacy's *Doppelgänger* had made an appearance. After feeble attempts to bury Witkacy, hampered by her semi-consciousness, Czesława gave up. She was discovered, along with Witkacy's body, the next day.

★

Both Benjamin and Witkacy were destroyed by the totalitarian regimes they tried to escape, in Benjamin's case the Nazis, in Witkacy's both the Nazis and the Soviets. The case of the Russian Futurist poet Vladimir Mayakovsky differs from both in that his suicide was brought on at least in part by a regime he embraced and had even helped to put into power. Supplementing his own self-destructive tendencies with revolutionary fervour, Mayakovsky's tragedy is that he was an example of the successful revolution's first rule of thumb: eradicate all other revolutionaries.

Like Witkacy, Mayakovsky had a flair for the theatrical, a personality trait that began at birth: he was born on his father's birthday, 7 July 1893, something that delighted the family and seemed to mark him for some special destiny. Vladimir's father was a hard working, good humoured forest ranger, a man who loved children and animals. He was a large man with a booming voice, and Mayakovsky inherited both of these characteristics from him. It's possible that he also inherited something less welcome from his father. Just before Vladimir's thirteenth birthday, his father died suddenly of septicaemia, from a pin prick on his finger that had become infected, and it's believed that Mayakovsky's later hypochondria and extreme fastidiousness stemmed from this incident; like Witkacy, Mayakovsky developed a compulsion about hand washing. From an early age, Mayakovsky had been separated from his father and siblings because of a lack of schools in their remote home village of Bagdadi (now renamed Mayakovski) in Georgia, near the town of Kutaisi; Vladimir had to be sent elsewhere for his education, while his father remained in the forest. The possibility of living together as a family again seemed imminent when the tragedy struck, and one outcome was that Mayakovsky was now the only male in the family (he had two sisters) and the responsibilities that accompanied this weighed on him. The family's financial prospects looked bleak; given that his father died before he had reached fifty, his dependents weren't entitled to a full pension, and they were faced with having to support themselves on ten roubles a month. It's from this time that "the famous Mayakovsky frown" first appeared. If photographs of Witkacy give the impression of an almost infinitely pliable face, Mayakovksy presents the polar opposite. As A.D. P. Briggs remarks, "Almost every adult photograph shows the poet with a severe expression, looking defensive, embarrassed, hostile, annoyed or merely preoccupied, but always serious minded and unrelaxed. [. . .] It was after the death of his father that Mayakovsky, otherwise a manly and handsome figure, first adopted the look of unremitting moroseness by which he is now known."[43]

Like most poets, Mayakovsky was precocious. He taught himself to read at an early age, enjoyed playing word games and displayed a remarkable memory; he was often asked by his father to recite some of his favourite poems. These performances were characterized by a strong sense of rhyme and rhythm, characteristics that would become a part of Mayakovsky's later popular readings. Being the son of a forest ranger might suggest that Vladimir was predestined to be a nature poet, but something happened at the age of seven that led to very different results. Accompanying his father on his rounds, they came across a rivet factory in a ravine. Vladimir was astounded by the electric lights illuminating the site. For the young boy it seemed that night had been banished and daylight was now available on demand. Man had improved on nature and was no longer its slave; machines, not nature, captured his imagination. A later incident cemented Mayakovsky's growing passion for the modern. In school, a large portion of the tsarist curriculum involved readings from the scriptures, and Mayakovsky was surreptitiously tested on his biblical acumen by being asked the meaning of the word *oko*, an archaic Church Slavonic equivalent of the modern Russia word for 'eye', *glaz*. In Georgian, however, it means 'pound' and this is what Vladimir answered. The incident stuck with him, and in an autobiographical sketch he remarked, "So I immediately detested everything ancient, everything churchy, and everything Slavonic. Perhaps that was where my Futurism, my atheism and my internationalism came from."[44] Although resolutely anti-church and anti-religion, Mayakovsky's poetry is full of references to God, some of them eerily prescient; in his poem "Man," he ascends to heaven, where he soon becomes bored and returns to earth, only to discover that a thousand years earlier he had shot himself.

Mayakovsky's rejection of everything ancient was given another prod in 1905 when Vladimir became involved in revolutionary activities. In Kutaisi, where he was going to school and living with his mother, Mayakovsky was infected with the revolutionary spirit; he took to reading subversive literature and attending underground anti-tsarist discussion groups, happy to be accepted as an equal by the older boys and adults. He passed around leaflets, put up posters and enjoyed singing the *Marseillaise*. The posters and leaflets had a profound effect, as many of them combined politics and poetry, something that Mayakovsky would soon do himself.

A few months after his father's death, his mother borrowed money from friends and moved the family to Moscow. Here they didn't escape poverty, but at least they were together – Vladimir's sister Lyudmila had been studying there already. Mayakovsky's struggle to survive strengthened his solidarity with the poor and quickened his disgust with the old regime. He was ecstatic about the move. Everything about the big city enchanted him; compared to the trams, cinemas, huge buildings and electric lights, nature was boring and slow, an appreciation forgotten by today's 'back to nature' sensibility. Mayakovsky met more revolutionary types and his increasing commitment to a new regime was validated by getting himself arrested three times, once for participating in a prison break, in which his whole family took part; his sisters and mother shared his anti-tsarist sentiments. Although only fifteen, he spent several months in jail, part of this in solitary confinement, and the experience affected him deeply. For one thing it effectively ended his career as a revolutionary activist: he was now known to the police and as a marked man was of no use to the underground. The loneliness and insecurity of a prison cell would haunt him in later years, yet his experience behind bars also suggested that there might be better ways of dragging Mother Russia into the modern world.

One benefit was that in prison he had the leisure to devote himself to reading. As a boy he exhibited a talent for art and while behind bars he was allowed to paint, read and write as he desired. He read the Symbolists Andrei Bely and Valery Briusov, but wasn't impressed. He then tackled 'world classics' like Shakespeare and Byron. He was halfway through *Anna Karenina* when he was released, and never bothered to finish it. Mayakovsky's attitude toward literary 'greats' is summed up in his remark that he had "no idea how the Karenin business turned out." Tolstoy, Dostoyevsky, and the rest were part of the corrupt old world and he had come to do away with all that.

Mayakovsky's 'futurism' received its final confirmation at Moscow's School of Painting, Sculpture and Architecture, where he met an older student to whom he took an immediate dislike. David Burlyuk was eleven years Mayakovsky's senior, and in some ways he was Jacques Vaché to Mayakovsky's Breton. Mayakovsky restrained his headstrong personality in order to benefit from his lessons, exhibiting a talent for self-subduing that would later prove a kind of suicide in itself. Burlyuk had no such inhibitions: he was a dandy who wore pretentious frock-coats and lorgnettes and sang to himself as he walked. Mutual disregard blossomed into inevitable friendship when the two discovered each other walking out of a Rachmaninov concert, bored to tears. Laughing, they spent the rest of the evening discussing how tedious everything in the art, literature and music of the time was and how it was up to them to do something about it.

Like the Dadaists, Italian Futurists, Surrealists and many other aesthetic movements of the early twentieth century, the Russian Futurists rejected practically everything that came before them, although perhaps because of the Russian temperament, which is given to exaggeration, they did so with a peculiar vehemence. The Russian Futurists – which, along with Mayakovsky and Burlyuk (who was more of an impresario and promoter than an artist) included the poets Vassily Kamensky and Velimir Khlebnikov – did their best to draw attention to themselves by dressing outlandishly and making outrageous statements. They wore spoons in their button holes, painted on their faces, and gave poetry readings with a grand piano suspended over their heads. Burlyuk once hired fifty young boys to run through the street shouting, "The Futurists are coming." (Along with Tristan Tzara, Dali and, much later, Andy Warhol, Burlyuk understood that modern art was as much about publicity as it was about the art itself.) Mayakovsky himself stood out in his famous yellow blouse (made by his mother), green overcoat and top hat, over six feet tall and booming challenges like, "The past suffocates us. The Academy and Pushkin are more incomprehensible than hieroglyphics. Throw Pushkin, Dostoyevsky, Tolstoy, etc. overboard from the steamship of modernity." One gets an idea of their aesthetic programme from the title of an early anthology of Futurist poetry, *A Slap in the Face of Public Taste*.

Mayakovsky is one of the most vain modern poets; the

personal pronoun "I" appears almost relentlessly in his poetry, and perhaps his best known poem, "A Cloud in Trousers," contains lines like "Glorify me!/ I'm beyond comparison with the great/ I above every created thing place *nihil*." An early work of this time, *Vladimir Mayakovsky: A Tragedy*, in which Mayakovsky portrays himself as a creature of supreme integrity and loftiness, gives an idea of what was in store for him. It's full of posturing and hunger for attention, but it also suggests loneliness and self-pity, as well as suicidal feelings: at one point he tells the reader that he will lay down on a railroad track, and "the wheel of the locomotive will embrace my neck.". One biographer called the work "a celebration of his genius as a poet, and the apotheosis of the Poet offering himself as a sacrifice for the sufferings of all mankind."[45]

Unlike Benjamin and Witkacy, Mayakovsky quickly enjoyed what many writers desire: early success. Yet it came with the usual price. In St. Petersburg he gave a reading at the infamous Stray Dog Café; the applause was loud and gratifying and a journalist for *Theatre Review* wrote of a "Mr. Mayakovsky who read several of his poems in which the audience immediately sensed a great genuine gift of poetry."[46] Future reviewers agreed. Although the Futurists were often incomprehensible, and generally provoked their audiences, Mayakovsky had a knack of speaking directly to his listeners, and the stentorian voice and powerful frame made an immediate impression. He quickly became something of a celebrity, his good looks and evident strength easily attracting women. But the attention soon turned into a habit, and when he didn't receive it, he grew petulant. His brief affairs were also less than satisfying. As with Witkacy, there were two Mayakovskys: one loud, aggressive, and boorish, demanding attention and often being insulting when he got it; the other a sensitive, lonely, insecure young man, who adopted his swaggering pose as a kind of protective colouring. Childhood feelings of being unloved – brought on, no doubt, by the long separations – and memories of his months in prison, added to his emotional confusion. Mayakovsky's hunger for love was abated for a time by meeting Elsa Brik, who later married the Surrealist

Louis Aragon. The two became lovers, but it was Lili Brik, Elsa's sister, who became the love of Mayakovsky's life. Lili was married to an older man, the scholar and critic Osip Brik, but this didn't stop her and Mayakovsky from becoming lovers. Osip Brik evidently had a very modern outlook on relationships; for the rest of Mayakovksy's life, the three lived in an on-again, off-again *ménage à trois*. Brik also became Mayakovsky's publisher.

Yet even his love for Lili Brik didn't provide emotional security. In a poem inspired by, written for and first read to her, "The Backbone Flute," Mayakovsky exhibits an attraction to suicide that will turn up more frequently in later poems. "More and more often I think" he writes, "Wouldn't it perhaps be best/To put the full-stop of a bullet/At the end of me?/Today I – just in case – am giving my farewell concert." (Later, in "Man," already mentioned, Mayakovsky cries, "Chemist let me take/My soul/With no pain/Out into infinite space," but is denied extinction and must suffer a kind of Christ-like fate.)

With the outbreak of WWI, Mayakovsky volunteered for service, even though as the only male in his family he was exempt. His political youth, however, branded him 'unreliable', and he spent the war years as a draughtsman for the Petrograd Military Automobile School. Then came the revolution, and Mayakovsky threw himself into it body and soul. He wrote poems supporting the Bolsheviks and worked for ROSTA, the Russian Telegraph Agency, where he designed pro-communist posters, wrote propaganda, political verse, children's poetry, plays and organized events and agitprop 'happenings', drawing on his experience as a Futurist. Most of his avant-garde companions didn't make the transition so smoothly; many had fled, some were silenced or suffered tragic fates, like Mayakovsky's fellow poet Velimir Khlebnikov, who starved to death while wandering the country, famously sleeping on a pillowcase stuffed with his manuscripts. Lenin and the Bolsheviks disliked modern art in general and Futurism in particular; the only future they had in mind was one in which they called the shots, and artists like Kandinsky and

Chagall quickly got the message and left for Europe. Maya-kovsky, however, believed in the revolution and would cut his cloth to suit its needs. He would soon jettison the egoism of his early work and convince himself that true poetry must serve the needs of the state. In a kind of psychological suicide he "changed his own character," and agreed with the Bolshe-viks that "this was no time for individualism or for writing pieces which could be called unintelligible," so "he ruthlessly suppressed those tendencies within himself and gave his all to the young state." In Mayakovsky's own words, "I mastered myself/Stepping on the throat of my own song," lines, ironic-ally, from a poem called "At the Top of My Voice."

But for a brief while, it seemed that political and poetic revolutions could work hand in hand. In 1922, Mayakovsky travelled to Berlin and Paris, and met with poets, artists and fellow travellers, among them Picasso and Leger. Returning to Russia, with Osip Brik he started two magazines, LEF and the New LEF; the idea was to corral all the Futurists, Formalists, Constructivists and other 'new' movements into a single cultural front, the Left Front of Art. It seemed that, as the Surrealists would try to do in the next decade, the forces of modernism could serve the aims of the new proletariat regime. But this honeymoon would be brief, and neither magazine lasted long; ironically, one of their main theoretical positions was that a proletarian society had no need of poetry – at the same time as Mayakovsky was filling its pages with the stuff. During this time Mayakovsky made a film adaptation of Jack London's *Martin Edin*, whose hero commits suicide. Called *Not Born For Money*, Mayakovsky played the lead. In it, he fakes a suicide to escape a false life, and becomes a worker. A gun used in the film would appear again later on in his life, sadly as something more than a prop.

Working in Lunacharsky's ministry, Mayakovsky became the poet of the revolution, but even with this official impri-matur, his position was always tentative. In 1924 he composed an elegy on the death of Lenin, which made him famous throughout Russia. He travelled again, this time to the United States, Mexico and Cuba – his popularity, as well as Osip

Brik's connections, granted Mayakovsky extraordinary liberties, and no doubt the Bolsheviks saw the advantages of sending their premiere poet on a public relations jaunt. His relations with Lili Brik began to break down – he had fathered a child in Paris and was in love with a much younger woman, and she also took other lovers – but when he heard of the suicide of the poet Sergei Yesenin, he criticised him for his narcissism. Yesenin, a popular poet, who was married for a time to Isadora Duncan, was an alcoholic and drug addict; in 1925 he slashed his wrists in a Leningrad hotel, wrote farewell poems with his blood, then hanged himself. Yesenin's last poem ended with the lines, "In this life, there's nothing new about dying/ But, of course, there's nothing newer about living." Mayakovsky wrote a rebuttal, changing Yesenin's last words: "In this life/ There's nothing hard about dying –/ To make a life/ Is considerably harder."

Yet, Mayakovsky, who seemed on top of the world, was not long to follow. Even though he forced his poetry to toe the party line, in the atmosphere of the late 1920s, he fell increasingly under scrutiny, and his work was criticized as being still too 'formal' and 'unintelligible' for the common man. Party hacks accused him of individualism, self-glorification and insincerity. His play *The Bedbug* was heavily criticized, and another, *The Bathhouse*, was a flop; this was understandable, as both were satires on the new ruling elite. Mayakovsky's problem was that he was unable to stop being revolutionary, and this was dangerous, especially after *the* revolution had finally inaugurated the new dictatorship of the proletariat. The party could use him, but once it had achieved its goal, he had to fall in line, like everyone else. No matter how much he tried to do this, Mayakovksy was too intelligent and honest not to recognize that the 'revolution' he had helped to make a reality, had only changed one set of masters for another. That he had prostituted his genius to hacks with a fraction of his talent, for whatever noble cause, could not have escaped him.

By the late 20s, Mayakovsky's health began to suffer, and his depressions returned. Although he still kept a room at the Brik's apartment, he and Lili were no longer lovers, and his infatuation with the much younger Tatiana Yakovleva, a White Russian whom he had met and fallen in love with in Paris, ended sadly when he learned that she had married, while he was stuck in Russia, for the first time denied a travel permit. When a major exhibition, "Twenty Years of Work," devoted to his life and writings was panned, or worse, ignored, by the party critics, Mayakovsky took it badly. Earlier he had performed an act of deadening self-abnegation by joining the Committee of Proletarian Writers (RAPP), a group that had opposed his earlier attempts with LEF. He did this, presumably, to end the isolation he had more and more been subjected to, but it did no good. The Committee quickly reorganized itself into an inner core of hardliners, and an appendage group, made of Mayakovsky and a few other 'minor' writers.

In early 1930, Mayakovsky's depression grew, and his health got worse. The Briks had left Moscow for an extended stay in London. Although he and Lili were no longer lovers, he depended on her and Osip, and this was the first time both had left him alone in the apartment. His readings and lectures went badly, and in March he was admitted to hospital suffering from a nervous breakdown, but in truth he was simply exhausted. When he left after a short stay, friends noticed that he looked haggard and distracted. He sent telegrams to Lili, complaining that she didn't write to him often enough; she replied, suggesting he find a "new text" for his telegrams. On 11 April, a week before the Briks were to return, Mayakovsky missed a lecture, something he hadn't done before.

Mayakovsky knew what was coming and tried to be with friends, but no one seemed to understand the state he was in; at one point he tried to telephone his friend from LEF, Nikoloa Aseyev, but was told he wasn't at home. "Well, it means that nothing can be done," he said and hung up. Other friends weren't able to meet him either, and things were not going well between him and his latest girlfriend, the actress Nora Polonskaya. She was again much younger than Mayakovsky, and he had argued with her, jealous over her young friends.

On 14 April, after spending the evening at a disastrous party, Nora and Mayakovsky argued again. He demanded she stay with him, but she insisted on going to a rehearsal. At 10:00 a.m. she finally managed to leave the small room Mayakovsky used as a studio in Lyubyansky Passage. She took a few steps down the hall then heard a shot. When she turned back and opened the door, the room was full of blood. Mayakovsky had kept the pistol he had used as a prop in *Not Born For Money*. It was loaded with one bullet. He had put barrel against his heart and fired. On his desk was a letter. It read:

"To All of You: Don't blame anyone for my death, and please don't gossip about it. The deceased hate gossip. Mama, sisters, comrades, forgive me. This is not a good method (I don't advise others to do it), but for me there's no other way out. Lili, love me. Comrade Government, my family consists of Lili Brik, Mama, my sisters, and Veronica Vitoldovna Polonskaya [Nora]. If you can provide a decent life for them, thank you."

"The incident is closed," Mayakovsky continued. "Love's boat/ smashed on the everyday./ Life and I are quits/ And there's no point/ In counting over mutual hurts, harms, and slights. Best of luck to you all!"

Notes

1 Quoted in *The Complete Correspondence 1928–1940 Walter Benjamin – Theodore Wiesengrund Adorno* editor Henri Lowitz; translator Nicholas Walker (Polity Press: 1999) p. 342.

2 No copy of the note exists; it was presumably destroyed by Henny Gurland during her journey to Lisbon, in fear, perhaps, that if found it would somehow compromise her. But on her arrival in New York, at Adorno's request she gave him a verbatim account of it.

3 Walter Benjamin, letter to Gershom Scholem, 17 April 1931.

4 Lee Siegel, Introduction to Gershom Scholem *Walter Benjamin The Story of a Friendship* (New York Review Books: New York, 2001) p. ix.

5 Adorno remarked of Benjamin's character that he was "so completely the medium of his work [. . .] that anything one might call 'immediacy of life' was refracted . . . his private demeanour

approached the ritualistic." In *On Walter Benjamin* ed. Gary Smith (MIT Press: Cambrigde, Mass., 1988) p. 329.

6 Walter Benjamin *Reflections* (Harcourt, Brace, Jovanovich: New York, 1978) p. 301.

7 Ibid. Peter Demetz, Introduction, pp. xxiv–xxvi.

8 Walter Benjamin *Illuminations* (Fontana Press: London, 1992) p. 249.

9 Momme Brodersen *Walter Benjamin: A Biography* (Verso: London, 1996) p. 197.

10 In spring 2002 I visited Port Bou and had the opportunity to see Karavans' work and also the cemetery where Benjamin is said to be buried. The memorial, although subject to the ravages of time and vandals (local teenagers making their own mark on history), is a fitting tribute to Benjamin, its sheer descent to the waters below eerily embodying Benjamin's own aimless and endless wanderings and fruitless bid for escape. In the cemetery, overlooking the Mediterranean, there is a grave with a plaque marked with his name, yet his remains aren't buried there. In his book on Benjamin, Gershom Scholem wryly comments that the grave is "an invention of the cemetery attendants, who in consideration of the number of inquiries wanted to assure themselves of a tip." He agrees with Hannah Arendt's remark that "the spot is beautiful," but considers the grave "apocryphal." I can concur that, as Arendt says, "It is by far one of the most fantastic and most beautiful spots I have seen in my life," but during my visit I had no occasion to proffer anyone a tip. (Gershom Scholem *Walter Benjamin: The Story of a Friendship* [Faber & Faber: London, 1982] p. 226.)

11 Jay Parini *Benjamin's Crossing* (Anchor Books: London, 1998) p. 280.

12 Huxley, too, is in the ranks of the literary suicides. His own youth was saddened by the suicide of his brother Trevenen, after he failed to meet the high standards of achievement set by the Huxley clan; Huxley based the suicide of Brian Foxe in *Eyeless in Gaza* on his brother's death. And *Brave New World* itself famously closes with the suicide by hanging of John the Savage, confronted with the choice between a primitive life on an Indian reservation, or the living death of conformity to the modern totalitarian state.

13 It may be mixing subjects here, but this analogy makes me wonder if Elias Canetti had Benjamin at all in mind when writing

of the bibliomaniac Peter Kien in his *Auto-da-Fé*, who, as mentioned earlier, burns himself to death amidst heaps of his collection. Benjamin was an obsessive bibliophile, and made a point of never reading many of the books in his library. Gershom Scholem admitted to being annoyed at the attention Benjamin would pay to bindings and other fetishes of the collector. "The enthusiasm with which he was capable of discussing bindings, paper and typefaces . . . frequently got on my nerves . . . I deny that metaphysically legitimate insights can arise from this way of evaluating books on the basis of their bindings and paper." (Scholem, p. 71.)

14   Peter Demetz, Introduction, *Reflections* p. xiii.

15   One of his fellow inmates was Arthur Koestler who, much later, was another literary suicide.

16   Walter Benjamin *Reflections* p. 4.

17   Elsewhere I have remarked that Benjamin's suitcase and Pessoa's chest, which contained, among many others, the fragments that constitute his *Book of Disquietude*, and which today is still not completely exhausted, strike me as warranting a comparative study. Another item would be the pillow case belonging to the Russian Cubo-Futurist poet Velimir Khlebnikov, in which he supposedly stuffed his numerous manuscripts and on which he allegedly slept during his last days, wandering through the chaos of the revolution.

18   Hannah Arendt, Introduction to Walter Benjamin *Illuminations* p. 11.

19   Walter Benjamin *Reflections* p. 303.

20   As in many cases discussed in this book, speculation and uncertainty surround Benjamin's last hours. For a detailed account, see Momme Brodersen's *Walter Benjamin: A Biography* pp. 250–262, which I have drawn upon for this chapter.

21   Erwin Loewenson, quoted in Momme Brodersen, *Walter Benjamin: A Biography* p. 70

22   Gershom Scholem, *Walter Benjamin: The Story of a Friendship* (Faber & Faber: London, 1982) p. 178.

23   Ibid. p. 179

24   Hesse in fact was one of the few well known literary figures of the time who praised Benjamin's work; at one point, he even tried to help him publish one of his books. This should be kept in mind by leftist critics who often target Hesse as a proto-Nazi because of novels like *Journey to the East* and *The Glass Bead*

Game, both of which employ the device of an esoteric, hierarchical spiritual society, a mark, for the politically correct and ideologically blind, of Hesse's incipient 'fascism'.

25 Ibid. p. 224.
26 Czeslaw Milosz, Introduction to Stanisław Ignacy Witkiewicz *Insatiability* (Quartet: London, 1985) p. viii.
27 It's been suggested that Jadwiga Janczewska, Witkacy's fiancée, committed suicide after an affair with Szymanowski.
28 Quoted in Gary Smith, ed. *On Walter Benjamin.*
29 For more on Gurdjieff see my *In Search of P.D. Ouspensky* (Quest: Wheaton, Illinois, 2004).
30 Jerzy Eugeniusz Płomieński, quoted in Anna Micińska *Stanisław Ignacy Witkiewicz: Life and Work* (Interpress Publishers: Warsaw, 1990) p. 288.
31 Ibid. p.110.
32 Ibid. p.292.
33 Ibid. p.294. Others shared Gombrowicz's feelings. The philosopher, mathematician and painter Leon Chwistek, a friend of Witkacy from childhood, remarked: "He is a degenerate individual, equally removed from true art as from life, a perpetual embryo crazed by megalomania." Bronisław Mailnowski, who maintained a rocky relationship with Witkacy throughout his life, said: "I respect his art and admire his intelligence and worship his individuality, but I cannot stand his character." Quoted in *The Witkiewicz Reader* ed. Daniel Gerould (Quartet Books: London, 1993) p. 341.
34 Witkacy seems a good example of the type of individual who has a constant need for something to be 'happening' around him, who throws his own life and those of his friends and acquaintances into constant disarray in order to keep at bay some feeling of stagnancy. Again, the parallel with Gurdjieff is suggestive. Both Witkacy and Gurdjieff seemed to have a need to have people around them and to constantly control their actions and reactions by indulging in some form of 'theatre'. For most of his career, Gurdjieff had a retinue of students whom he would submit to a variety of physical and psychological exercises, aimed at producing in them a sense of 'wakefulness'. Yet one can ask how much these tactics were to the students' benefit, and how much they satisfied a need in the teacher. Another character who falls into this category, although one less 'serious' than Gurdjieff, is the 'magician' Aleister Crowley, who adopted

numerous alter egos and who seemed intent on having as much attention as possible paid to him and his exploits. For more on Crowley see my *Dedalus Book of the Occult: A Dark Muse* (2003).

35 Anna Micińska, p. 157.

36 Quoted in *Witkacy*, Daniel Gerould (University of Washington Press: Seattle, 1981) p. 4.

37 Louis Iribane, Introduction to *Insatiability* (University of Illinois press: Chicago, 1977) p. xxxix.

38 The Russian novelist and essayist Yevgeny Zamyatin is credited with being the creator of the anti-utopian novel, a genre that, by the second half of the twentieth century, had become a mainstay of science fiction and 'speculative' literature. *We*, written in 1924, was first published in an English translation in the United States; a Russian edition was published in Prague in 1927. Although circulated in manuscript form, it was never published in the Soviet Union.

39 Louis Iribane, p. xxix.

40 Ibid. p. xxiii.

41 Ibid. p. vii. Witkacy's apprehensions about a coming totalitarian regime have been traced to his experiences in Russia during the Bolshevik revolution. Poland was under Russian rule in WWI, and when Witkacy joined the army he was made an officer in the elite tsarist guards. Although he had had his life spared during the coup, he lived in constant fear of reprisal, as the tsarist guards were known for their brutality. Another incident made a powerful impression on him. On his return to Poland from Russia, Witkacy is said to have witnessed the senseless murder of his friend and mentor, the Symbolist poet Tadeus Miciński, who was mistaken for a tsarist general and attacked by a mob. Some accounts consider this traumatic experience apocryphal.

42 Quoted in *Witkacy*, Daniel Gerould p. 19.

43 A.D.P. Briggs *Vladimir Mayakovsky: A Tragedy* (Willem A. Meeuws: Oxford, 1979) p.12. In this Mayakovsky resembles the beat writer William S. Burroughs, who in practically every photograph of him exhibits the same dead pan lack of expression.

44 Ibid. p. 8.

45 Ann & Samuel Charters *I Love: The Story of Mayakovsky and Lili Brik* (Andre Deutsch: London, 1979) p. 30.

46 Quoted in A.D. P. Brigss, pp. 30–31. The Stray Dog Café was the testing ground of pre-revolutionary Russian poets, artists and intellectuals. For more on this, see my *In Search of P.D. Ouspensky*.

The Manic-Depressive Suicide

In a grimly fascinating book, *Let Me Finish*, the German academic Udo Grashoff put together an anthology of suicide
notes, gathered from police records. Reading these, it's difficult to argue with A. Alvarez's assessment, quoted earlier, of
the "shabby, confused, agonized crisis which is the common
reality of suicide." The notes Grashoff collected suggest that
the motivation for most suicides fall within a fairly limited
purview: unrequited love, debt, shame, sickness, an intolerable
domestic situation. They also confirm that the only thing
to come of most suicides is a nasty mess for someone else
to clean up. Yet one note in particular expresses a sentiment
shared, I think, by the subjects of this chapter. In her last
words, a young woman, intent on ending her life, debated
with her friends and countered the arguments she believed
they would make in order to stop her. She agreed with them
that killing herself would "accomplish nothing." But this, she
explained, was precisely the point. That was exactly what she
wanted to accomplish: nothingness. Death offered the only
access to the oblivion she desired. The cessation of existence
was her goal and in the end she reached it. The pain of 'being'
was simply too great for her to bear and suicide was the only
way to avoid it.

Such psychic pain is of course associated with depression.
As William Styron writes in his account of his own depression, "mysteriously and in ways that are totally remote from
normal experience, the grey drizzle of horror induced by
depression takes on the quality of physical pain. But it is not
an immediately identifiable pain, like that of a broken limb.
It may be more accurate to say that despair, owing to some
evil trick played upon the sick brain by the inhabiting
psyche, comes to resemble the diabolical discomfort of being
imprisoned in a fiercely overheated room. And because no

131

breeze stirs this cauldron, because there is no escape from the smothering confinement, it is entirely natural that the victim begins to think ceaselessly of oblivion."[1] Styron remarks that in his case, the pain was "most closely connected to drowning or suffocation," and he goes on to comment that William James, who battled depression for many years, hit the mark when he wrote in *The Varieties of Religious Experience* that, "It is a positive and active anguish, a sort of psychical neuralgia wholly unknown to normal life."[2] James continues: "Such anguish may partake of various characters, having sometimes more the quality of loathing; sometimes that of irritation and exasperation; or again of self-mistrust and self-despair; or of suspicion, anxiety, trepidation, fear."[3]

As defined by the *Diagnostic and Statistical Manual of Mental Disorder IV* published by the American Psychiatric Association, depression is "a disorder of mood, characterized by sadness and loss of interest in usually satisfying activities, a negative view of the self, hopelessness, passivity, indecisiveness, suicidal intentions, loss of appetite, weight loss, sleep disturbances, and other physical symptoms." For Kay Redfield Jamison, whose own account of her manic-depressive illness, *An Unquiet Mind*, was a bestseller, "Manic-depression, or bipolar illness encompasses a wide range of mood disorders and temperaments." "Occasionally," she writes, "these changes reflect only a transient shift in mood or a recognizable and limited reaction to a life situation. When energy is profoundly dissipated, the ability to think is clearly eroded, and the capacity to actively engage in the efforts and pleasures of life is fundamentally altered, then depression becomes an illness, rather than a temporary or existential state."[4] A less specific account, embedded among the dozens he culled from a variety of sources, was offered by Robert Burton almost four hundred years ago, in *The Anatomy of Melancholy*. Melancholy, Burton writes, is, "A kind of dotage without a fever, having for his ordinary companions fear and sadness, without any apparent occasion." And with a succinctness rare for Burton, he went on to boil the malady down to a single characteristic, calling it "an anguish of the mind."

That the writers I look at in this chapter – Virginia Woolf, Sylvia Plath and Anne Sexton – suffered such an anguish, is clear from the accounts of their lives.

A reader may wonder at the wisdom of selecting three women writers as the subjects of a chapter on manic-depressive suicides. Although men clearly suffer from it as well, according to one authority, "major depressive illness is more likely to affect women"[5] than it is men; why this is the case still remains unclear. Yet there's another reason I've grouped these writers together. In the cases of Woolf, Plath, and Sexton, their depression and their writing were powerfully linked, so much so that one almost wants to say that if they weren't depressives, they might not have been writers, and *vice versa*. Virginia Woolf invested so much importance in her writing that even the mere *possibility* of a bad review was enough to plunge her into despair. In the case of Sylvia Plath, it's arguable that her reputation as a significant writer stems at least in part from the fact that she killed herself. And Anne Sexton is one of the few examples of a poet who discovered herself as a writer through using writing as a therapy to overcome her depression. In all three cases, writing, and the individual's mental and emotional state, her very *self*, were in a strange and ultimately final relationship with her death. About her friend Sylvia Plath, with whom she swapped stories of failed suicide attempts, Anne Sexton remarked that "she had the suicide inside her. As I do. As many of us do. But, if we're lucky, we don't get away with it and something or someone forces us to live."[6] Sexton herself was 'lucky' several times, as were Plath and Woolf; all three made many attempts to end their lives, and failed at them all – until, of course, their final attempts.

In *The Dynamics of Creation*, the psychologist Anthony Storr examines the psychological motivations at work behind creativity. Chapter titles like "Creativity as Wish-Fulfilment," "Creativity and the Schizoid Character," and "Creativity and the Obsessional Character," may be off-putting, but unlike many psychoanalytic approaches, his book avoids the reductionism and outright absurdity often associated with Freudian accounts of art and artists; it also has the merit of being well written. Of the manic-depressive temperament, Storr writes that "his principal concern is [. . .] to protect himself from the danger of loss of self-esteem; but unlike the schizoid person [who needs to detach himself from others], his self-esteem is much more dependent upon a 'good' relation with others. Like the schizoid person, he fears other people in some ways; but it is not so much the fear of attack or being overwhelmed, as the fear of withdrawal of love and approval."[7] Storr continues: "one could say that normal people become conditioned by receiving enough love as small children to expect that others will give them approval, and thus proceed through life with confidence. People who remain in the depressive position have no such built-in confidence. They remain as vulnerable to outside opinion as a baby is vulnerable to the withdrawal of the breast. Indeed, for such people, the good opinion of others is as vital to their well-being as milk is to the infant. Rejection and disapproval are a matter of life and death; for unless supplies of approval are forthcoming from outside, they relapse into a state of depression in which self-esteem sinks so low, and rage becomes so uncontrollable, that suicide becomes a real possibility."[8]

Anne Sexton, Sylvia Plath and Virginia Woolf all meet Storr's criteria. After one of Sexton's fits, which could include violence, random behaviour, and infidelity, she would often seek forgiveness and approval from her long-suffering husband; lying beside him as she did beside her great aunt as a child, her husband soothed her by stroking her back and saying, "That's my good girl." According to her friend and fellow poet Maxine Kumin, "Anne always had the notion that she was the most under-loved person in the universe. There could never be enough proof that she was loved."[9]

According to an account left by her neighbour – "the last person to see Sylvia Plath alive" – and who was himself poisoned by the gas she used to kill herself, Sylvia Plath gave the impression of being inept at the basic practicalities of life, and was always in need of help, yet "she tended to be a self-centred person, not letting herself become involved with other people's problems. [. . .] The world revolved around her," something her neighbour had observed "in other creative people."[10]

And according to her biographer Mitchell Leaska, Virginia Woolf "needed the care and protection of someone whose devotion was unquestioned."[11] By all accounts she received exactly that from her husband Leonard Woolf, with whom it is doubtful she had sexual relations, but who ministered to her emotional, psychological and medical needs through a long, demanding and heartbreaking relationship. All three women needed continuous helpings of unconditional love. In some cases they received this; in others not. But even in the case of Virginia Woolf, who had the at times saintly Leonard to look after her, love and care wasn't enough, and when the final descent came, she chose to kill herself, rather than face madness. Would Anne Sexton and Sylvia Plath not have followed her in suicide if they had received sufficient love? According to Anthony Storr, "the person of the depressive temperament behaves as if he were insatiable; as if he had never had enough." And he concludes, "It is reasonable to assume that this is in fact the case."[12] Sadly, reading the lives of these tragic characters, one comes away feeling that all the love in the world would not have been enough to fill the hole in their psyches.

Virginia Woolf was born into a family and environment that practically ensured she would become a writer; it also ensured that, like the children of other famous parents, she would have to struggle to overcome a sense of being overshadowed by them. Her mother, Julia Jackson Stephen, had previously been married to Herbert Duckworth, of the publishing family, and was descended from an attendant of Marie Antoinette; she was also related to a group of sisters, renowned for their beauty, who modelled for many of the pre-Raphaelite painters and photographers. Her father, Sir Leslie Stephen, was a respected literary critic, and founder of the *Dictionary of National Biography*. Virginia's home in Hyde Park Gate, London, was a centre for late Victorian intellectual life; Henry James, George Eliot, George Henry Lewes, and James Russell Lowell, were among some of the distinguished visitors, and this early familiarity with literary and scholarly people more than likely primed Virginia for her later celebrity as part of the Bloomsbury set.

It was a crowded house at Hyde Park Gate. Both parents had been widowed, and Virginia's siblings included children from three marriages: Julia's children from her first marriage, George, Stella and Gerald; Leslie's daughter Laura (who was mentally unstable and lived with the family until she was institutionalised in 1891); and Leslie and Julia's own other children, Vanessa, Thoby, and Adrian. Along with children the house was also crowded with books. Unlike her brothers, who received formal education, Virginia did not (a common practice at the time), but she made up for this by her prodigious and at times obsessive reading, devouring the better part of her father's huge library; like many sensitive, introverted children, what Virginia lacked in life she made up for in the world of her imagination. Although Virginia had to compete with her siblings for her mother's attentions, her father recognized her talent and encouraged her, and he declared early on that she was destined to make her living "writing articles."

The death of her mother from influenza in 1895, when Virginia was thirteen, was described by her as "the greatest disaster that could happen;" it led to the first of her many breakdowns, which were usually characterized by severe mood fluctuations, nervous irritability and paralysing melancholy, and often required medical attention and institutionalisation. Yet the early and recurrent sexual abuse that she and her sister Vanessa were subjected to by her older half-brothers George and Gerald – revealed to a correspondent only late in life – more than likely triggered the moods of self-loathing and low self-esteem that would characterize her later depressive states.[13] George, who was fourteen when Virginia was born, took to 'fondling' her when she was six, and apparently continued the practice until her late teens, camouflaging his furtive caresses with inordinate displays of brotherly affection. Although there is some debate over whether her marriage to Leonard Woolf was ever consummated – there is some indication in her diaries that it may have been, but the general belief is that it was not – Virginia's erotic predilection for women – as in her famous affair with Vita Sackville-West – is well documented and more than likely had its roots in her early mauling by her half-brothers. That the Bloomsbury crowd was noted for its sexual irregularities was no doubt also an encouragement in this direction.

Her mother's death plunged Leslie Stephen into a prolonged and effusive mourning; Julia was not yet fifty and Leslie couldn't come to terms with losing a wife a second time. The sight of her father reduced to tears and comforted by her sisters no doubt severely affected Virginia, who desperately craved his love and attention; she also secretly felt guilty over the fact that she had favoured him over her mother, with whom she felt she had competed for his affection. Her own relations with her mother had been difficult; deeply attached to her approval, she would fly into rages if she felt she was being slighted; for her part, Julia was sparing in the attention Virginia desperately craved, and was herself subject to dark, unresponsive moods. The family knew of 'Ginny's' mood-swings, but accepted them as part of the family dynamic; the idea that she was somehow emotionally or mentally disturbed was unacceptable to them – again, something common at the time. Her half-sister Stella, who became for Virginia a second mother, took over the reigns of the family, and was her step-father's comforter. Sadly, the emotional security provided by Stella was pulled out from under Virginia first by Stella's marriage, and then more severely by her succumbing to a sudden fever just after her honeymoon, only two years after her mother's death. In 1904, when Leslie Stephen died, Virginia had another, more catastrophic nervous collapse. It was also then that she made her first suicide attempt and was briefly institutionalised, a pattern that would repeat itself at different intervals throughout her life.[14]

With the death of their father, Vanessa, Adrian, Thoby and Virginia sold the house at Hyde Park Gate and moved to Bloomsbury, no doubt to exorcise painful memories (and the unwanted attentions of their half-brothers). They bought a house on Gordon Square, and in many ways recreated the atmosphere of their first home. At Cambridge, Thoby (who died of typhoid in 1906) had met Lytton Strachey, Clive Bell, Maynard Keynes and, most importantly, Leonard Woolf. Thoby began to hold regular 'Thursday evenings' at home, when he would gather with his friends, a tradition that first Vanessa, then Virginia would carry on after his death; it was out of these weekly meetings that the famous 'Bloomsbury group' would emerge. Virginia had begun writing and publishing book reviews for *The Times Literary Supplement*, a journal she would be associated with for many years. Vanessa would marry Clive Bell, and Leonard Woolf, who had joined the Ceylon Civil Service and had returned to London on leave, met Virginia and soon decided he wanted to marry her. At first hesitant, Virginia finally agreed. They were married in August, 1912, and were determined to earn their living through writing. Less than a year later Virginia suffered another nervous breakdown, plunged into madness and made another attempt to kill herself.

Virginia had by this time started to write novels. She had started *The Voyage Out* (originally titled *Melymbrosia*) in 1908, and had finished it by 1913. But her breakdown following her marriage meant the book wouldn't be published until 1915. Her second novel, *Night and Day*, soon followed. Both were conventional works; the 'experimental' novels she is most known for today – *Mrs. Dalloway, The Waves, Orlando* – were a decade away. But as with Sylvia Plath and Anne Sexton, Virginia increasingly came to associate writing with her own sense of self. Her self-esteem, her worth as person, became anchored in her work as a writer. In later life, finishing a book would bring her close to suicide: when finishing *The Years* she wrote, "That's the end of the book. I looked up past diaries . . . and found the same misery after *Waves* after *Lighthouse*. I was, I remember, nearer suicide, seriously, than since 1913 . . ."[15] Delivering the final draft would leave her feeling vulnerable and exposed, certain that her work would be recognized as worthless and herself as a fake, and she would agonize over changes she should have made. The slightest possibility of error induced intense feelings of self-revulsion, which she would project on to others. During one of these states, after meeting an acquaintance, she wrote in her diary, "I can imagine [. . .] how she (Mrs. Sydney Waterlow) cursed that dreadful slut Virginia Woolf."

On another occasion, hearing that the acerbic artist and novelist Wyndham Lewis, who was no friend of Bloomsbury,[16] had written about her in his book *Men Without Art*, which includes pungent criticisms of Hemingway, Faulker, and Eliot, Woolf slipped into a paralysing state of anxiety. She couldn't bring herself to read Lewis' remarks, which, admittedly, are written in some of his most waspish tones and include the assessment that "she is taken seriously by no one any longer today." (The book was published in 1934, after her 'stream-of-consciousness' novels had been published.) "Why then," she writes, "do I shrink from reading W.L.? Why am I sensitive? I think vanity: I dislike the thought of being laughed at: of the glow of satisfaction that A., B. and C. will get from hearing V.W. demolished: also it will strengthen further attacks: perhaps I feel uncertain of my own gifts . . . What I shall do is craftily to gather the nature of the indictment from talk and reviews; and in a year perhaps, when my book is out [*The Years*], I shall read it." She then makes an admission of a masochistic pleasure in feeling this way. "Already I am feeling the calm that always comes to me with abuse: my back is against the wall . . . and then there is the queer disreputable pleasure in being a figure, a martyr." The paralysis continues, as does the masochism, "When will my brain revive? In 10 days I think . . . and then there is the odd pleasure of being abused and the feeling of being dismissed into obscurity is also pleasant and salutary." Yet the real goal is the nothingness, a self-erasure more complete than mere obscurity: "I mind being in the light again, just as I was sinking into popular obscurity . . . I don't think this attack will last more than two days . . . And how many sudden shoots into nothingness open before me . . . if only for a time I could completely forget myself, my reviews, my fame, and sink in the scale . . ."[17]

Woolf's insecurity about her work seems excessive, but a milder form of it isn't unusual in most writers. All writers have second thoughts about a work, and it's common to feel insecure when presenting your efforts to an often insensitive public. To expose yourself to criticism takes some courage, and in order to actualise what talent they have, writers need an enormous amount of self-confidence and self-belief, as well as an ego sufficiently strong to quiet the doubts that plague them. And if, as seems likely, having your work accepted is a means of gaining approval, it's understandable that, as Anthony Storr points out, some writers become addicted to this. "Some writers," he writes, "are so driven to produce short works in rapid succession that they never do themselves justice. The immediate rewards of journalism are seductive in this respect. Seeing yourself in print every week, or even every day, is immensely reassuring to some characters."[18]

But although "many journalists cannot face the long period without reward demanded by writing a novel"[19] – or a book, for that matter – Virginia wasn't one of these. She was no beginner. She did devote herself to producing longer, more serious work than book reviews and articles; by the time she became a target for Wyndham Lewis' criticisms (which, on the whole, I find accurate) she had already published several novels, an important feminist essay (*A Room of One's Own*) and been applauded as a serious exponent of literary modernism. But even this wasn't enough to confirm her self-belief. After each book, the props holding her up would fall away, and she would drop into a terrifying and debilitating madness. As her biographer writes "without writing Virginia's world became unreal, menacing, and she herself reduced once more to a state of helpless passivity."[20]

It's no wonder then that she kept a journal for decades: the act of writing itself, although not foolproof, could at times keep the madness at bay. The danger with this, as with many obsessive journal writers, is that life then is no longer something to be lived; it becomes a source of material for writing – when, that is, it isn't too overwhelming and threatening. But that life was often overwhelming and threatening for Virginia is clear from her journals. Although even to the end she followed the journalist's credo to, "Observe perpetually.

Observe the oncome of age. Observe greed. Observe my own despondency. By that means it becomes serviceable . . . I will go down with my colours flying . . . Occupation is essential", it was precisely this acute observation that at times pulled her under. It was through this "inexplicable susceptibility to some impressions," she wrote, "that I approach madness."[21] Once, looking at a house to rent, she observed with disgust that the rooms were "rank with the smell of meat and human beings." Other people struck her as particularly offensive, "I begin to loathe my kind," she wrote, "principally from looking at their faces in the tube. Really, raw red and silver herrings give me more pleasure to look upon." Although when the illness was upon her she would deny that anything was wrong and would often refuse treatment, in her lucid moments she could recognize that things were not right. "She would discuss her illness," Leonard Woolf wrote. "She would recognize that she had been mad, that she had had delusions, heard voices which did not exist, lived for weeks in a nightmare world of frenzy, despair, violence."

It was in one of these lucid times that, feeling the darkness approaching again and no longer having the strength or the motivation to face it (her reputation, she felt, had diminished, as did her income from her books; after WWII it would decline sharply) she decided to follow one of those "shoots into nothingness" whose appearance comforted her. Leaving Leonard what must rank as one of the most heartbreaking farewells ("You have given me the greatest possible happiness," she told him. "You have been in every way all that anyone could be. I don't think two people could have been happier till this terrible disease came . . ."), on 28 March 1941, after filling her pockets with stones, Virginia walked into the river Ouse, near their home, Monks House, in the village of Rodmell in Sussex, and drowned herself.

On the night of Sunday 11 February 1963, after leaving them glasses of milk and slices of bread for breakfast, although they were too young to feed themselves, Sylvia Plath opened the window of her children's room in her maisonette at 23

Fitzroy Road, in the Primrose Hill area of North London.[22] Then she carefully sealed off her kitchen door on the floor below with towels and adhesive tape, left a note on the pram to call her doctor, laid out a cloth for a pillow, turned on the gas, and put her head deep inside the oven. When an *au pair* who had come to help with the children arrived the next morning, she heard them crying, but was unable to get into the house. Eventually, with the help of a builder, the door was forced. Immediately they smelled the gas. The children were shivering but unharmed; London then was in the grip of the coldest winter in 150 years and the house was barely heated.[23] They then opened the kitchen window, turned off the gas, and pulled Sylvia into the living room, where the nurse tried mouth-to-mouth resuscitation. It was too late. Sylvia was dead; according to the doctor at University College Hospital, who examined her body, she had died at around 8:00 am, although an earlier examination at the scene suggested her death had occurred sometime between 4:00 and 6:00 am. Trevor Thomas, who lived below her and was the last person to see her alive, claimed that at around 12:30 am he had seen her in the hallway of the house, "with her head raised with a kind of seraphic expression on her face." When he asked if she was well, she replied, "I'm just having a marvellous dream, a most wonderful vision." If this was so, then she must have finally decided to go through with it not long after Thomas spoke with her.

There's some speculation that Plath didn't really want to die that night, that, as in many attempted suicides, she really wanted to be saved. Most of the evidence suggests otherwise, but the uncertainty that still hovers around the facts of her death[24] is emblematic of the ambiguity surrounding her life as a whole, especially her marriage to Ted Hughes and Hughes' responsibility, if any, for her death. So much mystery, so many conflicting stories, and so much control over the 'official' account, first by Ted Hughes himself, and then by the Hughes estate, has accreted around Sylvia Plath's death that in 1993 Janet Malcolm published a book specifically about the difficulty of writing a biography of Plath.[25] Malcolm was prompted to write her book – an essay on the perils of biography – after reading her friend Anne Stevenson's 'authorized' biography of Plath, *Bitter Fame*; authorized, that is, by Olwyn Hughes, Ted Hughes' sister, who hated Plath but who strangely had control of her literary estate. Stevenson's book received bad reviews, precisely because it was written in close association with Olwyn Hughes, so close that she practically was credited as its co-author. Not surprisingly, it presented the official Hughes' view regarding Plath and Hughes, and was seen as little more than propaganda for the pro-Hughes, anti-Plath camp.[26]

On the other side of the debate is a book like Ronald Hayman's excellent *The Death and Life of Sylvia Plath* which, because he raised points that clashed with the official accounts, could not quote from Plath's and Hughes' work, outside of what is permitted by 'fair usage'. Hughes argued at different times that his actions were motivated by a desire to protect Sylvia's memory, their children's feelings, and his own privacy, but given that the lost diaries are indeed lost (or destroyed), we really have very little to go by to know how satisfying an explanation this is.

Sylvia Plath was born on 27 October 1932 in Boston, Massachusetts. For the first part of her short life she seemed the kind of girl that her classmates would choose as "most likely to succeed." By the time she was twenty, she was a top student, an editor and columnist for local journals, and had published short stories in popular girls' magazines like *Seventeen* as well as more weighty publications like the *Christian Science Monitor*. She won a scholarship to Smith College, an exclusive all-girl school, and also a competition to be a guest editor for *Mademoiselle*, which had recently published her prize-winning story "Sunday at the Mintons." Later achievements included a Fullbright scholarship to Cambridge. Yet, beneath the sparkling surface, things were not so bubbly.

When Sylvia was eight, her father died. Otto Plath was a lecturer in entomology at Boston University, and his book, *Bumblebees and their Ways* was highly regarded. Otto was, by the standards of the time, old for a father; he was forty-six when Sylvia was born, and when Sylvia's brother Warren

143

arrived he was fifty-one. Sylvia's mother, Aurelia, was twenty-five when Sylvia was born and had been Otto's student; she had a great love of literature and showed promise in it herself, but after her marriage devoted herself exclusively to Otto's needs, becoming his wife as well as his secretary. Sylvia loved her father and understandably desired his praise. And although Otto was an obsessive workaholic, a dominating type who despised small talk, vague ideas and sloppy thinking,[27] Sylvia was his favourite and until his illness she didn't feel any lack of the approval she needed from him. But then things changed.

In 1936, just before her brother was born, Otto developed a form of diabetes. If he had it treated then, it wouldn't have been fatal. Otto, however, had contempt for conventional medicine and had made his own diagnosis. He refused to see a doctor, and over the next four years his condition deteriorated; at the same time he kept up a gruelling work schedule. As Ronald Hayman points out, both Sylvia's parents exhibited an inordinate self-discipline, rooted in a kind of masochism. In Aurelia's case, its form was self-sacrifice, first of her own possibilities as a writer to Otto, then of her own pleasure, denying herself simple comforts in order to provide Sylvia and Warren with a good future. In later years, Sylvia would refer to her as a "martyr," and in accounts of her own attempts to excel and be a good wife and mother, it isn't difficult to find a family resemblance.

As Otto's condition worsened, and his work load increased, Sylvia felt him moving away from her. He had less patience with her and seemed less interested in her attempts to entertain him and win his favour. Her mother kept the children from pestering their increasingly irritable and suffering father, who often exploded in rage and pain at the muscle spasms gripping his leg. By October 1940, it was clear something was really wrong. One morning Otto stubbed his little toe; that evening it and the rest of his foot had turned black; red streaks shot up toward his ankle. His leg had turned gangrenous and had to be amputated. The surgeon asked, "How could such a brilliant man be so stupid." Aurelia may have asked this herself. Less than six months later he was dead.

Like many young children, Sylvia felt that her father's withdrawal must have been her fault; if he spent less time with her, she must be to blame. After his death, and in the months approaching her own, the seat of blame had shifted. As A. Alvarez writes of the poetry of her last days, "She seem convinced, in these last poems, that the root of her suffering was the death of her father, whom she loved, who abandoned her, and who dragged her after him into death." Eventually she would come to see both her mother and herself as responsible for his death. And although, as Ronald Hayman comments, Otto Plath didn't quite kill himself, he did set a suicidal example, following the dictates of his obstinacy rather than the indications of his health. In her relationships with men, the loss of her father drove Sylvia to an obsessive need to be in her lover's or husband's company practically all the time.

Although Sylvia had fantasized about her own death soon after her father's, fantasies that would dominate her poetry and her autobiographical novel *The Bell Jar*, the first visible sign of them becoming a reality occurred in 1953. During a skiing trip with a boyfriend she had decided she didn't want to marry, she fractured a fibula attempting a run that, for an inexperienced skier like herself, was 'suicidal'; the incident turns up in *The Bell Jar*. This 'accident' came just before she took up her guest editorship at *Mademoiselle*. It may have been a test run for the real thing, a few months later; or, as a story she told of her near drowning at two suggests, it may have been the surfacing of an urge that had been with her from birth. At the beach when a toddler, she said that she found herself crawling straight for the water; her mother snatched her just as her head pierced the "wall of green." Other test runs turn up in her life. In 1962, a year before her suicide, she 'accidentally' sliced off the tip of her thumb; not long after she drove her car off the road in an attempt, she said, to kill herself. But just two months after she had spent four weeks in New York guest-editing *Mademoiselle*, enjoying the kind of approval only real talent could attract (its one thing to have your parents' approval, quite another that of an upmarket, sophisticated glossy magazine), Sylvia took a shot at the real thing.

After disappearing for days, sparking a search by police, neighbours and even the boy scouts, and triggering headlines like BEAUTIFUL SMITH GIRL MISSING AT WELLESLEY, she was finally found hiding in a crawlspace in the basement. She had taken an overdose of sleeping pills; when they found her she was more dead than alive. This too found a place in *The Bell Jar*.

The sleeping pills were part of a regime started by a psychiatrist Sylvia had seen recently, recommended by her family doctor after Sylvia showed signs of depression. Her month at *Mademoiselle* by most accounts was successful, although Sylvia herself found much to criticize about her performance; she always found something lacking in her talents, even when they were being applauded by others. At the end of her month in New York, for example, she had felt such self-disgust that she threw her new, expensive clothes, bought for her trip, out of the hotel window. Before leaving she had applied for a place in a writing course given by Frank O' Connor; on her return she found she hadn't been accepted. The disappointment was devastating and her self-deprecation increased.

Like Virginia Woolf an obsessive diarist, she confided in her notebook: "You've failed to equip yourself adequately to face the world. You're spoiled, babyish, frightened. You must be more honest, more decisive, more constructive. You're not taking advantage of your freedom because you're incapable of deciding where you want to go. You're a hypocrite, plunged so deeply into your private whirlpool of negativism that the simplest actions become forbidding. When you see people who are married or happy or active, you feel frightened and lethargic. You don't even want to cope. You big baby! You just want to creep back into the womb or retreat into a masochistic hell of jealously and fear. Don't you see how selfish and self-indulgent it is to go on thinking about razors and suicide and self-inflicted wounds? Start writing. Be glad for other people and make them happy. Go out and do something. It isn't your room that's a prison, it's yourself."

This last remark is an echo of Hesse's Steppenwolf, his realization that what he seeks liberation from are the limits of his own personality. And although in this passage, Sylvia knows – as she more than likely did throughout – that suicide is no answer, like Harry Haller, she pursued it all the same.

Sleepless nights, horrible fantasies of killing her mother, shame over being unable to maintain the discipline and demanding work-schedule she had set herself – now geared toward winning Aurelia's approval – failure with men and in her friendships: all this and more harangued her guilty conscience. When her mother noticed fresh gashes on her legs, Sylvia admitted to self-harming. Then, gripping her mother's hand, she burst out: "Oh mother, the world is so rotten. I want to die. Let's die together."

The electro-convulsive therapy the psychiatrist prescribed did as much good for Sylvia as it did for Ernest Hemingway. But her mother, remembering Otto's deadly stubbornness, this time made the opposite mistake, and decided against a second opinion; the fact that she couldn't afford another doctor's fees was also a consideration. This was more material for *The Bell Jar*. Earlier, while in New York, Sylvia had become obsessed with the execution by electrocution of the 'atomic spies', Julius and Ethel Rosenberg. Now she knew what they must have felt. It's difficult to assess the effect on her already troubled psyche. Not only must the ordeal have been repeatedly horrifying and dehumanising. It was her mother who had put her into the hands of her torturer. She was put into psychiatric care at McLean Hospital, and the treatment seemed to work, but this was only on the surface; the urge was still there. Like Jacques Rigaut, Sylvia simply put her suicidal intentions on hold for ten years; eventually she'd get around to it.

Sylvia's treatment was successful enough that in 1955 she graduated from Smith *summa cum laude*; the same year one of her poems won another award, and she also started her classes at Cambridge. In February 1956 she met another young poet, Ted Hughes, at a Cambridge party. Four months later, on 16 June, 'Bloomsday' (the single day making up Joyce's *Ulysses*) they were married. For Sylvia, Hughes was "the best possible man to replace the father whose death had robbed her . . . of the man who could have been trusted never to withdraw his love."[28] Hughes was handsome, tall, strong, athletic, creative, competent, and successful, both as a poet and as a lover; tales of his seductions and affairs were plentiful. The attraction was immediate. After spying him at the party, Sylvia said he was the only man there big enough for her. They talked for a while, then Hughes ripped off her hairband and kissed her violently. She responded by biting Hughes on the cheek, drawing blood. Aggression was an ingredient in their relationship from the start. Although Plath gave the impression of a serious, sensible girl, sophisticated and poised, below the surface was a deep, insatiable hunger. Hughes, she thought, might be able to satisfy it.

For a while the marriage worked. They travelled, first to Spain, then to meet his parents in Yorkshire. Sylvia took her final exams for her degree. In August 1957 they went to America, vacationing in Cape Cod, Maine. In September she began teaching at Smith College. But by May 1958, after less than two years of marriage, the first signs of a rupture appeared; they quarrelled after Sylvia had found Ted with a girl. The pit of insecurity started to open. The major event of that year, however, was the seminar given by the poet Robert Lowell, himself a sufferer of manic-depression, that Sylvia attended and where she met and became friends with Anne Sexton. It was after this that her poetry took on a new urgency and depth. It was then that she also decided to resume the analysis she had broken off when she left for Cambridge.

In 1959, Sylvia became pregnant. After travelling through the states and spending time at a writers' colony, they returned to England. Their first child, Frieda, was born on 1 April 1960, in London, where they settled. Later that year, her first collection of poems, *The Colossus* was published; reviews were modest, but respectful. In 1961 she began work on what would become *The Bell Jar*; soon after, however, her second pregnancy ended in a miscarriage. That August they moved to Court Green, in Devon. In January 1962, Nicholas, their second child, was born.

In June that year, the womb that Sylvia had wanted to creep back into almost ten years earlier had started to attract her again. This is when she purposely drove her car off the road. Perhaps she was subconsciously aware that the man she could trust to never withdraw his love was doing precisely that. In July she discovered that Hughes was having an affair with Assia Wevill, the wife of another poet.[29] Hughes himself was feeling constrained by Sylvia's possessiveness. In September they separated and in December, at the start of one of the worst winters in memory, Sylvia and the children moved into 23 Fitzroy Road.

It was hard. Sylvia did her best. But the children were demanding, the flat was barely furnished, she had very few friends and it was very, very cold. On top of this, the man who was supposed to be there for her, as her father had been, had abandoned her, as her father had. She tortured herself, thinking of the fun he and Assia were having, while she was here, in a half-empty, freezing house, alone with the children. She tried. She set herself an impossible work schedule, as she had done before. She would paint, repair, put the house in order, take care of Frieda and Nicholas, *and* write. But it didn't work out that way. She couldn't find the time. She had an *au pair*, but she didn't last. One friend she did have was A. Alvarez, who met her and Hughes in 1960, and who remembers that Christmas Eve in 1962 when she asked him to come by for dinner and to hear some of her new poems. They had a lot in common. They were both poets and they had both attempted suicide. And not so long ago he had been through a divorce. Alvarez had already been invited to a friend's for dinner but it must have been clear to him that she was terribly lonely, so he said he would come for a drink. When he did he was surprised. She seemed different. He had never seen her so strained. He listened to her poems in the cold, bare flat, and the proximity of death was palpable. He thought she was in some kind of 'borderline psychotic' state, but because he was dealing with his own depression, the responsibility of dealing with hers too wasn't appealing. He stayed for a while, then left, knowing he had "let her down, in some final and unforgivable way."

Some other friends were Jillian and Gerry Becker, a South African couple who lived in Islington. Sylvia and the children stayed with them the weekend before she killed herself. Jillian remembers her alternately talking calmly and raving. At times she was lively and rational; at others, depressed and bewildered. Although she felt that she had been overshadowed by Hughes' more prominent success, things were going well for her, she had commissions and had been invited to broadcast. But she couldn't get over Ted's betrayal, and her sedatives, stimulants and other medication couldn't have helped her mood. She was expected to stay until Monday morning, when she would leave early, in time to be at the house when the new *au pair* arrived. But that Sunday she changed her mind and, convincing them she was fine, she returned home.

One other friend was Trevor Thomas, although at first he didn't take to her. She was a bad neighbour, leaving her pram blocking the hallway, filling up his rubbish bin instead of buying her own. But he was beginning to like her better and soon realized she was in a bad way and needed help. One evening she had rung his bell and when he answered was in tears. "I'm going to die," she told him. "Who will take care of the children?" Then she went off into a fit about Hughes and the Scarlet Woman, the Jezebel who had taken him away from her. *She* was responsible for all this. *She* was to blame. They were so happy until *she* arrived. Her husband was a famous poet, but she was a poet too and she should be celebrating: her book (*The Bell Jar*) had just been published (under the pseudonym Victoria Lucas) and had got good reviews. But he had left her with the children and no money and no help and had gone off with *that woman*. It was all *her* fault. His too . . .

Thomas didn't quite understand but it was clear she was upset and was in distress. But when he saw her the next morning he apologized for being so silly. Nothing was wrong. She was fine. Everything was all right.

What she didn't tell him was that she would get back at them, both of them. Her ten years were up. And that Sunday, when she returned from the Beckers, she did.

By the time Anne Sexton met Sylvia Plath at Robert Lowell's poetry seminar, she had already tried to kill herself three times.

By the time of her death by carbon monoxide poisoning, sitting in her car in her garage, after having lunch with a friend, she, like Plath, had acquired some considerable accolades: a Pulitzer Prize for her book *Live or Die*, honorary doctorates as well as a full professorship – although she lacked any academic training – a Fellowship of the Royal Society of Literature, as well as ones from the American Academy of Arts and Letters and the Guggenheim Foundation. She had been nominated for the National Book Award, had received several scholarships and grants and had won literary prizes. She had even formed a rock band[30]. All this however did little to dent her basic lack of self-esteem. When asked by her therapist at their first session what she thought she might be good at, she replied that the only thing she might be good at was being a prostitute; that way she might be able to help men feel sexually powerful. "It is difficult," her therapist wrote, "to communicate fully how pervasive Anne's profound lack of self-worth was and how totally unable she was to think of *any* positive abilities or qualities within herself."[31] Like Virginia Woolf and Sylvia Plath, Anne Sexton received more objective confirmation of her own talent and abilities than most people do. Yet, like them, she had a kind of inner vacuum, a perpetual emptiness that sucked away any approval as soon as it was granted.

Sexton's trouble, her therapist concluded, was her "total inability to live the life she believed was demanded of her. She felt helpless, unable to function as wife or mother . . ."[32] She came of age in post-WWII America, when women were supposed to be content with marriage, children and domesticity: the house, garage and 2.5 kids. Given this, its understandable that Sexton has become an important figure for feminists, and that her career, spanning the 'swinging sixties', would make her for a time something of a counter-cultural figure; a common remark about her is that she was read by people who didn't usually like poetry, but felt her voice 'spoke' to them. Sexton's first doctor diagnosed her condition as 'postpartum depression', following the birth of her second child, but she had already sought therapy before this, troubled by her infidelities while her husband was in the army during the Korean War. From the beginning, sex, often incest, was a central ingredient in Sexton's problems. She confessed to an incident of incest with her daughter, and her childhood relationship with her great-aunt Nana, with whom she would 'cuddle' while ignored by her parents, and for whose death she felt responsible, may have included an element of incest. It's also possible that she was sexually abused by her parents. She had many lovers and affairs, including one with one of her psychiatrists and also possibly with Sylvia Plath, and seemed to seek emotional security in sexual relationships. Her actual condition, although often described as bipolar or manic-depressive, seemed to defy definition; according to her therapist, she exhibited "a mental disorder that eluded diagnosis or cure." Symptoms included trance states, manic and sometimes violent behaviour, dread of leaving her house, dread at being left alone, especially with her children, multiple personalities, memory loss, faulty memory (or outright lying), compulsive infidelity, and an inclination toward and fascination with suicide.

At bottom though, Sexton comes across as someone, like Virginia Woolf, who "needed the care and protection of someone whose devotion was unquestioned." As her biographer remarked, once her madness was out in the open, "she took on the role of patient, which she did not abandon for the rest of her life."[33] Not only her doctors, but her family, friends, and acquaintances were all drawn into the impossible and unrewarding task of saving her.

Sexton's symptoms began with her becoming a mother. Although in her last days, Sylvia Plath found taking care of her children a burden and a prison, she had been abandoned with them by Hughes in a cold, empty house; when their marriage was going well, she loved being a mother. Not so Anne Sexton. Sexton lacked Sylvia's determination to excel, and her application to practical tasks. (Like Virginia Woolf, with whom she felt a connection, Sylvia used domestic chores to fight off her fears; in her last journal entry, Woolf comments on the virtues of cooking haddock and sausages.) Sexton was hopelessly undomestic. She felt inadequate in everything, especially when her husband was away on one of his many business trips. On one occasion, on a day when he had driven eight hundred miles, he called and asked her to put potatoes in the oven; he would fix the rest of dinner when he got home, as he usually did. When he returned, he discovered the potatoes were where he had left them. When he asked why she hadn't put them in the oven, she replied that she didn't know how. Helplessness is often a ploy for drawing attention and care, and whether or not Sexton was really as inept as she appeared, her impracticality, reminiscent of Walter Benjamin's, had the desired effect.

Six months after entering treatment for her 'postpartum depression', Sexton's condition worsened. She experienced a morbid fear of being alone with her babies. It began when she returned late from a party; her husband was away and a neighbour had offered to baby-sit. Joy, her second daughter, had croup, and when Sexton returned she was choking; it was clear she couldn't breath. Sexton turned on the hot shower and held Joy in the bathroom all night, hoping the steam would help. After that she had a terrible fear that the children would die. Now whenever her husband went away, she went through terrific agonies. She wouldn't eat, and she would cry ceaselessly. Only when he returned did her symptoms stop.

These fears turned into attacks of rage against the children. She would seize Linda, her two-year old, and slap her. Once, when she found Linda playing with her excrement, she picked her up and threw her across the room. After this she became afraid that she would kill them. Her family stepped in, taking care of the children while her husband was away, hiring a woman to do the chores, even paying her psychiatric bills. It didn't help. One night near the anniversary of her great aunt's death, Sexton fell into a deep depression. She took a portrait of Nana and the diary she kept when the family had finally decided to put her in a nursing home. Then she took the bottle of sleeping pills her doctor had given her and went to the back porch. She sat there, the pills in one hand, the portrait in another, thinking it over. The idea that she would let her doctor down if she killed herself made her hesitate. Her husband woke up, found her sitting there in the dark, and called her psychiatrist. Sexton said she wanted to get to the place where Nana was; as with Sylvia, the womb was inviting her to crawl back inside.

Sexton was hospitalised for three weeks; her sister took Linda, and Joy lived with her grandmother; Sexton was separated from her children for the next three years. In November 1956, the day before her twenty-eighth birthday, Sexton made another suicide attempt. She took an overdose of barbiturates, Nembutal, which she later called her 'kill-me pills'. She would carry a supply of them in her handbag ever after, ready at any time to join Nana; for a backup, she also had a razor. When she felt she was drifting off, she phoned her mother-in-law. The failed attempt resulted in a stay at Glenside, a forbidding mental institution, grim and depressing compared to the first clinic she had stayed at. At this point she and her family accepted that she was officially 'sick', possibly insane. Sexton explained: "I was trying my damnedest to lead a conventional life, for that was how I was brought up, and it was what my husband wanted of me. But one can't build little white picket fences to keep nightmares out. The surface cracked when I was about twenty-eight. I had a psychotic breakdown and tried to kill myself." The notion of the 'desperate housewife' is by now a cliché, but Sexton seems to have invented the role.

It's tempting to suspect she took extreme steps to avoid her unwanted responsibilities. "My feeling for my children," she wrote, "does not surpass my desire to be free of their demands on my emotions." And even her first doctor expressed doubts that she had a true organically based depression. But breakdowns on both sides of the family history suggest some inherited predisposition, as do the severity of her symptoms: radical mood shifts, anorexia, insomnia, suicidal impulses, wild rages.

Anne may have sunk into complete madness, or she may have killed herself much earlier than she did, if not for a suggestion by her therapist. Anne seemed to have reserves of energy, but, like Dostoyevsky's Stavrogin, had no idea what to do with them. She talked about walking from room to room, thinking of something to do, feeling like a caged animal, feeling "this almost terrible energy in me." She had to fight not to masturbate all day, and twined her hair into knots as she read a magazine. She made the beds, cleaned the bathroom, baked cookies, but it was all 'displacement activity', even the masturbation, although sex isn't that far removed from creative work. Her feelings of inadequacy were rooted in the lack of attention she received from her mother, a lack she was now passing on to her own children. Her obsession with Nana was understandable: she was the one source of approval, a position that was now occupied by her husband. What Anne needed was to find some means of feeling capable *herself*. When she told her therapist that the only thing she could be good at was prostitution, he disagreed. His diagnostic tests showed she had a great deal of unrealised potential. Why don't you write about your feelings, your experiences, he asked. If nothing else, it might help other people facing similar problems.

Soon after Anne began to bring her doctor her poems. He was impressed. They were polished, accomplished, and showed surprising technical mastery. She had finally found something she was good at.

By 1960, her collection *To Bedlam and Part Way Back* was published to good reviews. The seminar with Robert Lowell and the other poetry workshops she attended had paid off, although she was too frightened to make the telephone calls to ask to join them, and had to get a friend to do it. Throughout the rest of her life, Sexton did practically nothing by or for herself, except write and give her poetry performances. These were more of an entertainment than a traditional poetry reading, and were not always to the cognoscenti's liking: at one event, an academic asked, "How about more Anne Sexton and less Phyllis Diller," the name of a popular comedienne of the time. She refused or was unable to do the simplest things, like go shopping, unless accompanied by a close friend. The only activities she could manage were her doctor's appointments, and those with her hairdresser. (Sexton always managed to keep her appearance elegant, and in her early years had been a model.). Any other need to leave her house threw her into a panic. She once agonised for weeks over the need to get the children some new shoes.

She became associated with the 'confessional' school of poetry; as her biographer wrote "all that was 'sick' or 'hysterical' about her behaviour in day-to-day life could be turned into something valuable through the act of writing poetry."[34] Understandably, her central theme was death. Her poems had titles like "Godfather Death," "The Death of Fathers," "For Mr. Death Who Stands with His Door Open," "The Death Baby." Her last book published in her lifetime was *The Death Notebooks*. The posthumously published *The Awful Rowing Toward God*, which showed her later, more religious pursuits, suggests the tension and strain of her experience; this, however, was less popular with her readers.

As the sixties moved on Sexton's achievements accrued, and she moved away from strictly 'confessional' verse to cultural criticism. She lived a kind of double life. A public figure, publishing books, accepting awards, receiving distinctions, on one hand; on the other, her intractable self-hatred led to repeated breakdowns, suicide attempts and the inevitable hospitalisation. Her dependencies and neuroses increased. Among others she developed an obsession with constipation, and wouldn't travel without a supply of laxatives. In Detroit, after a performance, she discovered she'd ran out, and asked a friend to find some. The friend refused; Sexton got a cab and at midnight prowled the streets, looking for an open pharmacy. Other, more necessary medications became a routine. Like many performers, she developed a stage persona that contrasted sharply with her 'real' self. Confident, glamorous, commanding before an audience, in the dressing-room she was a wreck, dependent on alcohol to induce the manic mood necessary for her act. Heavy drinking had always been part of her adult life and in the end would lead to her final depression. Some of her 'fans' also noticed another duality. While on stage, Anne could speak about the 'truths' of human relations, the insights that made her poetry so meaningful to her readers. Yet in her own life, she was unable to make much use of these.

Throughout her rising success, and repeated breakdowns and suicide attempts, her husband and children tried to cope, but the situation was unstable and at times exploded into violence, followed by forgiveness and reassurance. Yet Sexton's infidelities were a regular part of their marriage, and in 1973, she asked for a divorce. Their break-up precipitated her final decline. Her daughters, now young women, found it difficult to handle their unpredictable mother, and many friends had been used up, their supply of affection and concern gone. Increasingly, Sexton depended on drink and affairs to keep her going, but her health had visibly declined. Of Ernest Hemingway's suicide she said "to shoot himself with a gun in the mouth is the greatest act of courage I can think of." Her friend Sylvia's death fascinated her. They were, she had felt, in a kind of competition, and Sylvia had got there first. "I'm so fascinated with Sylvia's death: the idea of dying perfect, certainly not mutilated . . . Sleeping Beauty remained perfect . . ." It was time to join her.

Divorced, living alone, estranged from friends and family, she had been emptied by her misery, and her alcoholism had deadened her creativity. Her suicide, though not unexpected, was a surprise. There was no note, no warning. After a final lunch with her long time friend Maxine Kumin, at which she seemed normal, at least for her, Anne Sexton got into her car in her garage and turned on the ignition. The radio was playing. It was the act, her therapist wrote, "of a lonely and despairing alcoholic."[35] In a tribute to her in the *New York Times*, Erica Jong wrote, "Anne Sexton killed herself because it is too painful to live in this world without numbness, and she had no numbness at all."[36]

Notes

1 William Styron *Darkness Visible* (Picador: London, 1991) p. 50.
2 Ibid. p. 17.
3 William James *The Varieties of Religious Experience* (Collier Books: New York, 1977) p. 129.

4   Kay Redfield Jamison *Touched by Fire* (Free Press Paperbacks: New York, 1993) p. 13, 17

5   Ibid. p. 17.

6   Quoted in Carolina King Barnard Hall *Anne Sexton* (Twayne Publications: Boston, 1989) p. 7.

7   Anthony Storr *The Dynamics of Creation* (Atheneum: New York, 1972) p. 75

8   Ibid. p. 76.

9   Quoted in Diane Wood Middlebrook *Anne Sexton: A Biography* (Virago Press: London, 1991) p. 259.

10 Trevor Thomas *Sylvia Plath: Last Encounters* (privately printed, Bedford, England, 1989) p. 4.

11 Mitchell Leaska *Granite and Rainbow: The Hidden Life of Virginia Woolf* (Picador: London, 1998) p. 179.

12 Storr p. 82.

13 Kay Redfield Jamison points out that depression ran in Virginia Woolf's family. "Her grandfather, mother, sister, brother and niece all suffered from recurrent depressions, her father and another brother were cyclothymic [a milder form of the ailment], and her cousin James, who had been institutionalised for mania and depression, died of acute mania." (Jamison, p. 225). Clearly, there is evidence to suggest that manic-depression and other mental and emotional disorders can be inherited. It is also highly possible that such inherited traits remain latent unless released by a 'trigger', which in Virginia's case seemed the death of her mother and the incestuous attentions of her step-brothers.

14 Although Virginia Woolf has been retroactively diagnosed as having bipolar (manic-depressive) illness, some of her symptoms seem to suggest similarities to schizophrenia. On a disastrous Italian holiday, she heard voices ordering her to do "all kinds of wild things," King Edward spouting obscenities, and the birds singing in Greek. Other symptoms included violence, incessant talking ending in gibberish, coma, anorexic body image, delusions, fear of being seen in public, and the belief that strangers were talking about her.

15 Virginia Woolf *A Writer's Diary* ed. Leonard Woolf, (The Hogarth Press: London, 1953) p. 229.

16 As his satiric novel attacking the clique, *The Apes of God*, made clear.

17 Woolf, *A Writer's Diary* pp. 228–231.

18 Storr, pp. 78–79.

19 Ibid. p. 79.

20 Leaska, p. 433.

21 Quoted in Herbert Marder *The Measure of Life: Virginia Woolf's Last Years* (Cornell University Press: 2000) p. 55.

22 There is a blue plaque on the house, announcing, understandably, not that Plath killed herself there, but that W. B. Yeats had lived there. Plath, who lived for a time in nearby Chalcot Square (this house does have a blue plaque noting that fact) came across the house by chance, saw that flats in it were to let, and quickly arranged a five-year lease, of which Hughes paid a year's rent in advance. Later, Plath opened a volume of Yeats at random, half-hoping for some kind of sign. The passage she found read, "Get wine and food to give you strength and courage and I will get the house ready," which she took to mean she had made the right decision. Like Plath, Trevor Thomas, who himself had come across the house first and wanted the maisonette that Plath, he felt, stole from him (he wound up renting the garden flat below), was also attracted to the idea of living in a house that Yeats had inhabited, because of his interest in the occult, something, as is well known, Yeats was devoted to. In his memoir mentioned above (n. 10), Thomas speculates some vague connection between Yeats' occult interest and Plath's sad end. Yet, as Yeats lived in the house as a child and only briefly, he could hardly be responsible for the "forces for good and evil" that "may have been evoked in the séances possibly held in No. 23 Fitzroy Road," the effects of which, Thomas hints, "linger on and affect others there." Yeats' mother, who also lived in the house, was, it is true, a believer in ghosts and fairies, but not, as far as we know, a practitioner of black magic, nor, for that matter, was Yeats.

23 The bedrooms were in the upper part of the house, and as the coal gas used in the oven is heavier than air, and so sinks, the children were free of danger. Not so Trevor Thomas, who lived below her. He inhaled the fumes as he slept, woke up sick very late that day, and was later diagnosed with carbon monoxide poisoning.

24 For example, the autopsy report states that she died on 11/2/63, but that her body was examined on 10/2/63.

25 Janet Malcolm *The Silent Woman: Sylvia Plath and Ted Hughes* (Granta Books: London, 2005). Highly recommended. Although the personal and literary complications and cover-ups that

Malcolm untangles arose after Plath's death, and are slightly tangential to my purposes here, some indication of what is involved can be gleaned from the fact that Hughes destroyed (or lost or misplaced – both were offered at different times as explanations for what happened to them) Plath's last journals, even though, like Woolf, she was an obsessive diarist and clearly these last volumes would be of value in understanding her motivations and state of mind leading up to her suicide. Likewise unusual is the fact that Hughes, and later Olwyn Hughes, gained complete control over Plath's letters, even those written to her mother and which were already in her possession. When Aurelia Plath wished to publish a collection of her daughter's letters, she had to seek permission from the Hughes estate; not surprisingly, the letters published were subject to the same restrictions as was Anne Stevenson's biography. Mrs. Plath was also denied permission to read the last letter Sylvia wrote to her, only hours before she killed herself – at least she was strongly advised not to, and accepted this.

Hughes also took legal action against both Trevor Thomas, stopping the circulation of his privately printed memoir of Plath's last days, as well as forcing him to retract a statement about a party being held at 23 Fitzroy Road on the evening Plath killed herself at which bongo drums were played; and A. Alvarez, for publishing the first chapter of his book, *The Savage God*, in *The Observer* under the title "Sylvia Plath's Road to Suicide;" Hughes subsequently tried to stop publication of the book, which gives an account of Alvarez's friendship with Plath in the weeks leading up to her death. Hughes changed the selection of her poems made by Plath herself for her collection *Ariel*, published posthumously; he retained only twenty-seven of her original forty-one poems; the poems excised make uncomfortable suggestions about their relationship.

Strangest of all, as already mentioned, Hughes placed Plath's literary estate into the hands of his sister Olwyn, who disliked Plath, and who had an inordinate influence over Hughes himself. Hughes, like Yeats, was a keen student of the occult, initiated into the dark arts by Olwyn, who was a devotee of astrology and other magical pursuits. After Sylvia's death, Hughes remarked, "It was a fight to the death. One of us had to die," implying that some kind of contest of wills was involved in their relationship, and he was concerned that Sylvia may have

160

used black magic against him; there is a story that Sylvia had once skimmed a knife across the top of Hughes' desk, collecting, among other things, his dandruff, fingernails and dead skin. Hughes was deeply interested in shamanism, and the 'bongo drums' Trevor Thomas reported hearing on the evening of the day of Plath's death, may have been a means of exorcising whatever unwanted influence of Plath that remained in the house.

26 An idea of the Hughes' take on Sylvia can be garnered by the fact that the family's chief concern was over how the scandal of her suicide would affect Ted's reputation.

27 Ronald Hayman points out that in order to prove that human behaviour consisted almost completely of prejudices, Otto Plath would skin, cook and eat a rat in front of his students.

28 Ronald Hayman *The Death and Life of Sylvia Plath* (Sutton Publishing: Phoenix Mill, 2003) p. 91.

29 On 25 March 1969, Assia Wevill copied Sylvia Plath by gassing herself and her two year old daughter by Ted Hughes, Shura, in the kitchen of their flat. Although 'with' Assia at the time, Hughes was having an affair with yet another woman, Brenda Hedden. Hughes himself remarked, "All the women I have anything to do with seem to die." One wonders if he ever asked why that may have been. Like Freud and Valery Briusov, Hughes seems to me to be one of my 'agents of suicide'.

30 Anne Sexton and Her Kind.

31 Martin T. Orne, foreword, Diane Wood Middlebrook *Anne Sexton: A Biography* (Virago Press: London, 1991) p.xiii.

32 Ibid.

33 Ibid. p. 35. As with Virginia Woolf, there was a history of mental illness in Sexton's family. Her great aunt received electro-convulsive therapy; her grandfather was hospitalised for a nervous breakdown; her father was an alcoholic; her aunt committed suicide.

34 Ibid. p. 63.

35 Ibid. p. xx

36 Erica Jong "Remembering Anne Sexton," *New York Times* 27 October 1974.

Ten Suicides

Yukio Mishima

Probably the most spectacular literary suicide, certainly of recent times, was that of the Japanese novelist Yukio Mishima, who was born Kimitake Hiraoka on 14 January 1925 in the Yotsuya district of Tokyo. On 25 November 1970, before a literally captive audience, Mishima performed *hara-kiri*. His lover and disciple Masakatsu Morita, who would also attempt *hara-kiri*, after several attempts failed to decapitate Mishima as planned, leaving incomplete the *kaishakunin* part of the ritual, aimed to relieve the agony of disembowelment. Both received their finishing touches at the hands and sword of a third member of Mishima's *Tatenokai* ("Shield Society"), a kind of private army that Mishima hoped would be a model for a new, right-wing Japan, recapturing the samurai glories of old.

That day Mishima and his followers had taken hostage an army general at a *Jieitai* (self-defence forces) military base at Ichigaya. On threat of death, Mishima compelled the general to assemble the garrison, some 1,000 men. He then addressed them from the balcony, hoping to instil some of the patriotic and military fervour that, along with his narcissism and strange sadomasochistic fantasies, had become a central part of his self-image. He called for a coup d'état, a rejection of the 'Americanization' of Japan that had begun following WWII, and a reinstatement of the emperor. His harangues failed; the soldiers shouted abuse and obscenities. They had no interest in Mishima's samurai dreams. As the abuse grew, Mishima shouted "Listen! Listen! Listen!" No one did, and by this time police helicopters were drowning out both him and his hecklers.

Humiliated, Mishima returned to the room where they held the general. He tore off his jacket, revealing his naked torso. The general begged him to stop. "I was bound to do this,"

162

Mishima replied. Then he knelt on the carpet, loosened his trousers, and grabbed the *yoroidoshi*, a foot-long, sharply pointed dagger. With his left hand he rubbed a spot on his lower left abdomen, then brought the point of the blade to its target. Behind him his lover Morita, shaking and sweating, raised his sword. Mishima shouted a final salute "*Tenno Heika Banzai!*" (Long live the Emperor!), then emptied his lungs. Taking one last breath, he exhaled powerfully and sent the dagger home. He made a deep horizontal cut across his stomach; blood poured onto the floor. Completing the incisions, his intestines exposed, he waited for Morita to end it. But as the shaking student hesitated, Mishima collapsed, and the blow only dug deep into his shoulders. Two more attempts failed to decapitate him. Finally, another follower, a student of *kendo* (Japanese fencing), grabbed the sword and finished the job. When it was Morita's turn at disembowelment the panicky student did little more than scratch himself. The *kendo* student again took charge and quickly dispatched him as well. Then Mishima's followers untied the general and surrendered themselves to the police.

Its tempting to allocate Mishima's death to the Political Suicide category – a right-wing offering to balance Mayakovsky's leftist sacrifice – and indeed it belongs here to some degree, but Mishima's politics were themselves an expression of his deeper narcissistic and morbid sexual fantasy life. Mishima's interest in the samurai, the military and tradition have much more to do with his fascination with death, blood and beautiful male bodies than with any real insight or concern with politics. From his childhood, Mishima had a morbid fascination with "death and night and blood" and the gruesome debacle of his gory death was something he had looked forward to for some time. His suicide was much more an aesthetic than a political act.

Some idea of Mishima's psyche can be gleaned from the fact that his first orgasm was occasioned by his discovery of a reproduction of a Renaissance painting of St. Sebastian, the Christian martyr, tied to a tree and shot with arrows. In his early autobiographical novel *Confessions of a Mask* he writes,

"A remarkably handsome youth was bound naked to the trunk of a tree . . . Were it not for the arrows with their shafts deeply sunk into his left armpit and right side, he would seem more a Roman athlete . . . The arrows have eaten into the tense, fragrant, youthful flesh, and are about to consume his body from within with flames of supreme agony and ecstasy." The young Mishima unconsciously plays with himself while gazing at this sight, and is surprised when his 'toy' "burst forth, bringing with it a blinding intoxication." Years later, Mishima would famously pose for a photograph recreating this treasured scene.

As a child, Mishima was raised as a girl by his authoritarian and neurotic grandmother, who kept him close to her side in her darkened sick room; he later admitted that he enjoyed being secluded with her, and like Mayakovsky and Witkacy, Mishima later developed hypochondria, specifically a food phobia. Returned to his parents at 12, he developed a semi-incestuous relationship with his mother, and his father, a brutal military type, tried to root out any incipient literary impulse he may have had. His favourite fairy tales were those which ended in a gory death of the hero – "I was completely in love with any youth who was killed" – and he had a particular fascination with Hans Christian Andersen's "Rose-Elf," whose hero is stabbed to death and decapitated while kissing a rose given to him by his love. While playing with his schoolmates he discovered a "force" within him, "bent . . . upon the complete disintegration of my inner balance . . . a compulsion toward suicide, that subtle and secret impulse." During the war, as a teenager he worked at a *kamikaze* factory; realizing the planes were designed to be destroyed, he was enchanted by the fact that the factory was "dedicated to a monstrous nothingness." As Japan was losing the war, with destruction all around, he felt "free." "Everyday life had become a thing of unspeakable happiness. It was in death that I had discovered my real 'life's aim'." These early images and thrills had a profound effect on Mishima, and his huge literary output, only a small fraction of which has been translated into English, can be seen as an attempt at working out the implications of these youthful experiences.

Suicide among Japanese writers is not uncommon. Osama Dazai, with whom Mishima was for a time in a kind of competition, and with whom he shared remarkable similarities, drowned himself and his mistress in 1948. Yasunari Kawabata, Mishima's mentor, and the first Japanese author to win the Nobel Prize for literature, gassed himself 18 months after Mishima's suicide. The list goes on.[1] Yet, as Henry Scott Stokes' brilliant biography of Mishima makes clear, "Mishima endlessly rehearsed his own death."[2] In 1960 he wrote a story, "Patriotism," which glorifies *hara-kiri*. Five years later, he turned the story into a film, in which he took the part of an army lieutenant who disembowels himself, reminding us of Mayakovsky's part in the film *Not Born for Money*, a striking parallel. In his novel *Runaway Horses*, the protagonist, a right-wing terrorist, kills himself. And in the film *Hitogiri*, Mishima took the part of a man who slices open his stomach. The bloody scene in the *Jietai* headquarters that late November morning was something Mishima had practised quite a bit.

Like Witkacy, an irredeemable self-dramatiser, Mishima adopted many roles: a *yakuza* gangster, cross-dressing stage magician, body builder, family man, leather-jacketed motor-cyclist. He was addicted to seeing images of himself, as the book of photographs of him posing in the nude on the sea-shore, or with a white rose in his mouth, *Torture by Roses*, suggests. All these examples of his inherent exhibitionism damaged his literary reputation, and are indications of his basic lack of identity. But the role he embraced more than others was that of the soldier. This was prompted by guilt over his avoiding military service during the war by telling the army doctor he was tubercular; Mishima seemed to wallow in masochistic shame over this, and it gave justification for his eventual self-martyrdom. He was also ashamed of his weak, short body and sickly childhood, and in his thirties devoted himself to physical fitness, a discipline he continued to his death. But unlike the German novelist Ernst Jünger, a decorated war hero, Mishima's militarism was another expression of his fantasy life. The gruesome end of this particular fantasy was preceded by other gory displays. Initiation into his *Tatenokai* included drinking blood gathered from the cut fingers of the initiates, which Mishima flavoured with salt and passed around in a cup. Mishima's fascist tendencies, ill-judged humour and determination to tempt his critics came together in one of his last plays, *My Friend Hitler*. One recognizes that the English initials of his "Shield Society" are SS.

Most of Mishima's novels have an underlying sadism. In *The Sailor Who Fell from Grace with the Sea*, schoolboys murder one of their mothers' lovers. In *Temple of the Golden Pavilion*, a monk burns down a temple because of its beauty. In *Kyoko's House*, a narcissistic actor commits suicide with his mistress. In *Thirst for Love*, a widow falls in love with a young farm boy but kills him when he returns her interest. There is also a fundamental pointlessness. In the play *The Damask Drum*, the drum in question makes no sound when hit, a typical symbol. The essential emptiness and nihilism of Mishima's work is often obscured by the jewelled language, reminiscent in many ways of another sadistic nihilist, Valery Briusov (see Agents of Suicide). At the time of his suicide, he had completed a vast tetralogy, *The Sea of Fertility*, which has reincarnation as its theme, an attempt to infuse his work with something more than "night and blood and death." But the characters involved in this saga of sixty years of Japanese history, are caught in the same pointlessness of his earlier works. Kiyoaki, the central character, is only certain of his love for Lady Satoko when she gets engaged to someone else; he then seduces her and makes her pregnant, which forces her to enter a monastery, where he can never see her. Similar predicaments await him in future incarnations, including that of the right-wing terrorist who kills himself in *Runaway Horses*. Like many morbid romantics, Mishima believed the only love worth having is an unattainable one. A better title might have been *The Sea of Futility*.

Mishima's fantasy of a new samurai age had nothing to do with politics, but was his attempt to impose his obsessions on reality, an attempt he more than likely knew would fail. As one writer put it, it was "rather as if Tolkien had organised a plot to overthrow Queen Elizabeth and put Gandalf on the throne of England."[3] That this fantasy included real blood and death is an expression of his capacity to compel others to share his solipsistic vision; it doesn't take much to realize that, like many aesthetic suicides, Mishima had a strong belief that he was really the only person in the world, or at least that his subjectivity, his needs and appetites, were more real than anything else. While this may make for a powerful asset in writing, it leads to a dangerous disregard for other people, or at least to a tendency to see them as actors in your tale. The Japanese public, however, who had hailed Mishima as one of their greats in the 1950s, were embarrassed by his posturing and camp antics, such as starring in a trashy gangster film, and even singing the title song. By the time of his suicide, the general reaction was mild disgust, or an echoing of the response he received at the hands of his captive audience.

Harry Crosby

Like Mishima, the poet manqué Harry Crosby enjoyed an elaborate fantasy life, which culminated in a dual suicide on 10 December 1929, at a friend's studio in the Hotel des Artistes in New York City. There is, however, some speculation that Josephine Bigelow, the recently married woman he was having an affair with, wasn't as keen on ending her life as he was. For Malcolm Cowley, who knew Crosby in the Paris of the 'Lost Generation,' his suicide "was the last term of a syllogism: it was like the signature to a second-rate but honest and exciting poem."[4] And like Mishima, Crosby is a good example of the aesthetic suicide's disinterest in other people. For Cowley, Crosby was "self-centred without being introspective, and devoted to his friends without being sympathetic." The son of one of the richest banking families in Boston and the nephew of the financier J.P. Morgan, Crosby had a considerable inheritance, which he had no qualms about exploiting in his pursuit of excess; as his biography makes clear, Harry "appreciated waste," a sentiment he shares with the renegade surrealist and friend of Walter Benjamin, Georges Bataille[5]. Reckless, indifferent to consequences, and with a "talent for carelessness," Crosby is today seen by some as a great 'transgressive'; most readers, however, will simply recognize a spoilt narcissist.

Along with the usual retinue of extravagance enjoyed by rich kids everywhere – drink, drugs, sex, fast cars, fascinating hangers-on, including some of the literary greats of the time – Harry's peculiar delight was the contemplation of death, his own, which he associated with and built up into a personal mythology of sun worship, patched together from as many sources as he could find. "I ponder death more frequently than I do any other subject," he wrote, "even in the most joyous and flourishing moments of my life."[6] Although his poetry received some half-hearted applause from his more esteemed acquaintances – Lawrence, Eliot and Pound all contributed appreciations of his work to a posthumous collection, *Torchbearer*, admittedly commissioned and published by his own press, Black Sun – his poems are really one long suicide note. If he hadn't shot himself and his mistress, he would probably be less known today than he is; even his biographer Geoffrey Wolff admitted that were it not for his suicide, he wouldn't have written a book about him.

Again like Mishima, fantasies of his death were sexually stimulating. "Mutual suicide," he believed, was "the most sublime of couplings."[7] From the age of twenty-two, he repeatedly announced his intention to kill himself, and he had long planned to achieve *la grande mort* with his wife Caresse, preferably by flying a plane into the sun on the day he had chosen to cash in his and her chips: 31 October 1942. In the end, however, two days after a party given for him and Caresse by the poet Hart Crane – who would himself commit suicide two years later – and whose guests included William Carlos Williams, e.e.cummings and Cowley, he took his leave with another woman. While it is true that he made suicide pacts with practically every woman he was involved with, and these were many, why he decided to do it ahead of schedule remains a mystery. The event, which made the headlines, inspired cummings. "2 boston dolls;" he wrote, "found with holes in each other's lullaby"

Harry's fascination with death began in WWI, when he served as an ambulance driver. On 22 November 1917, during the second battle of Verdun, after heavy shelling had destroyed his vehicle, he was amazed to find himself still alive. His good fortune shifted into guilt and afterward he commemorated the death of his fellow driver Andrew Davis Weld each year, on his 'death day'. As his biographer wrote, "he formed his closest and most enduring friendship with a corpse . . ."[8] Harry swore that if he should "escape this peril" he would "ever after lead a virtuous, uncomplaining life."[9] Like many such near-death resolutions, it came to naught.

Harry continued to make similar grand resolves to change his life, which were generally forgotten the next day, and he invariably returned to indulging in every excess he could think of. These were considerable. He took to wearing all black, painted his fingernails black, and wore a black cloth carnation. On a trip to North Africa, he had a cross tattooed on the sole of one foot, and a pagan sun symbol on the other.[10] He became a devotee of Poe, Baudelaire and other morbid, decadent writers. Drink became a particularly favourite pastime and Harry developed an amazing capacity for intoxication; later this included other *de rigueur* items like opium, absinthe and hashish. His capacity for revelry was legendary. He would throw lavish dinner parties in his bed, often ending with everyone in the bath. He arranged carriage races in the streets of Paris. Inheriting a huge collection of rare books, he gave them away after reading them, sometimes pencilling in ridiculously low prices and slipping them into bookstalls along the Seine. Like the equally excessive Aleister Crowley, Crosby developed a unique signature, attaching the image of a black sun to his name.[11] An insight into his attitude toward life can be gleaned from this telegram, sent to his outraged Back Bay, Boston parents: PLEASE SELL $10,000 WORTH OF STOCK WE HAVE DECIDED TO LIVE A MAD AND EXTRAVAGANT LIFE. He did.

Again like Crowley, Crosby never grew out of an adolescent desire to shock the folks back home. His attack on Boston provincialism began with his marriage to the older Mary Phelps ("Polly") Jacobs, later re-christened Caresse. She was already married and when Crosby fell in love with her, he threatened suicide unless she left her husband. She did and their subsequent marriage outraged both families. The couple didn't care, as two days after their wedding they left Boston for Paris.

For a time Crosby worked at his uncle's bank, but the financial life bored him, and, fascinated by the bohemians of Montparnasse, he soon quit, announcing his plan to become a poet. Along with writing highly derivative decadent verse, this included pursuing Rimbaud's "systematic derangement of the senses" with alacrity. As Malcolm Cowley writes, "he had set himself the goal of going crazy in order to become a genius."[12]

In 1927 Harry and Caresse started the Black Sun Press. Originally titled *Éditions Narcisse*, an apt name for a vanity press, along with their own works, Black Sun went on to publish some of the most important writers of the time, and it is this, with his suicide, that has established Crosby in literary history. D.H. Lawrence, Archibald MacLeish, James Joyce, Kay Boyle (friend of René Crevel), and Hart Crane are some of the names associated with Black Sun, which specialized in producing lavish and highly collectible editions.[13] Yet Harry wasn't satisfied with simply enabling other writers to produce beautiful work. He was determined to be a poet himself, and although his autobiographical journal, *Shadows of the Sun*, displays neither an acute observation of the outer world, nor any profound insight into his inner one, Crosby applied himself to the task with tenacity. Again like Crowley, he 'willed' himself to become a poet, and while his work lacks any sign of natural talent, the sheer doggedness is at times admirable. Like Aldous Huxley, he read through the encyclopaedia, in order to "become an intellectual;" unlike Huxley though, the learning was superficial.

Although Harry moved from his earlier *fin-de-siècle* obsessions into a kind of modernism – he was associated with the avant-garde literary magazine *Transitions* – his fascinations remained the same. In "Lit de Mort" he writes: "I shall die within my lady's arms/And from her mouth drink down the purple wine/And tremble at the touch of naked charms/With silver fingers seeking to entwine./ My dying words shall be a lover's sighs/Beyond the last faint rhythm of her thighs."[14] A later poem, "Assassin," which Wolff describes as "a sometimes brutal, sometimes suicidal, sometimes visionary poem of more than a hundred lines," begins "*The Mad Queen commands: Murder the sterility and hypocrisy of the world, destroy the weak and insignificant, do violence to the multitude in order that a new strong world shall arise to worship the Mad Queen, Goddess of the Sun.*"[15] Further on, "*the mirror crashes against my face and bursts into a thousand suns*" and "*I crash out through the window, naked, widespread upon a Heliosaurus . . . and plunge it into the ink-pot of the Black Sun . . .*"

Although the influence of Rimbaud is clear, and the dying fall of Dowson has been jettisoned, Crosby is fixed on the same point. As Wolff says, "Assassin" is "less a poem than a testament, and its art is almost overwhelmed by its pathology." One last quotation seems to clinch this. "I the Assassin chosen by the Mad Queen I the Murderer of the World shall in my fury murder myself. I shall cut out my heart take it into my joined hands and walk towards the sun without stopping until I fall down dead."

How he could continue walking once his heart had been cut out is unclear, but its doubtful Crosby ever considered making sense. In another poem "Sun-Death," (later titled "Hail Death!"), Harry name checks great suicides of the past: Socrates, Sappho, Cleopatra, Jesus, Van Gogh and others, and repeats Nietzsche's injunction to "die at the right time." The right time, according to Harry, was when "your soul and your body, your spirit and your senses are concentrated, are reduced to a pin-point, . . . the point of finality, irrevocable as the sun . . ." Only then can we "penetrate into the cavern of the sombre Slave-Girl of Death," and "enjoy explosion" with her. And he warns against the stupid death of the Philistines, which can be nothing more than a whimper, and whose bodies and souls are "dumped unceremoniously into the world's latrine . . ."[16]

How running off to a friend's studio in New York's Hotel des Artistes with a newly married woman qualified as his "point of finality, irrevocable as the sun," remains an open question. A few days before his death he had invited Caresse to jump with him from the twenty-seventh floor of the Savoy-Plaza Hotel. She declined. Although she may have agreed to fly a plane into the sun in late October 1942, that was more than a decade away. Caresse, like Harry, had many other lovers and perhaps she was enjoying them too much to want to call it quits. Josephine Bigelow, however, seemed mad on the idea, although how much this was sincere and how much it was morbid pillow talk is unclear. They were extravagant people and they said extravagant things. A poem from her to Harry relates their shared delights: orchids, caviar, champagne, the number 13, the colour black. It also said what she knew Harry wanted to hear: "Death is our marriage." At the time Harry was in love with at least four women: Caresse, Josephine, and two others, Constance Coolidge, otherwise known as the Comtesse de Jumilhac, and a woman he called the Sorceress. But then Harry was always in love with someone.

He had bought an automatic a year earlier, had a sun engraved on it and took to carrying it. While Caresse, Harry's mother and his uncle J.P. Morgan waited for Harry to arrive at Morgan's townhouse for lunch, he and Josephine had other plans. When he didn't turn up, J.P. was miffed and Caresse concerned. Later, at dinner with Hart Crane, there was still no word, and Caresse, knowing of Harry's frequent rendezvous' at his friend's studio, telephoned the friend and asked if he would see if Harry was there. The friend knew he was; he had let Harry and Josephine in earlier that day, and he agreed to go and tell Harry to get in touch. When he arrived the door was bolted from the inside; when he knocked, no one answered. Eventually the building superintendent used an axe. Inside, they discovered Harry and Josephine fully clothed in bed. A fresh bullet hole was in his right temple, another was in Josephine's left temple. In Harry's hand was the Belgian automatic, engraved with the sun. A doctor who examined the bodies said that Harry had lived for two hours after Josephine. He had shot her, then, two hours later, shot himself.

Accounts of their relationship differ. For some they were desperately in love; for others, she was a nuisance Harry was eager to get rid off. For still others, especially Josephine's husband, she was happily married and the idea that she was serious about suicide was absurd; it was clear Harry had murdered her. What exactly happened is still uncertain. Perhaps, dared to do it, he acted on impulse, produced the pistol, and followed through. Then, realizing he would be charged with murder, he decided that after all, now was the right time to die. There was no suicide note, except, of course, his poems, and this disappointed the press and the police. The tabloids had a field day in any case, but less than a week later the deaths were old news and were forgotten. As Geoffrey Wolff writes: "Harry's shot was not heard round the world, nor did its bang reverberate beyond the merest instant."[17]

Georg Trakl

On 2 November 1914, in a Cracow hospital in the early days of WWI, the Austrian poet Georg Trakl injected an intentional overdose of cocaine, after earlier being prevented from blowing his brains out.[18] Traumatised by the carnage on the eastern front, by his drug addiction and by life in general, Trakl fell into a coma and died the next day. Three days later, the philosopher Ludwig Wittgenstein, who had anonymously given a large part of his inheritance to Trakl (another recipient was the poet Rilke), responding to a request to visit him in hospital, arrived only to find Trakl's grave. It was perhaps provident that Trakl and Wittgenstein did not meet. Constitutionally incapable of handling any responsibility, even one as cheering as accepting a large sum *gratis*, when attempting to draw on the money Wittgenstein had given him, Trakl had run out of the bank in a panic, unable to deal with his windfall.

The shyest of men, on trains Trakl preferred to stand in the corridor, rather than share a compartment with a stranger, and for much of his time he led a feral, vagabond existence, choosing to sleep in the woods around Innsbruck, rather than face contact with a landlord. In a letter to his friend Karl Heinrich, a year before his death, Trakl wrote: "I do not have easy days at home now and I drift between fear and helplessness in sunny rooms where it is unspeakably cold. Strange shudders of transformation, bodily experienced to the point of vulnerability, visions of mysteries until the certainty of having died, ecstasies to the point of stony petrifaction, and a continuation of dreaming sad dreams." To another friend he wrote, "It seems to me that I wander around daily like a vagabond, at times in the forests which are already turning red and where marksmen harass the wild life to death; or I explore disconsolate streets in the bleak areas of town, or simply lounge around and watch the seagulls . . ." Dissolution, death, decay, madness, loneliness, and fear are some of the standard themes in Trakl's dark, sombre verse. As one critic put it, Trakl's life displayed the trajectory of a "progressively deteriorating personality," and his death was the "culmination of a grimly logical pattern."[19]

Georg Trakl was born in Salzburg on 3 February 1887, the fifth of seven children of a successful ironmonger. Although brought up in a prosperous, bourgeois family, Georg's childhood had its share of dissonances. His mother was Catholic, his father Protestant, and in his early years Georg went to a Catholic school in the morning, and received instruction in the Protestant faith in the afternoon. Neither of his parents had much time for him. His father, who was fifty when Georg was born, paid him little attention, especially in later life, when he might have benefited by his intervention. His mother, who suffered from depression and took opium to relieve the strain, spent most of her time locked in her rooms, caring for her antiques. Georg's strongest bond was with his sister Grete, and there's reason to believe their relationship was incestuous. She too, like her brother, became addicted to drugs at an early age, and like him she also committed suicide, shooting herself at a party in Berlin three years after Georg's death. There's little evidence Trakl had an emotional relationship with any woman beside Grete. He hated his mother, and at one point confessed that he could strangle her. His other contact with women came from his visits to brothels, and he is said for a time to have maintained a platonic relationship with an aged prostitute who would listen to him talk.

It's possible the suicidal impulse that ended his life appeared early on. As a child he's said to have thrown himself in front of a frightened horse, and to have stepped in front of a moving train. On another occasion, this death instinct resulted in a darkly comic incident. Sometime between the age of five and eight, Trakl walked into a pond until it was over his head. He was only saved because someone saw his hat floating on the surface. Apocryphal or not, this image seems to convey some essence of Trakl's brief and failure-prone existence. With Walter Benjamin and Anne Sexton, Trakl comes across as a master of ineptitude. A poor student, he had to repeat classes, and eventually had to leave school, failing to complete his courses at the *Gymnasium*. Poor academic results are not unusual in poets, but in Trakl's case the tendency was amplified by the drug habits he picked up in his teens. By fifteen he carried a flask of chloroform, and was dipping his cigarettes in an opium solution. This early indulgence later led to continuous use of morphine, veronal and the cocaine that eventually killed him. Alcohol, too, became a frequent crutch, and Trakl once described his life as "days of delirious drunkenness and criminal melancholy."[20] There's a story of Trakl's parents coming home one afternoon and finding Georg laid out on the sofa, stoned; on a later occasion, he slept outside overnight in the winter, drunkenly insensate to the cold and snow.

Like Anne Sexton, aside from poetry, there was very little Trakl was good at. As the poet Jeremy Reed remarked, Trakl was reluctant "to accept responsibility for living." "Unable to commit himself to life, and constantly delaying the process, [Trakl] reverted psychologically to states supported by primal, mythic consciousness."[21] A kind of poetic Peter Pan, Trakl was sent into a panic by any need to deal with the necessities of life. His poetry, Reed writes, "anticipated apocalyptic catastrophe on an inner plane, but he was little physically qualified to deal with the reality."[22]

Trakl was probably introduced to drugs by a pharmacist's son, who pilfered them from his father's supplies. Failing to complete his schooling, Trakl hit on the idea of apprenticing himself to a pharmacy, thereby insuring a steady source while incidentally learning how to make a living. (Throughout

Trakl's brief mature life – if we can call it that – the need for money to buy drugs was a constant concern.) In 1905 he began his three-year term at the White Eagle pharmacy in Salzburg. Around this time he became friends with a local bohemian, Gustav Streicher, a playwright who seems to have put Trakl on the road to becoming a *poète maudit*. Streicher encouraged him to write, and Trakl produced two plays. Both were performed, but received bad reviews. Trakl also had his first work published in a Salzburg newspaper, a piece of impressionistic prose, lost to us now. By this time he was looking the part of the Rimbaudesque bad boy – long hair, sideburns, unkempt dress – drinking and smoking almost continuously. A friend at the time described him as "sullen, testy, arrogant, self-conscious and tired of life."[23] He announced that he had decided to kill himself so frequently, that one exasperated friend replied, "Please, not while I am with you."

Finishing his apprenticeship, to complete his training Trakl entered the University of Vienna. Here he spent most of his time carousing with friends. One important contact was with the critic Hermann Bahr, who helped Trakl place three poems in the *Neue Wiener Journal*, his first publication outside of Salzburg. In 1910 he completed his university training, and that year Trakl was faced with the necessity of fending for himself. His father died, and with this the small allowance he was granted ended. Trakl faced the poverty he would know for the rest of his life. One way to avoid the horrors of everyday life was, ironically, to enter the military, and Trakl began a one-year term of service in the army. But this was only temporary, and after his year he was faced with the same problem. He tried to work at a pharmacy in Salzburg, but the experience was catastrophic: dealing with customers so unnerved Trakl that he would sweat through several shirts in a day; finally he quit. He would, more or less, remain unemployable for the remainder of his life. After finally getting a position he sought in the Viennese bureaucracy, he quit after only two hours. Other jobs fared similarly, and his attempts to emigrate to Borneo or Albania in search of work also failed. From this time on, Trakl's search for some secure perch in life was coupled with his need and inability to establish a firm identity.

In 1912, Trakl returned to the military, and was sent to work in an army hospital in Innsbruck. Here he had his first and only stroke of good luck. At the Café Maximilian, Trakl met Ludwig von Ficker, publisher of the literary journal *Der Brenner* (which, among other things, was in part responsible for the Kierkegaard revival in the early twentieth century.) Predictably, the meeting took some effort; Trakl sat apart from the group around Ficker for hours, paralysed by shyness. Finally, he asked a waiter to deliver his card. Ficker invited him over, and from then on until his death, *Der Brenner* would publish a Trakl poem in every issue. Through Ficker Trakl met the only men of genius equal to his own that he would know: the satirist Karl Kraus, the painter and playwright Oscar Kokoschka, and the architect Adolf Loos. Through *Der Brenner* the novelist Franz Werfel (who followed the trail Walter Benjamin took through the Pyrenees; see "The Political Suicide") read his poems and was so impressed that he convinced his publisher, Kurt Wolff, to publish them. In July 1913, *Gedichte (Poems)*, the only collection published in Trakl's lifetime, appeared; a second collection, *Sebastian in Traum (Sebastian in a Dream)* was also accepted, but appeared after his death.

Yet although his time in Innsbruck and his association with Ficker was probably the happiest and most promising of his life, Trakl was never really happy and its clear he suffered from some form of mental imbalance, most likely schizophrenia. To a friend at this time he was "silent, reserved, shy, entirely turned inward . . . sensitive, sick." He had "hallucinations" and "raves."[24] One hallucination, which he said had also come to him as a child, was of a man standing behind him with a drawn knife. Later, when under observation by army physicians, Trakl confessed that he heard bells; he also told them that his real father was a cardinal and that he himself was destined for some greatness – a not unusual remark from a poet, and in part justified. Trakl probably had visions throughout his life and, as in the case of the French poet Gérard de Nerval, his friends may have simply chalked these up to his temperament. At a country fair, for example, he once pointed to a calf's head and announced, "That is our lord Christ!" He would also sit for hours in company without saying a word, then suddenly erupt into a monologue having nothing to do with whatever anyone else had been talking about.

That he himself had doubts about his sanity can be seen in a letter Trakl wrote to Ficker, ostensibly about his concern over his sister's marital problems and recent miscarriage. (She had married an older man for security, but soon realized her mistake, and, like Georg, had used drugs to compensate.) He told Ficker, "I no longer know in from out," a concise description of a schizoid split. "It is such an indescribable disaster when one's world breaks apart. Oh my God, what a judgement has broken over me. Tell me that I must have the power to live on and act truthfully. Tell me that I'm not insane. A stony darkness has broken in. Oh my friend, how small and unhappy I have become."[25]

Although it's difficult to see Trakl ever overcoming his difficulties, the outbreak of WWI made this more or less impossible. Trakl was sent to Galicia, on the eastern front, and, with no medical training, was single-handedly responsible for the care of ninety badly wounded soldiers following the battle of Grodek. Trakl could do little to help and the screams and shrieks of pain were terrifying. A soldier who could no longer stand it shot himself in the head, and Trakl could see pieces of his brain sticking to the wall. He ran outside, but there, in the courtyard, he saw the corpses of partisans hanging from the trees; it's possible he may even have seen one place the noose over his own head. This was too much, and at dinner that evening he announced that he would shoot himself, and ran outside. He was stopped before he could pull the trigger and put under arrest. He was sent to Cracow, where he shared a room with a lieutenant suffering *delirium tremens*; understandably, his condition worsened.

Trakl's suicidal impulse may have broken out earlier than this. At Grodek he's said to have tried to rush to the front line; it took six men to disarm him, a resurgence, perhaps, of the same urge that had him step in front of a moving train. While in Cracow he expressed concern that he would be tried for cowardice, and perhaps this led to his final attempt, although a military that could put as unstable an individual as Trakl in charge of ninety badly wounded men should itself have faced a court martial. A doctor in charge of Trakl remarked that his case represented an interesting example of "genius and madness," and noted that his patient " 'wrote poetry' ", the inverted commas suggesting the dubious character of the practice. Ficker managed to see Trakl in Cracow; it was then that he suggested writing to Wittgenstein, who was also at the front, to ask him to visit. (Ficker had been chosen by the philosopher to distribute his donations.) Ficker also asked Trakl if he had any drugs. "Would I be alive otherwise?" the poet replied, ironically making clear that they were the only thing keeping the horror of reality from overwhelming him. Evidently they couldn't do this for long, and on that November day, Trakl used them for another, more lasting release from an unbearable situation.

Heinrich von Kleist

Immanuel Kant was perhaps the most influential philosopher of the last few centuries and his *Critique of Pure Reason* is one of the most important philosophical works in the canon. By the time of his death in 1804 he was clearly aware of his achievement and of the enormous impact his work had on his contemporaries. What Kant wouldn't know was that seven years after his death his ideas about epistemology, the study of how we know what we know, would lead to a suicide, a double one in fact. On 21 November 1811[26], on a grassy knoll overlooking Lake Wannsee just outside Berlin, the playwright and novelist Heinrich von Kleist put a bullet through the heart of his companion Henriette Vogel, a 31 year-old woman with an incurable cancer, and then placed the barrel of the gun in his mouth and fired. Although Kleist, like Harry Crosby, had shown an inclination to form suicide pacts, with both male and female friends, from an early age, it was his study of Kant that sent him over the edge. "My one supreme goal has vanished, and I am bereft," he wrote after reading the sage of

Königsberg. Kleist read Kant in 1801, and in that year, legend has it, he and some friends walked along the Wannsee, discussing the best methods of killing oneself. Ten years later, at the age of thirty-four, Kleist decided to put some of their ideas to the test.

Kleist's 'supreme goal' was to order his life according to the Enlightenment ideals of reason and logic. Like many of his time, he strove to organize a methodical 'life plan' and to put it into effect. Knowledge, understanding, and planning, he believed, could master life's chaos and reduce the wild and arbitrary to the controlled and orderly. Happiness could be attained, provided one pursued it rationally. But Kant, as far as Kleist was concerned, had pulled the rug out from under this project by showing that we can never know the world as it is *in itself*, but only as our perceptions show it to us; only, that is, as appearance. All we can know is the world of the senses, and they are by no means infallible. What the world is *really* like is a mystery. Our knowledge, and the certainty it provides, is, Kant argued effectively, severely limited. This troubled Kleist. "We cannot decide if what we call truth is really truth, or whether it only seems that way to us," he despaired in a letter of 1801, the year of his 'crisis'.

Such abstruse metaphysics may leave most of us unperturbed, but their effect on Kleist was devastating. "Regardless of whether this interpretation tallied exactly with Kant's teaching," Kleist's biographer Joachim Maass writes, "it pierced Kleist's heart like a poisoned arrow and sent him staggering."[27] The result, or so Kleist believed, was a shattering insight into life's fundamental uncertainty, its dissonance with our own hopes and aims, a discontinuity that carried through down to the individual and society. This dark, disturbing vision became the essence of Kleist's work, seen in his novel *Michael Kohlhaas*, in stories like "The Earthquake in Chile," and even in comedies like *The Broken Jug*. Writing of Kleist's plays, E.L. Doctorow remarked that their "overwhelming sense [. . .] is of immense disorder, teeming madness, an infernally wild fluctuation of feeling and event."[28] Kafka, he says, loved Kleist's work, and read him aloud to his friends.

Such a vision is by now commonplace. Epistemological, moral and cultural relativity reign; it's the so-called 'post-modern condition'. But in Kleist's time it was radical, and many, including Kleist's older contemporary Goethe, who affirmed the harmony between personality and the world, took it as a sign of madness. Goethe is said to have burned his copy of Kleist's play *Das Kätchen von Heilbronn*, about shared dreams and somnambulism, because it was "tainted with an incurable disease."[29] Like his other contemporary, E.T.A. Hoffmann (who Goethe also disapproved of), Kleist had an interest in trance, dreams and other altered states of consciousness, an expression of his rejection of reason and inherent mysticism.

Today, like his near-contemporary Thomas Lovell Beddoes, Kleist is seen as ahead of his time, a precursor of contemporary literary themes like the theatre of the absurd, existentialism and post-modernism. After Kant, consciousness for Kleist, as for many of us, became a burden; it no longer illuminated the path to rational perfectibility, but the unavoidable descent to the abyss. Hence, in his brilliant and beautiful essay, "On The Marionette Theatre," Kleist argues that no adult human being possesses the grace and unself-conscious ease of movement we find in puppets. He posits some future state in which this innocence may be recaptured, denied us since our exile from the garden and, more recently, our loss of childhood. "Grace," he writes, "appears in that form which either has no con-sciousness or an infinite consciousness. That is, in the puppet or in the god." Another form of unconscious grace, one that Kleist in the end would avail himself of, is, of course, death.

Bernd Heinrich Wilhelm von Kleist – to give his full name – was born on 18 October 1777 in Frankfurt-on-the-Oder; Kleist himself, however, celebrated his birthday on 10 October, an indication of the ambiguity associated with his life. Kleist's Prussian family was well known, and he came from a long line of generals, although there was one poet, Ewald von Kleist, a friend of Lessing's, whose death fighting for Frederick the Great at the hopeless battle of Kunersdorf can be seen as a kind of suicide. Like many romantic young men, Kleist thought little of his family's standing, and he said that he would gladly abandon honour, nobility and class, in exchange for love and happiness. There's little known about Kleist's childhood, which he thought of as 'joyless', and which, he claimed, was attended by 'musical hallucinations'. His tutor spoke of him as a fiery spirit, provoked into rages by trifles, but also possessed of generosity and chivalry. An inordinate response to everyday incidents is a characteristic of both Kleist's life and work, and early on he made a suicide pact with his cousin, agreeing to take their lives if "anything unworthy" should befall them.

In this Kleist seems one of Hesse's 'suicides,' who are ready at a moment's notice to give up their self. There was, as Maass argues, "not a single work in which he did not treat explicitly or implicitly of this alternative, not a single defeat to which he did not respond with a yearning for self-destruction." Like Jacques Vaché and Harry Crosby, he didn't want to die alone; "the death drive and love were for him inseparable, a longing, as it were, for the ultimate embrace."[30] His closest relationship seemed to be with his half-sister Ulrike, from his father's first marriage; in later life, after the failure of his own relationships, she provided some measure of emotional ballast, as well as frequent financial support. In his last days, however, a falling out with her precipitated his release from this world.

At 14, Kleist joined a regiment of guards at Potsdam and had achieved the rank of second lieutenant before he decided to leave the military eight years later, after seeing service in the Rhine campaign against revolutionary France. He entered Frankfurt University, studying physics, mathematics, philosophy, cultural history and law. "I have set myself a goal that will require the unremitting exertion of all my powers and the use of every minute's time," he wrote, embarking on his project of self-betterment with the kind of intensity that would in the end undermine him. In the same year, 1799, he confided to Ulrike that he found it "incomprehensible how a human being can live without a plan for his life; the sense of security with which I employ my present time and the calm with which I look to the future make me profoundly aware

of just what inestimable happiness my life plan assures me."
Yet, this confidence concealed an insecurity. "Existing without a life plan," he continued, "without any firm purpose,
constantly wavering between uncertain desires, constantly at
variance with my duties, the plaything of chance, a puppet on
the strings of fate – such an unworthy situation seems so
contemptible to me and would make me so wretched that
death would be preferable by far."[31]

Ironically, a wavering, unstable life was precisely what was in
store for Kleist; again like Thomas Lovell Beddoes, he would
find himself shifting back and forth between several cities:
Dresden, Paris, Frankfurt, Leipzig, Berlin, Basle, Prague. In
1800, in an effort to anchor himself in respectability, he initiated an engagement with Wilhelmine von Zenge, the daughter of a regimental commander. The two were unsuitable and
the engagement was another part of his 'life plan'. It had little
time to succeed, as Kleist soon left Frankfurt for Leipzig and
Dresden. In Würzberg he underwent some kind of surgery
which, he informed his fiancé, would make him 'worthy' of
her. There's suspicion that Kleist was impotent and/or homosexual, or that he had some deformity (he did suffer from a
speech defect, which made him uneasy in company); in any
case his sexual life remains mostly obscure (he seemed to
exhibit a lifelong abstinence), and the engagement was soon
broken off. Not, however, before Wilhelmine tried to refute
the new scepticism that had overtaken him. She was concerned
that his obsession would interfere with him obtaining some
position that would enable them to marry. He was concerned
that it had undermined the entire foundations of life. In 1802
he abruptly ended the engagement and, more or less, jettisoned
any claim on normality. That same year he began to write.

In 1803 Kleist moved between Berne, Milan, Geneva and
Paris. At some point on his return to Prussia, he had a nervous
breakdown. He contemplated following Rousseau's philosophy and thought of living as a peasant while getting 'back
to nature'; at the same time he considered joining Napoleon's
army in the hopes of being killed during his planned invasion
of England. His first play, *The Schroffenstein Family*, appeared

anonymously, and he began work on *The Broken Jug*. He also started work on a tragedy, *Robert Guiscard*, but burned the manuscript in disgust. Kleist had by this time met Goethe, Schiller and Wieland and his literary profile, if not his professional one, was rising. In 1805 he tried for a second time to enter the Prussian civil service, but was predictably unsuccessful. In 1807, while trying to enter occupied Berlin without a passport (the year before, Napoleon had routed the Prussians and had occupied the country), he was arrested by the French and spent six months in prison. Here he wrote *Penthesilea*, which anticipates Nietzsche's savage vision of the Dionysian character of Greek tragedy, rejecting the received notion of Apollonian serenity embraced by Goethe. On his release from prison, his first short stories started to appear.

In Dresden, with the philosopher Adam Müller, Kleist started a literary journal, *Phoebus*; here he published perhaps his best known story, "The Marquise of O," about a woman who discovers she is pregnant but has no idea how it happened or who is responsible. The journal however soon went bust and Kleist and Müller parted on bad terms. Kleist suffered another failure at the hands of Goethe, who staged an unsuccessful production of *The Broken Jug*; Kleist was so enraged he wanted to challenge Goethe to a duel. Perhaps prompted by his imprisonment, Kleist had become fanatically patriotic and he devoted himself to writing political poems and tracts. But in 1809, Austria was trounced at Wagram and Kleist fled to Prague where he fell seriously ill with some unspecified complaint. Rumours that he had been admitted to an insane asylum competed with others that he had planned to assassinate Napoleon; he did, indeed, ask a friend to procure arsenic for him, but this probably had more to do with a planned suicide attempt than a political murder. At any rate, Kleist felt at an end; writing, he said, had become pointless. "How shall I ever pull myself together?" he asked Ulrike in a letter. The "imperfect state of the world, the fundamental irreconcilability of the social order with justice and decency" that Thomas Mann saw at the centre of Kleist's vision had, it seemed, triumphed.

1810 was a better year, at least at first. He finally settled in

Berlin and there started the city's first daily newspaper, the *Berliner Abendblätter*. Initially successful, it was later censored by the government, and its readership dropped. By early 1811, it folded, and Kleist was again left adrift. Financially insecure, his work, although acknowledged by his peers, having little public success, Kleist again tried to gain a toehold in the civil service, but again failed. He had by this time met Henriette Vogel, one of the 'interesting' women courted by the Berlin romantics; she had already been one of Müller's lovers, but he left her to marry a woman Kleist had been in love with.

At 33, Henriette was no longer pretty. But she had wit, an appetite for knowledge, was an accomplished pianist and singer and, perhaps most resonant with Kleist, was given to spiritual exaltation. She was also suffering from a terminal uterine cancer, and had not concealed her yearning for a quick death, to avoid a certain slow and painful one.

Although Kleist found her unattractive at first, Henriette pursued him; her husband, a good natured accountant, apparently accepted the affair. Recently, Marie von Kleist (no relation), a woman Kleist had great feeling for, had left Berlin, and Henriette moved to fill the void. At one point, Kleist dramatically promised that he would do whatever she asked of him. Soon after this, listening to her sing to her own accompaniment, Kleist enthused: "It was so beautiful I could shoot myself!" Their eyes met and Henriette reminded him of his promise. He assured her he would keep his word. She then asked him to shoot her.

The couple decided on a plan. They needed an accomplice, and Henriette chose a close friend of her husband's, whom she assured Kleist would perform the requisite duties. Writing their farewells and placing them in a sealed box, they chose a popular inn near the Wannsee, the appropriately named New Jug, as the site of their last days. In his final letters to Marie von Kleist, whom he had on several occasions asked to accompany him to the next world (and who had obviously declined) Kleist wrote, "Since my childhood days, in my thoughts and in my writing, I have been in constant contact with beauty and morality and that has made me so sensitive that the most

trifling aggressions [. . .] are doubly and trebly painful."[32]
Like Anne Sexton, Kleist killed himself because he had no
'numbness'; like Werther, he could find no place for himself
in the world, and his idealism left him bruised at the slightest rebuff. It's no wonder Goethe recoiled from him. Like
Kierkegaard, Kleist could see the world only in terms of an
'either/or': either total triumph or a quick departure. His
last letters display remarkable insight into his inability to
reconcile himself with the world, and a delicacy of feeling
toward those he was leaving behind. He also asked that his
barber be paid what he was owed. For her part, Henriette
left detailed instructions for a Christmas gift for her
husband.

The couple arrived at the New Jug on the afternoon of
the 20th. To the innkeeper and his wife, they seemed happy
and carefree, but that night they were heard pacing the floor.
The next morning they awoke early, and asked if a letter
could be sent to Berlin. A messenger was found and the letter
dispatched. They asked about the lake and if a boat could take
them to the further shore. There was no boat, they were told,
but it wasn't a long walk. They seemed in fine spirits and in
the afternoon asked if the messenger would reach his destination soon. They were assured he would; at this they seemed
glad. They then asked that coffee be brought to them at a grassy
spot, not far from the inn, overlooking the lake. This was
surprising, as the weather was cold and a fog was settling. But
they insisted and were generous with their thalers; as they
walked away, the housekeeper wondered what might be in
the basket Henriette carried and which was covered by a white
cloth. She soon found out.

When the housekeeper brought the coffee, Henriette wondered if they couldn't have a table and chairs as well. The
housekeeper said the coffee would be cold by the time she
could do this, but she insisted again. When these too were
brought, Kleist asked for a pencil; when this was brought,
Henriette gave the woman one of the coffee cups, asked her
to wash it, and to bring it back. As the woman walked away,
baffled by these requests, yet happy with the guests' largess, she

186

heard a shot. "A funny couple," she thought, "playing with guns." Then she heard another one.

When she returned with the washed cup she found them. Henriette lay on her back, her coat open and a small dark hole showing on her blouse. Kleist knelt by her feet, his left arm hanging over his left leg, his right hand, still clutching the pistol, on her hip, his head resting on it. The housekeeper understood what was in the basket. Bloody foam oozed from Kleist's mouth. By seven that evening, Henriette's husband, accompanied by the friend entrusted with the gruesome charge, had arrived; they had received the letter as the couple consummated their tryst. The instructions, detailed, considerate, and not unreasonable, included a request to be buried side by side. They were, but not before an autopsy performed on Kleist reached the conclusion that his brain showed clear evidence of "mental unbalance;" Kleist would have been pleased to know that the saw used to open his skull had broken. A failure by all accounts in his lifetime, today the Kleist prize is one of the most honoured literary awards in Germany.

Thomas Lovell Beddoes

Like the Hungarian writer, physician and suicide Géza Csáth[33], the poet, dramatist and doctor Thomas Lovell Beddoes combined a career in medicine with one in literature. In Csáth's case, the appeal of a medical career had much to do with his drug addiction; for Beddoes it was a combination of his obsession with death and dead bodies – he was, for Ezra Pound, "the prince of morticians" – and his strange conviction that the study of physiology and anatomy would lead to a new era in drama. Sadly, Beddoes' careers in both medicine and literature were practically non-starters. Although he received his MD in 1831 from the University of Würzberg, he never practised professionally. And although he completed the work for which, if at all, he is known today, *Death's Jest-Book*, in 1829, he spent the remaining twenty years of his life revising it, and publishing nothing. His 'messterpiece' itself, as it might be called, only appeared after Beddoes' death. Although peppered with lyrical, if macabre beauty, it remains more an oddity than anything else and is, as one critic put it "perfectly adapted to remain unread."

An uncomfortable air of frustrated energies surrounds Beddoes, partly rooted in his often thwarted homosexuality; among his several neuroses was an inability to finish his projects, hence Graham Greene's sobriquet of "the filibustering medical poet." Delay even followed him to the grave. After his death, his friend and editor Thomas Forbes Kelsall bequeathed his collection of Beddoes' papers to the poet Robert Browning. Although Browning announced that if he ever became a professor of poetry, his first lecture would be on Beddoes, "a forgotten Oxford poet," he himself stashed the MSS in a box and left them untouched for a decade; Beddoes, then, was doubly forgotten. The box, the MSS and Beddoes' interminable revisions are reminiscent of the Portuguese poet Fernando Pessoa, who kept a similar collection of scraps, fragments, and jottings in cramped, crowded handwriting in a similar chest; like Beddoes', Pessoa's best known 'work', *The Book of Disquietude*, remained unfinished. Like Pessoa, Beddoes committed his work to an unwieldy mess of notes, and like his MSS, Beddoes' life was one of fragments and pieces.

For Harold Bloom, "Beddoes, in despair of his time and of himself, chose to waste his genius on a theme that baffled his own imagination."[34] That theme was death, and like Harry Crosby, Beddoes seemed to have little else on his mind. He made more than one suicide attempt. As one of the characters in *Death's Jest-Book* says: "O Death! I am thy friend, I struggle not with thee, I love thy state: Thou canst be sweet and gentle, be so now; and let me pass praying away into thee . . ." In 1848, after failing to open an artery sufficiently enough for him to bleed to death – a sad showing for an anatomist – Beddoes' leg became gangrenous, and had to be amputated below the knee. A year later, in 1849, at the age of forty-six, in his third suicide attempt, Beddoes finally managed to kill himself in a Basle hospital by ingesting a dose of curare, the Orinoco arrow-tip poison that a century later would become an accessory to general anaesthesia. There is a certain irony in this: one of Beddoes' early tragic works was entitled *Love's*

Arrow Poisoned, an expression of the macabre black humour that coloured his life. In his suicide note, Beddoes wrote: "I ought to have been, among a variety of other things, a good poet." He also added, in a bit of doggerel justifying the first remark: "I am food for what I am good for – worms." Like the note pinned to René Crevel's chest, "Please cremate me. Disgust," this ranks as a searing expression of profound self-contempt.

Thomas Lovell Beddoes was born in 1803 in Clifton, Shropshire, and came from an illustrious and eccentric family. His mother was the sister of the novelist Maria Edgeworth and his father was the doctor Thomas Beddoes. Friend of Coleridge, Erasmus Darwin, and Humphry Davy, Beddoes senior was among the early self-experimenters with nitrous oxide, inhaling the 'wild gas' and discovering its anaesthetic properties.[35] He also had the strange habit of dissecting animals with his son in attendance. This was in order to teach children "accurately to distinguish the parts of the body." Beddoes senior's pedagogical zeal no doubt influenced his son's later preoccupations, although he wouldn't be aware of them; he died when Beddoes junior was only 5. Eccentric ideas were not unfamiliar to the maternal side of Beddoe's family too. His maternal grandfather is said to have tried to divert the course of the Rhône, and to have invented a kind of carriage that supplied its own road, the so-called 'walking barrel'.

This eccentric strain appeared in Beddoes as his afore-mentioned inability to complete a work, and in a predilection for creating or finding himself in unenviable situations. After attending Bath grammar school he was sent to Charterhouse where he proved "wilful, perverse, independent and precocious,"[36] and where he occupied himself writing verse, Gothic tales, a novel in imitation of Fielding, and in inventing a slang language. A story told of this time gives us an idea of his character. Unhappy with the work a locksmith did on his bookcase, when Beddoes next met the man he gave him an impromptu hair-raising dramatic performance of his own death and descent into the pits of hell; the locksmith, terrified, rushed out, and it took much persuasion to have him ever return.

Beddoes' independent streak carried over to Pembroke College, Oxford, where he once appeared at a tutorial with a large butcher knife to cut the pages of a book he hadn't yet read. At Oxford he published *The Improvisatore* in his first year, a clearly immature work which was later suppressed. In 1822 *The Bride's Tragedy* — his only completed verse tragedy — which showed his affinity with the Elizabethan and Jacobean dramatists, appeared and was something of a success. According to Lytton Strachey, "In a single bound, he had reached the threshold of poetry, and was knocking at the door."[37] Unfortunately, Beddoes seemed to have stopped knocking before the muse opened up. He tried to follow *The Bride's Tragedy* with other works, but his projects stalled, and he at one point proposed to continue writing under the pseudonym Theobald Vesseldoom.

In 1824, called to Florence by the ill health of his mother (she died before he arrived), he met Walter Savage Landor and Mary Shelley, with whom he shared an interest in corpses: *Death's Jest-Book* is often called a kind of 'Frankenstein's monster,' put together from bits and pieces.[38] In 1825 he completed his degree at Oxford and began work on what he called "a very Gothic styled tragedy," yet, rather than pursue a literary career, he decided to study anatomy and physiology. The 'Gothic styled tragedy', *Death's Jest-Book*, was completed four years later. But Beddoes, insecure about his creativity and highly susceptible to others' opinions, agreed to revise it as friends suggested, and spent the rest of his life doing so.

After leaving Oxford he went to Göttiingen, the beginning of his long self-exile in German speaking lands. There he proved brilliant but unruly. In 1829 he was expelled from the university for being drunk in the street. It was also in Göttingen that he made his first suicide attempt. He had become obsessed with discovering the mythical 'Bone of Luz', a kind of osseous Philosopher's Stone, spoken of in Talmudic lore, and which was supposed to hold the key to immortality. Located in the coccyx, it was said to revive the dead. Pursued by Faustian furies, Beddoes was compelled to search for "every shadow of a proof or possibility of an after existence, both in the material and immaterial nature of man." When his investigations into the seat of the soul proved futile, he tried to take his own life.[39] His attempt failed, but he left Göttingen "penetrated with the conviction of the absurdity and unsatisfactory nature of human life."[40]

He moved on to Würzberg to complete his degree, but was deported from Bavaria the next year for being a political agitator; he never received his diploma. Along with his interest in bodies and poetry (which Beddoes senior also wrote), and his knack for eccentricity, Beddoes junior had inherited his father's taste for radical politics: this, death and his unfinishable work would occupy him from now on. He studied German philosophy, became a member of the *Germania Burschenshaft*, a radical student political society, and wrote inflammatory pamphlets in his adopted language. Indeed, Beddoes took to German so well that he remarked that English seemed a foreign tongue to him; linguistically, as in other ways, Beddoes became a "psychic alien . . . a man so essentially modern that his wandering existence becomes an appropriate metaphor for the contemporary human condition."[41] He settled in Zürich, where he was elected a professor of comparative anatomy, but the university authorities refused to recognize his election. His years in Zürich were relative happy, but antiliberal riots forced him to flee once again: he witnessed an army of six thousand peasants armed with pitch forks, scythes and knives depose the liberal government. His friend, one of the liberal leaders, was killed, and Beddoes barely escaped himself. From this point on, he had no fixed home and, like another seeker of immortality (and appreciator of death), the Renaissance alchemist and physician Paracelsus,[42] Beddoes drifted from place to place, a strange solitary figure, with long tangled hair and his ever present meerschaum pipe.

During a ten month stay in London, Beddoes expressed his contempt at the state of English theatre by attempting to burn down the Drury Lane playhouse with a lit five pound note. Visiting Kelsall in Southampton, he locked himself in his room for days, smoking constantly, sinking into deep depressions. Visiting relatives, he arrived at their country house astride a donkey. Understandably, friends and family began to think he had gone mad. He himself remarked in a letter that he had become "a non-conductor of friendship." In 1847 he returned to Frankfurt where he began a homosexual relationship with Konrad Degen, a baker nearly thirty years his junior. Beddoes' affection for Degen was considerable: he once hired a theatre in Zürich for a night so that Degen, who we assume had thespian aspirations, could play Hotspur, with Beddoes the sole audience. A falling out with Degen led to Beddoes attempting suicide. At the Cigogne Hotel, he slashed his leg with his scalpel, one he may have used in dissection. When he failed to bleed to death, he was taken to the hospital where, like Cato, he tore off the bandages; he did this so often that eventually, as mentioned, his leg developed gangrene and had to be amputated. Beddoes told his family that he had fallen from a horse and the real reason for his amputation and later death was only revealed sometime after he was dead.

A reunion with Degen followed, and things seemed to be going better; they spoke of an Italian holiday, of literature and politics. Beddoes was able to walk and there seemed little to suggest that he would make another stab at killing himself. But during one walk, at a chemist's Beddoes purchased the curare. When his doctor was summoned to his bed on the evening of 26 January, he found the poet-doctor insensible. He never regained consciousness and died that night. Among other things, his last note asked that a case of Moet Champagne – fifty bottles – be drunk in honour of his death, and that one of "Reade's best stomach pumps" be purchased and given to his physician as a gift. Appropriately for Beddoes, when death came for him, it left a few jests in parting.

Otto Weininger

On 26 March 1827 one of the undisputed geniuses of western civilization, Ludwig von Beethoven, died in his room at Schwarzspanierstrasse 15 in Vienna. Seventy-six years later the address would become famous once again for another death. In the same room on 3 October 1903, shortly after the publication of his *magnum opus, Geschlecht und Charakter (Sex and Character*), the twenty-three year old Austrian philosopher Otto Weininger shot himself in the chest. He was found the next morning, fully clothed and covered in blood, and was taken to hospital but died soon after. Weininger had only recently returned from Italy, where he had gone for a holiday, after completing the work for which, if at all, he is remembered today. That he banked a great deal on the book's reception is evident from a remark he made to a friend shortly after finishing it. "There are three possibilities for me," he declared. "The gallows, suicide, or a future so brilliant that I don't dare to think of it." What actually happened can be seen as a self-fulfilled prophecy. Weininger had expected his work to excite critical acclaim, and while it was cordially received, it failed to make the stir he had hoped for. Disappointed in his masterpiece's reception, and troubled by his own depressions, Weininger, who considered himself a kind of 'Redeemer', decided to end his life where one of his greatest heroes had ended his, thus forging a link between Beethoven's genius and his own, genius in general and his own in particular being one of Weininger's central themes.

Predictably, following his suicide, *Sex and Character* became a best-seller, ironically creating precisely the kind of heated debate and sensational notice Weininger had wished for. This isn't surprising, given that the book made some startling assertions. Although Weininger begins with an idea that today, coming after Jungian psychology, doesn't seem that radical – that everyone is really a mixture of both masculine and feminine psyches – from this point on he enters some very turbulent waters.[43] Notoriously, Weininger argued that women were an inferior species, immoral, soulless and uncreative, who were basically interested only in sex and child-bearing. Men, on the other hand, were spiritual beings who were responsible for practically all the virtues and achievements of culture and civilization. While women are only concerned with sexual relations – they are, he said, 'matchmakers' by instinct – men have a mission to create and promote works of genius. This, of course, is hampered by the cunning and deceit of women.[44] Equally inflammatory were Weininger's remarks about Jews, or more precisely, Jewishness, which he saw as a decadent strain in human nature, not limited to one race, although in the Jews, Jewishness is understandably more prominent than in other races. As a Jew himself who had converted to Christianity, Weininger provided anti-Semites with much metaphysical ammunition, and to Jews he seemed a virulent case of Jewish self-hate. Embedded in these explosive views were Weininger's exhortations to pursue the difficult task of becoming a genius, which he believed was possible through an effort of will and which, we can assume, Weininger believed he had accomplished in producing his work.

Not surprisingly, Weininger became a kind of a cultural hero among the many aspiring young Viennese geniuses and his work became a *cause célèbre*; his death triggered a string of imitations, and achieved in reality what Goethe's *Werther* only did in myth. Like many in this book, suicide was something Weininger had contemplated throughout his life, although his views on it, like much else in his life, were often paradoxical. In a letter to a friend, Arthur Gerber, written in the time leading up to his death, Weininger wrote, "The man who fails in suicide? He is the complete criminal, because he wants life in order to revenge himself. All evil is revenge!" Yet in a series of brilliant aphorisms he wrote while contemplating killing himself, Weininger remarked that, "The suicide is almost always a sadist, because he alone wants to get out of a situation and can act; a masochist must first question all eternity whether he may, should, take his own life." (Like Man and Woman, Sadist and Masochist were for Weininger Platonic Ideals or characterological types.)[45]

Of death itself Weininger wrote, "I cannot comprehend life so long as I am living it . . . Only death can teach me the meaning of life," an insight echoed a decade later by the philosopher Ludwig Wittgenstein. A great reader of Weininger, in his *Tractatus Logico-Philosophicus* Wittgenstein wrote, "Death is not an event in life: we do not live to experience death . . . The sense of the world must lie outside the world . . . The solution of the riddle of life in space and time lies *outside* space and time."[46]

Although Weininger is reviled today as an anti-Semite and misogynist, Wittgenstein, like August Strindberg, Edvard Munch, James Joyce, Ford Maddox Ford, and others recognized his importance. The poet William Carlos Williams was so impressed by Weininger's ideas that he decided to marry a woman he didn't love, because Weininger argued that sexual affinity, rather than love, formed the true bond between Man and Woman. He also believed that he himself fell short of Weininger's criteria for genius, precisely because of his weakness for women. In *The Female Eunuch*, the feminist Germaine Greer offered an ageist and sexist backhanded complement to Weininger, calling *Sex and Character* "a remarkably rigorous and committed book by a mere boy." Hitler, too, had a high opinion of him; speaking of Weininger, who he more than likely did not read, he is reported to have said, "There was only one decent Jew, and he killed himself."[47] Obviously, such remarks could not have helped Weininger's reputation, and others were understandably less impressed. Elias Canetti refused to write an introduction to a reprinting of *Sex and Character* on the grounds that it was racist and sexist.

Otto Weininger was born in Vienna on 3 April 1880 to a successful Jewish goldsmith. Weininger's father, Leopold, was a strict parent who, recognizing Otto's precocity, encouraged it. At an early age he took Otto to concerts, introducing him to the work of Mozart, Weber and, above all, Wagner; in later life, Wagner would become Weininger's favourite composer. He promoted Otto's facility with languages, and by the time he was eighteen, Otto had an excellent command of Latin, Greek, French, English, Italian, Spanish and Norwegian, not to mention his native German. He was also early on addicted to books, so much so that his father remarked, "There was one thing Otto would never share with anyone – his books. He lived in complete isolation with them."[48]

This youthful evidence of genius had the usual effect: Otto had little time for games and rarely played with other children. His father's strict character had an equally powerful effect, and most accounts suggest that the rigid and hyper-serious Otto inherited his inflexible demeanour from his father. Of Otto's mother we know very little, other than that Otto never mentioned her in his letters, that she was good at languages and that she, like the rest of the family, suffered under Leopold's dominance, enduring his criticisms and demands while suffering from tuberculosis. If Weininger's later musings on the Sadist and the Masochist have a basis in his history, its safe to say his parents provided the models.

Weininger's brilliance was evident in school, but, as with Thomas Lovell Beddoes, so was his unruliness. He often disrupted class work and followed his own inclinations, rather than that of his teachers, rejecting assignments and working on his own. This predilection for his own path was clear outside school as well. Otto's friends remarked that he never read a newspaper and that "happiness was not part of his nature." Young Otto had a haughty, sensitive personality and, like Heinrich von Kleist, would react violently if he felt his dignity was at stake. He was dedicated to ideas though, and liked nothing more than to stay up all night discussing them. As a friend recalled, "Abstract regions, from which others would turn away with a cold shiver, were his real home."

In 1898 Weininger graduated from secondary school and, after an argument with his father, who wanted him to put his multilingual abilities to practical use by entering the Consular Academy, registered at the University of Vienna. Here he studied philosophy, psychology, natural sciences and medicine, and again like Kleist, seems to have thrown himself into a massive self-improvement programme aimed at solving the big riddles of human existence. This resulted in his thesis, "Eros and the Psyche," an early version of his major work. In 1901, looking for a publisher for it, he approached Freud. Although Freud later recalled Weininger as a "slender, grown-up youth with grave features and a veiled, quite beautiful look in his eyes," and that he "could not help feeling that I stood in front of a personality with a touch of genius," he declined to suggest Weininger's work to his own publisher. He advised the young genius, whose work was much more metaphysical than scientific, to spend the next ten years gathering empirical evidence. "People want facts, not thoughts," Freud said. Weininger replied that he'd rather write ten different books in that time. Freud also pointed out that he himself was working on a similar theme – suggesting a possible proprietary interest in publishing first – and passed on some of his own thoughts on bisexuality. One result of this was that when *Sex and Character* appeared, Freud's friend and collaborator William Fliess sued him for giving *his* ideas about bisexuality to Weininger, and Weininger himself was accused of plagiarism.

When Weininger received his Ph.D, his first act was to renounce the faith of his fathers and convert to Protestantism. Although a not uncommon career move for many assimilated Viennese Jews – one famous convert being the composer Gustav Mahler – Weininger had more philosophical reasons. Judaism, for him, exemplified the "extreme of cowardice;" the Jewish faith, he argued, was feminine, soulless, and lacked a sense of good and evil, something, he believed that could not be said of Christianity. Christ himself became something of an ideal, and Weininger increasingly adopted an ascetic lifestyle, specifically focusing on inhibiting his sexual urges.

Weininger's own sexual life remains something of a mystery. Some have suggested that his appearance precluded anyone falling in love with him. His father remarked that Otto didn't have sex until his twenties, but there's little evidence for this. There's practically nothing about his relations with women in accounts by friends, aside from a single meeting with a "Miss Meyer," whom, his sister reported, after an hour with Weininger said, "I have been with Jesus Christ."[49] Nietzsche remarked that ascetics adopt their stringent disciplines because of powerful sensual appetites; given the vehemence of Weininger's remarks about women, and his powerful creative drive, one suspects he was profoundly attracted to them, but his dedication to his ideal demanded abstinence. There is also reason to suspect an element of homosexuality in Weininger, and that, like his Jewishness, his effeminate traits were something he had to fight against. There was also a possible masochistic strain in this; as his biographer says, "He seemed to enjoy using the ugliest self-hatred to destroy his own life through ascetic practices."[50] Nietzsche again:

asceticism aimed at destroying sensuality often becomes a source of it. Weininger seemed to combine both the Sadist and Masochist in himself.

By this time, Weininger had undergone a kind of psychic shift; he seemed to take the exact opposite of the course suggested by Freud, and abandoned empiricism entirely and embraced a kind of universal symbolism. "The scientist," he believed, "takes phenomena for what they are; the great men of genius for what they signify" – a remark that could have been made by Swedenborg, Goethe or Blake. Plato, Plotinus, Augustine, Kant, Wagner and Beethoven were his pantheon, and introspection became a central methodology; at twenty Weininger lectured at a Conference on Psychology in Paris on its importance. He became his own subject: he would look at his image in the mirror when he felt inspired, to see if the state made any change in his appearance. This increasing inward turn, combined with his inordinately high standards and iron discipline began to take its toll. He began to feel criminal urges, along with his sexual ones, and to have hal-lucinations – or, as he believed, to recognize the significance of otherwise banal incidents. Talking to his friend Gerber about suicide, Weininger told him about the link between a dog barking and death. Sitting in the Münchener Gasthoff, Weininger "suddenly heard a dog bark in a very peculiar, pene-trating way which was then quite new to me, and at the same moment I had the inevitable conviction that someone was dying at that very moment." The use of the word 'inevitable' prompts wonder. Months later, "in the most terrible night of my life . . . I literally had to fight against death . . . Just as I was falling asleep, I heard a dog bark three times in just the same way as that time in Munich."[51]

As the dog began to symbolize death for Weininger, the horse did the same for insanity. "With the surety of a guiding thought," he wrote, "I had the feeling that the horse represents insanity."[52] Death and insanity began to preoccupy him. "The danger of insanity," he confided in his friend, "is always present in those who try to penetrate the discipline of logic and pure knowledge," something that Weininger had clearly engaged in. One sign of his mental strain was the appearance of his *Doppelgänger*, or double, which he began to see very often; as the legend of the *Doppelgänger* goes, if you see him, you are nearing death. He asked his friend Gerber, "Have you ever thought of your own double? What if he came now? Your double is the man who knows everything about you, even that which nobody tells."[53] What nobody was telling, but what his friends could have little doubt about, was that the stress of pursuing genius, battling his lower urges and confronting an oblivious world was becoming too much for Weininger.

In a strange document entitled "Condemnation," written in November 1902, about a year before his suicide, Weininger likened his interior world to a house. Of what was going on inside it Weininger wrote: "A wild desperate activity, a slow terrifying realization in the dark, an eternal clearing out of things. Do not ask how it looks inside the house." Shortly after this he made a kind of formal farewell to his family.

Weininger seems to have had insight into the roots of his radical views. "The hatred of woman," he wrote in *Aphorisms*, "is always only the not yet overcome hatred of one's own sexuality." And if, as he believed, "All genius is a conquering of chaos and mystery," it was sadly also becoming clear that, "The genius which runs to madness is no longer genius." In a perceptive essay on Weininger, one writer summed it up: "It may be that his passionate pursuit of truth led him to envisage a standard of maleness which he felt he could not sustain, and that this was what led to his suicide."[54] It's reported that a partial lunar eclipse took place during his funeral: a fitting emblem, one that Weininger himself would no doubt have sought the meaning of.

Arthur Koestler

In 1999 female students at the University of Edinburgh, along with members of the Scottish Women's Aid Centre, as well as some politically correct males, succeeded in removing a bust from the psychology department that had resided there for years without causing the slightest controversy. Most likely the many students who passed the likeness of the Hungarian-born English novelist, essayist, and journalist, whose estate at the time of his death in 1983, estimated at just short of a million pounds, had been bequeathed to the university, didn't even notice it. Or if they did, they saw it as only one more monument to one more dead white European male, a breed whose collective cachet had depreciated considerably throughout the 80s and 90s.

But the recent newspaper serialization of sections of a new biography of this particular dead white male had caused a stir – not surprisingly, as the excerpts published dealt with the scandalous and, if the assertions they made were correct, criminal sex-life of a highly respected literary and political figure. Sex scandals are commonplace in the British press, but rarely do they result in a university changing its décor. These scandals, however, centred around a charge of 'date rape', then, as now, an incendiary if ambiguous subject. And if the 'series' of such assaults on women the biographer placed at his subject's door were substantiated by little more than his assertions – meaning he provided little, if any, corroboration for them – this was a negligible detail. Then, as now, the mere accusation was enough for the self-righteous to demand immediate action, especially as the female students involved complained that they felt 'uneasy' beneath the bust's salacious stare. The university felt compelled to take steps, and to this day the bust rests in some undisclosed spot, where it is safe from attack and, perhaps more to the point, where its unseemly gaze can harm no one. The financial contribution associated with it suffered no such indignation.

The bust in question is that of the polymath Arthur Koestler, most famous for his anti-Stalin political thriller *Darkness at Noon*, but also the author of a number of books in an embarrassingly wide spectrum of subjects, ranging from creativity, biology and behavioural psychology to capital punishment, ESP and the history of the Jews. The biography is David Cesarani's massive tome of academic gossip, *Arthur Koestler: The Homeless Mind* (1998), described as both "richly documented," and an "erratic" work of "moral prating". The 'date rape' in question is that of the filmmaker Jill Craigie, wife of the later Labour leader Michael Foot, and allegedly took place in 1951. Craigie did not make it public until forty years later.

Cesarani claims that Koestler raped other women as well, but it's the circumstances surrounding Koestler's suicide in 1983 that possibly places him in the same category as Harry Crosby and Jacques Vaché. On the morning of 3 March 1983, a housekeeper employed by Koestler and his wife Cynthia arrived at their house at 8 Montpelier Square in Kensington and found a note pinned to the door. "Please do not go upstairs," it read, "Ring the police and tell them to come to the house." Amelia, the housekeeper, telephoned friends of the Koestlers instead, who then rang the police. When Inspector David Thomas and a colleague finally entered the house they found Koestler in the sitting room, dead, upright in an armchair, a glass of brandy in his hand. Cynthia was lying on a sofa, facing Arthur, a whisky beside her on a coffee table. She was dead too. Also on the table were two wine glasses, both with a powdery residue, and a jar of honey, used to sweeten the drug they had taken. The powder was the remains of the Tuinal they had dissolved, a powerful barbiturate. An examination suggested they had been dead for thirty-six hours, which means they must have taken the drug on the evening of the 1st.

At the time of his death, Koestler had been suffering from Parkinson's disease and leukaemia for years, although he had kept this a secret for a long time, and, as his friend and fellow parapsychology investigator Brian Inglis remarked, he was "falling apart." Others, like the writer Julian Barnes, who became a friend and chess-mate late in Koestler's life, were also struck by his condition. His hands shook, he had difficulty concentrating, could barely walk, his eyesight was failing, and a recent swelling in his groin suggested the cancer was spreading.

Koestler was a very vocal advocate of euthanasia; he was vice president of the Euthanasia Society (now EXIT) and had even written a 'how-to' pamphlet on killing yourself. That he would take his own life rather than allow himself to deteriorate further seems understandable. Indeed, his editor and literary executor Harold Harris, who saw Koestler for the last time a week before his suicide, knew, as most of his friends did, that he would not "quietly submit to the final removal of his physical and mental faculties." Harris was even concerned that Koestler "might have left it too late."[55] "He was unable to stand, his speech was disjointed, and he clearly found it difficult to concentrate on what was being said to him." What caused an uproar and remains today a controversial subject is the fact that Koestler's wife, Cynthia Jeffries – his third – decided to join him. Unlike Koestler, Cynthia was in good health, and at 55 wasn't yet facing the ravages of old age which Koestler, at 77, had begun to confront years earlier.

Although up until her death friends believed she gave no indication of wanting to kill herself, when the facts emerged practically everyone agreed that it made sense that she had. By all accounts, including her own, Cynthia was absolutely devoted to Arthur – pathologically so, according to some observers. She had been in love with Koestler since they first met in Paris in 1949, when he hired her as a secretary, and she had worked for him on and off until they married in 1965, when she was thirty-eight, and he was fifty-five. George Mikes, a fellow Hungarian and close friend of the two said, "No one knows or will ever know what exactly happened between Arthur and Cynthia. No one knows how and when Cynthia decided to die with him. But everyone who knew them well can see the logic, almost the inevitability of her decision."[56] Harold Harris, who edited the unfinished joint autobiography of Koestler and Cynthia, published posthumously as *Stranger on the Square*, wrote that, "It is hardly an exaggeration to say that his life became hers, that she *lived* his life. And when the time came for him to leave it, her life too was at an end."[57]

Yet not everyone was happy with this assessment, especially not David Cesarani. Cesarani's motive in writing his book was initially to explore the question of Koestler's Jewish roots – roots Cesarani, a professor of modern Jewish history, believed Koestler had vigorously and egregiously rejected. Cesarani gained access to the Koestler papers at Edinburgh on the strict condition that he was *not* writing a biography, a condition he agreed to and which the university believed he would honour. The task of writing Koestler's biography was already given to Michael Scammell, whose authorized work is scheduled for publication in 2007, although it has already missed a few deadlines. Cesarani's subsequent book, which, using Koestler's jettisoning of his Jewishness as a peg, hangs on it a plethora of personal faults and flaws, has itself caused a literary storm. Scammell, Barnes and the novelist Frederick Raphael have accused Cesarani of lying, of selecting his facts to suit his argument, of making unsubstantiated claims, and of engaging in a malicious exercise in character assassination. That Cesarani depicts in tabloid detail the many sexual escapades Koestler engaged in – it was common knowledge even before Cesarani's 'expose' that Koestler was an obsessive and aggressive womaniser – as well as incidences of violence, suggests that something more than academic interest fuelled his study. His most controversial assertion, however, is that, after a relationship and marriage built on domination and submission, Koestler bullied Cynthia into taking her life with him, in a form of 'suttee'. "It is this negation of another human being," Cesarani writes, "that casts a pall over the life, work and reputation of Arthur Koestler."[58]

That life, work and reputation were considerable. Koestler had the kind of life most writers only write about. And, as is borne out by the titles of many of his books – *Arrival and Departure, The Yogi and the Commissar, The Lotus and the Robot*, and perhaps most succinctly in one of his last works, *Janus: A Summing Up*, Janus being the two-faced Roman god – it was characterized by the tension born of two opposing forces. In Koestler's case, it was a clear, rigorous and supremely logical mind, linked to a fiery, impulsive and often violent emotional life.

Born in Budapest in 1905 to a prosperous father who had success with inventions like 'radioactive soap' and an envelope-opening machine, and a mother who visited Freud because of her persistent violent headaches, Koestler went on to have a life that exemplified "a typical case-history of a Central European member of the educated middle classes, born in the first years of our century."[59] Koestler could be seen as a kind of ideological impulse-buyer, were it not for the incisive intellect he brought to each of his infatuations. In a series of sudden shifts, starting with burning his matriculation book and abandoning university before receiving his degree, which he described as a "sudden enamouredness with un-reason itself,"[60] and which would reappear consistently throughout his life, Koestler embraced and rejected Zionism, Communism, Marxism, politics, scientific materialism, and Darwinism. In his last years he engaged in an eloquent if highly criticized exploration of the possibilities of parapsychology and its links to quantum physics, which included having a weighing machine installed at Montpelier Square, so he could test the possibility of levitation.

Although in books like *The Lotus and the Robot*, a study of Indian philosophy and Zen, he is critical of mysticism, and although he was one of the first to experiment with and reject psychedelic drugs – calling their effect "confidence tricks played on one's own nervous system"[61] – Koestler himself claimed that "it was always the 'oceanic' type of experience that dictated the really important decisions of my life, and determined its abrupt zigzag course."[62] One incidence of the 'oceanic' came to him while he sat in a Franco prison, during the Spanish Civil War, waiting to be executed. Whiling away the time by working out the mathematical proof that there is no ultimate prime number, Koestler experienced a "wordless essence, a fragrance of eternity, a quiver of the arrow in the blue." This serene detachment was interrupted by a vague nagging thought, which he recalled was the realization that he might be shot, and to which he replied, "So what? Have you nothing serious to worry about?"

It was experiences like these that led Koestler, at the height of his fame and influence in the 1950s as a passionate anti-Communist, to startle his critics by abandoning politics and plunging into detailed examinations of the flaws in Darwinian theory, the dangers of behavioural psychology and the roots of human creativity in a series of brilliant books like *The Sleepwalkers, The Act of Creation* and *The Ghost in the Machine*, now classics of anti-reductionist thought. By the time of his death, Koestler was a best-selling author, a respected journalist, had received numerous honours, organized dozens of symposia (so many that his last novel, *The Call Girls*, satirized the conference life) had hobnobbed with intellectual celebrities like Bertrand Russell, and was courted by Margaret Thatcher.

Yet alongside his cultural achievements, Koestler had acquired a reputation as a hard-drinking, bullying male chauvinist, a dark side that Cesarani had no qualms about revealing, although, as many reviewers of his book pointed out, many of his revelations had been made in previous books about Koestler. Koestler's marriages, to Dorothy Ascher, Mamaine Paget, and Cynthia, were characterized by his domineering personality, forced abortions, and appalling behaviour, mostly centred around his wives' need to accept his philandering, as well as his heavy drinking and general abusive treatment. Most bullies suffer from an inferiority complex and Koestler, incorrigibly competitive, would not be outdone: he once said that his inferiority complex was "as big as a cathedral."

His friend George Mikes broke off relations with Koestler when he tried to bully him into drinking more during their get-togethers. Koestler had a habit of smashing up his cars, and on one occasion, arrested for drink-driving in Paris, he took a swing at a policeman; something similar happened in the 1970s in London as well. During the Hungarian uprising in 1956, Koestler threw bricks through the window of the Hungarian legation. He was also prone to depression and attempting suicide and prior to his death, made several botched attempts. Once, on hearing that Walter Benjamin, who he had met in Marseilles, had killed himself, he swallowed the morphine Benjamin had given him, but his stomach refused it and he only vomited. An early attempt to gas himself, triggered by the Party's rejection of an early novel, failed when a book fell off a shelf and hit him on the head, leading him to change his mind. On another occasion in another Spanish jail he again tried to poison himself, but his body again rejected it. He even wrote a book about a suicide. In *The Case of The Mid-Wife Toad* Koestler investigates the tragic story of the Viennese Paul

Kammerer, a brilliant biologist and believer in the Lamarckian theory of acquired characteristics, who killed himself in 1926 when it was discovered that some of the test results supporting his work had been faked. Kammerer himself was not responsible for the forgery but his reputation was ruined and in despair he blew his brains out.

Cynthia, too, an attractive South African girl – shy, awkward and painfully self-conscious – was no stranger to suicide. Her father killed himself when she was thirteen and she herself considered it years later when she had been working for Koestler for some time. The two had become intimate, and she believed he was trying to get rid of her. "I knew he did not want me to be his 'slavey' for ever and that he thought I should find a husband and lead a life of my own. [. . .] I was confronted by my empty self from whom there was no escape even for an instant. At last I found a solution to this intolerable existence. [. . .] I would kill myself."[63] She thought of slipping into Kensington Gardens at night and taking an overdose of sleeping pills. She was pulled out of this despair by getting involved with another man. But the affair didn't last long and she was soon sending Koestler postcards, hoping he had lots of work for her.

That Cynthia was something of a cipher, and that she willingly gave herself over to Koestler, becomes clear from reading her sections of *Stranger in the Square*. That he took professional advantage of her devotion to him is also clear. Speaking of their first meeting, Koestler wrote, "More important, from a professional point of view, was a quality in her of unobtrusiveness, almost of self-effacement . . ."[64] Whether this is acceptable or not is debatable, but most writers as busy as Koestler would have been happy with the catch.

For Cynthia, working for Koestler was a dream come true. "It had long been my ambition to work for a writer. As a child I was happiest when reading and my favourite people were the imaginary heroes of books rather than those living around me." She had even fantasized about being like Arlova, the doomed Rubashov's secretary in *Darkness at Noon*. "I decided that she was the kind of secretary Arthur wanted. She never spoke, she never reacted in a distracting way." She even wished she could wear "an embroidered Russian blouse like hers."[65] When Koestler had sent her away for a time she was inconsolable. "I was longing for the past – for the days when I had worked for him and for the thrilling moments when we happened to be alone. I could not face the fact that life would never be the same again." That this devotion carried over into their emotional life and marriage, and that Koestler often, but not always, abused it – he did have a generous, affectionate side – is also difficult to ignore in the accounts of their life, both by Cesarani and by people sympathetic to Koestler.

But that he purposely browbeat her into killing herself, when by all accounts he could barely do the job himself, is a different question. In his pamphlet for the Euthanasia Society, Koestler spells out the many reasons why one *shouldn't* commit suicide. One of these is the loss of a loved one. Koestler makes clear that it's possible to survive this, providing one had strong outside interests. Yet it doesn't take much to see that Cynthia lacked these, even though, in her suicide note, she wrote, "I cannot live without Arthur, despite certain inner resources." The fact that she says this has led many, not only Cesarani, to believe that Koestler's grip on her lasted until she drank the honeyed Tuinal. Yet it was a grip she willingly endured, and even went out of her way to submit to.

The scenario of their last days raises some questions. If she didn't really want to join him, wouldn't it have been easy to fake taking the drug, especially in the company of a man dying in bits and pieces anyway? Cesarani indicts Koestler of not ensuring that she *wouldn't* kill herself after his death, and of not taking his own life in some way without her being present. "It is an indictment of Koestler," he writes, "that he lived with a woman who was a vacuum."[66] But if the "vacuum" loved him for some thirty-four years, was she really a vacuum? Yet even Cesarani doesn't see her as such. "She was woman of intelligence and humour, who saw through Koestler and knew exactly what she was doing with her own life."[67] This doesn't sound like a "vacuum." Friends who knew them said that in his last years, Koestler was in Cynthia's thrall, and was helpless

207

without her. Perhaps Koestler did try to talk her out of it, and failed? Barely able to walk or to speak, how could he have stopped her?

As George Mikes said, no one will ever know what exactly happened between them, but when Michael Scammell's biography appears, things may possibly become clearer. That his wife felt compelled to join him in death is surely tragic, yet it's possible that Koestler's bust, languishing in a closet in Scotland, may yet again see the light of day.

Thomas Chatterton

Even before Werther, the teenaged Thomas Chatterton was the original tragic Romantic genius. "The marvellous boy," as Wordsworth called him, abandoned poetry at an even younger age than Rimbaud, and in a more dramatic manner, committing suicide at seventeen, defeated in his battle against an uncaring, philistine London, which he had hoped to conquer after leaving his provincial, mercantile Bristol.[68] Ignored or rejected by those who should have recognised his gift – Horace Walpole in particular became the villain of this piece – Chatterton was left to starve in the archetypal garret, too proud to beg or even to accept help when it was offered. He struggled valiantly and defiantly, writing his poems, articles, and stories, sending them to editors, only for them to become lost in the wash of hackwork flooding Grub Street, or worse, printed without payment. Finally, his fate became unbearable and he decided to end it all, tearing his last poetry to bits in his death throes, succumbing to the arsenic he took that dreadful night of 23 August 1770 in Brooke Street, Holborn.

Unknown and practically unmourned when he died – he was buried in a pauper's grave – Chatterton soon became the symbol of the rising Romantic new guard, and an early death the trademark of that generation. Keats, who would himself die young, would dedicate his *Endymion* to Chatterton. Rossetti would later dedicate sonnets to his memory. Coleridge wrote a monody on his death, Blake spoke of him with praise, and Henry Wallis' painting of his corpse – with George Meredith as model – flame-haired and fallen in his attic room, still prompts

208

sighs and muted appreciation from viewers at Tate Britain. Across the channel, Alfred de Vigny's *Chatterton* was a success and, to its author's chagrin, triggered a spate of imitation suicides, causing Théophile Gautier to remark that in those days across Paris "you could hear the crack of solitary pistols in the night,"[69] as starving poets agreed that killing oneself was "still the best way to prove one's genius."[70] Vigny's play was so successful in fact, that the French government held a debate to argue the best way to halt its deplorable effect. To give Vigny credit, he was appalled at the suicide craze and pointed out that he had written the play in order to plead the cause of young writers, not to encourage them to kill themselves.

As in the case of Goethe's *Werther*, the dual themes of youth and neglected genius struck a chord in the public's sentiments. There were Chatterton handkerchiefs and Chatterton engravings. Odes were written in his honour, concerts given, and even a Gothic ruin erected in his name. A decade after his death, a best-seller by Herbert Croft, *Love and Madness* (a title reminiscent of a Woody Allen film), combined a recent *crime passionel* with Chatterton's story and more than anything else secured his place in the public consciousness as a doomed angel, a songbird too sensitive for this rough clime.[71] A year earlier, an English translation of Goethe's *Werther* included a note explaining to its readers that Werther's feelings, "like that of our Chatterton, were too intense to support the load of accumulated distress; and like him his diapason ended in death." Although the Chatterton craze ended with WWI, a trickle of it carried on into the new age, with works by Vita Sackville-West and a German writer, Ernst Penzoldt, carrying on the myth.

Chatterton's ghost has even played a saving hand in the lives of other poets, dissuading at least two of them from following in his tragic footsteps. During the *fin-de-siècle*, the wretched Francis Thompson – penniless, starving, drug addled and sleeping rough beneath the Covent Garden arches – having spent his last pence on a fatal dose of laudanum, was stopped from killing himself by Chatterton's spirit. Having swallowed half the dose, Thompson was about to down the rest when he felt a hand on his wrist. It was Chatterton, staying him, providentially, as the very next day, Thompson received news that the editor Wilfred Meynell had published one of his poems and wanted to contact him. The result was that Thompson spent his last years under Meynell's care, writing the poetry he is known for today.

Chatterton's biographer, the eccentric E.H.W. Meyerstein, a figure as fantastical as his subject, was plagued by depressions and thoughts of suicide throughout his life and, like Chatterton, was fated to be denied recognition in his lifetime; even today, although the author of many novels and books of poetry, he is known solely through his massive account of his hero's short life, and this by only a few. Meyerstein, though, deserves to be better known, and not only for his eccentricities, although these do spark curiosity – among others he was said to wave his false teeth to make a point, and he had an obsession with crime scenes, and would walk for miles to view one. Meyerstein's dedication to Chatterton brought him to live for a time beneath the poet's beloved Saint Mary Redcliffe in Bristol, where, aside from his last four months in London, he spent all of his brief life. And in a small room in Holborn, similar to the one in which Chatterton gave up his ghost, Meyerstein too faced the demon of self-destruction. Although in his journal he had written, "There is one ethical command: YOU MUST NOT KILL YOURSELF. However unbearable your environment is you must not do that,"[72] the loneliness, doubt and stung pride that afflicted Chatterton visited him too. But the ghost of Chatterton appeared again and, as with Francis Thompson, moved Meyerstein to take heart and endure. Meyerstein was so affected he wrote a poem, "Chatterton in Holborn: A Vision."

> Not many yards from this your lonely bed
> A lonelier than you broke life's locked door,
> And when the shades of fatal night were fled
> They found his papers piecemeal on the floor,
> The limbs and face distorted of the dead,
> Who had no sense of what his days were for,

But now remembers and bids you live on,
Your guardian angel Thomas Chatterton.

Ironically it was Meyerstein's *A Life of Thomas Chatterton*,
published well past the prime of Chatterton's posthumous
fame, that dissolved the romantic myths about him and made
him a more human and more interesting figure, making clear
his less than attractive sides, his spite, his quarrelsomeness, and
his ambitions.

Thomas Chatterton was born in Bristol on 20 November
1752. It was not a propitious start. According to his horoscope,
provided by Meyerstein, he had Mercury in the sixth house,
which presented "an infallible argument of a wretched life
and fatal end."[73] Whether Meyerstein worked back from
the known facts to arrive at this assessment is unclear, but
Chatterton's life was certainly not happy. His father had died
two months before Chatterton was born, and what we know
of him suggests an interesting character. He was a school-
master by trade but a musician by inclination who, among
other works, composed an anthem for his own funeral; he was
also a dabbler in the occult with an interest in the past, and,
apparently, a drinker.

Chatterton's mother, twenty and with an older daughter
born out of wedlock, was left penniless and was forced to set up
house with her mother-in-law. She brought in money from
starting a sewing school. Chatterton's family had held the
office of sexton in Saint Mary Redcliffe, a parish church, for
nearly two centuries – the position was then held by Thomas'
uncle, Richard Philips – and the church, with its atmosphere of
mystery and times long gone, was the single most important
influence on the boy. Although he was deemed backward at
first, Mary, Chatterton's sister, taught him to read. He scorned
modern books but was fascinated by ancient texts, their
illuminated capitals attracting him like some talisman. He
learned to read from a Black Letter Bible, and roamed the
church grounds, becoming familiar with the inscriptions on
the tombs, spelling his way through these traces of a lost
world.

Around this time we find an early appearance of what was probably Chatterton's central character trait. When his sister asked him what he would like painted on his bowl, he replied, "Paint me an angel with wings, and a trumpet to trumpet my name over the world." Early on fame and all that comes with it was his goal. Yet years later he would lament, "It is my pride, my damned native, unconquerable pride that plunges me into distraction."[74] "Proud as Lucifer" was how a cousin he lived with in Shoreditch, before his last days in Holborn, described him, when he chastised her for calling him "Tommy."[75] "When was a poet ever named *Tommy*?" he asked. Not being very knowledgeable about poets, his cousin said she didn't know.

Once he had mastered it, reading became his life's blood; Chatterton devoured books whole, gorging on metaphysics, mathematics and works on antiquities. He haunted bookshops and was a regular at the circulating libraries – and this, we must remember, as a boy. He was also prone to trance states, or at least deep abstraction, and he would sit for hours, contemplating some inner world. He would also cry for no apparent reason. He seldom played with other children, and his sole amusement seemed to come from the old parchments his father had taken from the muniment room of the church. His father had used these to cover books, and his mother used them in her sewing, but Chatterton saved them from this abuse and secreted them away in a lumber room in the attic. Here he also brought paper, inks, and charcoal. His mother wondered what he did there, locked away for hours. Soon enough, the world would know.

At eight Chatterton was sent to Colston's Hospital, a charity school. Here the basics in reading, writing and arithmetic were taught. While these did little to satisfy Chatterton's appetite for learning, the school's dress code had a deeper effect. The students wore medieval dress: a bluecoat, long surcoat, yellow stockings, and their hair was cut in a kind of tonsure. The curriculum depressed him but his sister noted that he seemed happier once he had begun to write poetry. At 10, his first poem was published in a

Bristol paper. Soon after he had also completed a "Hymn for Christmas Day."

His father's talent for composition seemed to be resurfacing, but Chatterton put it to a peculiar use. He had spent the hours locked away in his lumber room with the ancient parchments performing a kind of resurrection – or, to put it less romantically, he brought his love of the past and his knack for poetry together and invented an idealized Medieval Bristol poet-priest, one Thomas Rowley, producing a series of poems which he claimed to have discovered among the church's ancient texts. An audacious act for a boy not yet in his teens, but it was successful, and the authenticity of the 'Rowley poems' became a matter of debate for decades.

It was in fact an age of forgeries and frauds. The Scot James Macpherson had gained fame as the true author of the Ossian poems, seminal Romantic works by the 'Celtic Homer' that were translated by Goethe and formed the favourite reading of Napoleon. Palamazaar, a Frenchman who posed as a native of Formosa, wrote a book in Latin about his life; when his ploy was discovered, no one thought the less of him, the formidable Dr. Johnson remarking, "I should as soon think of contradicting a bishop." And Horace Walpole, who played a major part in Chatterton's fortunes, originally published his *Castle of Otranto* as a work "translated by William Marshall, Gent., from the original Italian of Onuphrio Muralto." Chatterton may only have been trying to hit the popular note.

Chatterton presented his forgeries to some local antiquarians, who were delighted with his discoveries and, more importantly, asked no embarrassing questions about them and wondered if there were more. He obliged and for a time his hunger for achievement and distinction was satisfied. But not for long. At 14 he left Colston's and was indentured to John Lambert, a Bristol attorney. Although the work was light – simple copying – and Chatterton was lucky to get it, he hated the routine and disliked having to eat with the servants. His attempts at poetry suffered as well; a servant found him writing poems and unceremoniously tore them up and threw them in the fire. As the years passed his misery increased until he spoke openly of suicide; when a letter he wrote to a friend saying that he planned to kill himself was discovered, his employer asked one of the antiquarians to speak with him – the last thing Lambert needed was a suicidal teenager on his hands.

Chatterton, who by this time was writing political satires for London papers, quickly realized the true power of the word. He realized that he had no future in Bristol, and his attempts to gain recognition by writing to well known figures, like Horace Walpole, were failures. Walpole questioned the authenticity of the Rowley poems, but more importantly was miffed at the idea of a teenage indentured servant speaking to him as an equal and said as much, forever after casting himself as the man who could have 'saved' Chatterton, but didn't. Chatterton knew he had to get to London and so wrote an even more desperate suicide note and left it in plain view. Lambert took one look at it and was eager to wash his hands of the boy. Chatterton soon left for London, armed with five pounds, his notebook, the address of his cousin in Shoreditch, and his titanic pride.

Yet, in a brilliant essay, Richard Holmes argues that Chatterton didn't commit suicide, but that his death was from an accidental overdose of arsenic, taken as a curative for syphilis, a common, if dangerous treatment at the time, a notion that Peter Ackroyd employs in his novel *Chatterton*.[76] Holmes points out that traces of opium were found on Chatterton's teeth when his body was discovered, and that he had more than likely been a user for some time, both his last letters and works like the weird, near hallucinogenic "African Eclogues" suggesting a state of consciousness associated with the drug. One of Chatterton's friends in Brooke Street was a Mr. Cross, a chemist, and he more than likely supplied Chatterton with the narcotic. Opium was used widely as a cure-all until the late nineteenth century and it was often cheaper than alcohol. Chatterton was also living on his own for the first time in the few weeks leading up to his death. In Shoreditch he shared a room, a bed even, and had relatives around him. But on Brooke Street he was alone.

Poverty, hunger, pride and that strange sensibility which would soon be called Romantic would lead him to reject the brutal world around him – Brooke Street was known for its prostitutes and cut-throats – and to seek comfort in some realm closer to his heart's desire, a realm accessed by himself and many others since through drugs. His friend the chemist Cross also told the scholar Michael Lort, who began to investigate the Chatterton story in the 1770s, that Chatterton "had the foul disease which he would cure himself." The 'foul disease' was syphilis and that Chatterton would 'cure himself' is in character; he had pretensions to medical knowledge and at one point in his last days wrote Dr. Barrett – one of the antiquarians to whom he delivered the Rowley poems – to help him get work as a surgeon on a ship bound for Africa: a mad dream, perhaps, occasioned by the poppy? The usual cure for syphilis involved calomel and vitriol, but a quicker, if more dangerous method employed arsenic in small doses.

Arsenic for the disease and opium to kill the pain. Alcohol more than likely as well. For anyone a dubious brew, but for Chatterton, according to Holmes, a deadly one. Drunk, stoned, impatient and unsure of his dose, Chatterton's death may have been the result of a tragic miscalculation, rather than that of neglected genius. He left no suicide note, other than the phoney one which freed him from Bristol four months earlier. And from the tone of his writings in London, which jettisoned the pre-Morris medievalism for the barbed satire of political taunt, and the barbaric splendour of the "African Eclogues," one doesn't get the sense that Chatterton – proud, unbending and as convinced as ever of his genius – wanted to "fall upon the midnight with no pain." Wild and unsupervised as never before, he may have just taken too much and the cure, as often is the case, may have simply turned out deadlier than the disease.

It's a shame that unlike Francis Thompson and Meyerstein, Chatterton had no guardian angel to stay his hand, or at least to lessen his dose. Like Walter Benjamin, he seemed plagued by bad luck; money that would have saved him from starvation without curdling his pride came the day after his death, and a fed Chatterton would have faced the world with a different outlook. Who knows what might have come of it, and what the loss of such a powerful symbol would have had on the starving poets and neglected geniuses that followed?

Cesare Pavese

On the evening of Sunday 27 August 1950, the body of the Italian poet, novelist and translator Cesare Pavese was found in a room he had taken the day before at the Hotel Roma in Turin, a few blocks from his own apartment. He had swallowed the contents of over a dozen packets of sleeping pills and was fully clothed and lying on the bed. He was only 42. Pavese had spent the weeks prior to his suicide arranging as neat and orderly a death as he could, burning letters and documents on a brazier in his room, even going so far as to make sure that *L' Unità*, the Communist Party newspaper, to which he contributed, had a good photograph of him in its files, presumably for his obituary. He had always believed that one should "seek death of one's own free will, asserting one's right to choose," and now he had put that belief to the test. Not long before, Pavese had won the prestigious Strega Prize, the most sought after Italian literary award, and the novels he wrote just before his end, like *The Moon and The Bonfires*, probably his best known outside Italy, show a craftsman and artist at his peak.

The ostensible prompt for taking his life was his rejection by the American B-movie actress Constance Dowling[77], but any reader of Pavese's remarkable journal, published as *This Business of Living*, soon recognizes that suicide, what he called his "absurd vice," was something he was moving toward practically all of his life – inexorably, one wants to say, aware of the cliché, but conscious of its aptness. Writing of Pavese, A. Alvarez remarked that he was the kind of suicide that is born, not made, and it's clear that Pavese was one of those whom the "Treatise on the Steppenwolf" describes so accurately. "I know that I am forever condemned to think of suicide when faced with no matter what difficulty or grief," he wrote.[78] His suicide note, left on the first page of his copy of his philosophical *Dialogues with Leucò*, found open in the room, was a plea for those he left behind to make no fuss. "I forgive everyone and ask forgiveness of everyone," he wrote. "O.K.? Not too much gossip, please."[79] The calm and nonchalance of these last words, reminiscent of Mayakovsky's, contrast powerfully with the tortured final entry in his journal. "The thing most feared in secret always happens . . . All it needs is a little courage. The more the pain grows clear and definite, the more the instinct for life asserts itself and the thought of suicide recedes. It seemed easy enough when I thought of it. Weak women have done it. It needs humility, not pride. I am sickened by all this. Not words. Action. I shall write no more."[80]

The chasm between words and action, or art and life, plagued Pavese endlessly. It's almost too obvious to point out that when he finally succeeded in crossing it, what he achieved was death.

Cesare Pavese was born in 1908 on a farm where his family spent their holidays, near the small village of Santo Stefano Belbo, in the Langhe area of Piedmont between Turin and the Alps. Although he spent most of his life in Turin, where he worked as an editor and translator for the publisher Einaudi, the landscape of his early years made a deep, perhaps fatal impression. Pavese believed in destiny and his destiny was shaped by the rugged, austere hills of his birth, on which he loved to wander on long, solitary walks. The contrast between the city and the country, which, like other dichotomies in his life, he was never able to reconcile – "I am made up of many parts that do not blend," he told his friend and biographer Davide Lajolo – became a mythic theme for him. The people of these hills were as rugged as they are, taciturn and reticent, and Pavese's mother was no exception. When his father died from a brain tumour when Pavese was six, his undemonstrative mother offered little tenderness and warmth, though he got some measure of this from his older sister, with whom he would live for most of his adult years. Throughout his life, Pavese had difficulty with women, and although his dissatisfaction with Italian Communism, with which he belatedly but without real conviction became involved, joining the party after WWII, is often cited as an equal element in his suicide, it was really his inability to find love that turned him toward indulging in his "absurd vice." As one critic remarked, "At the centre of his life there appears to have been an emotional vacuum which he tried repeatedly to fill, always without success."[81] Throughout his life, Pavese remained "the contemplative observer of himself who seeks . . . to break out of his solitude and yet continually fails to do so."[82]

In his later years Pavese would try to recapture some sense of the innocence of his early days; yet, by most accounts his childhood wasn't happy. He gives the impression of being an 'outsider' from early on — someone who, like the figure in Poe's poem, "does not see as others do"[83] — and, like the contrast between city and country, that between solitude and human contact is a central theme in both his life and work. Like many sensitive, intelligent children, Pavese stood apart from the life around him, exercising a capacity for distance that is essential for most writers, yet which would soon create a gulf between himself and the world.

Pavese's first experience with rejection happened, as it does with most of us, in his teens. Like most romantics, Pavese was attracted by the lure of the inaccessible. Thin, scholarly, and not particularly handsome, throughout his life Pavese was drawn to glamorous, overtly sexy women, and although on occasion a Marilyn Monroe might be attracted to an Arthur Miller, the kind of woman that Pavese desired usually wasn't interested in him. His first timid attempts at meeting girls resulted in fainting fits and when a cabaret singer he had met while in high school stood him up, he was sick for three months; their date was for six, but Pavese waited until midnight before admitting she wasn't going to show. Pavese also seems to have been plagued by some sexual inhibition or self-consciousness: impotence and premature ejaculation turn up frequently in his journal; "The man who ejaculates too soon," he writes, "had better never have been born. It is a failing that makes suicide worth while."[84]

Although his novels have an existential air, and its understandable that film-makers like Michelangelo Antonioni would be drawn to his work, Pavese's outlook is fundamentally romantic. Women are infinitely desirable, yet the real stuff of sex is nasty, dirty and ugly, and is always a disappointment. He is drawn to it, but repelled at the same time, and it's clear that the social and political concerns in Pavese's writings are an expression of his recognition that his detachment from life is essentially a product of immaturity. Yet he is not really a political writer, his association with Communism notwithstanding. His focus on the working class and the peasants in his novels is really an attempt to break through his isolation into 'life', yet it could never provide the kind of intensity that 'really' living does. It's instructive that he speaks of living as a 'business'. As one critic commented, Pavese saw life "as a necessary performance, as an artefact to be constructed, rather than a process to be accepted."[85] Self-conscious, awkward, rarely at home with himself, Pavese lacked that unconscious grace that many less thoughtful people seem to enjoy.

If life was, as Pavese thought, a business, it wasn't one he was very good at. Like others we have met – Trakl, Anne Sexton, Benjamin – Pavese seemed adept at being inept. In a letter written to a friend the young Pavese confesses that he is "incompetent, timid, lazy, uncertain, weak and half mad," and that he lacks any potential to "settle into a permanent job and make what is called a success in life."[86] And in a poem he sent the same friend, Pavese makes an early reference to suicide. He says that "one evening in December" he walked along a deserted road, with "turmoil in my heart," and also a gun. He fires a blast into the ground, feeling the recoil. He then imagines "the tremendous jolt it will give on the night when the last illusion and the fears will have abandoned me and I will place it against my temple to shatter my brain."[87] This is a reference to an incident in real life, when Pavese's best friend committed suicide, and Pavese was determined to do the same. He got a gun and went to the tree where his friend shot himself, but found he couldn't repeat the act; he fired shots into the tree instead. The inability to complete the suicidal gesture stayed with Pavese, adding to his sense of incompetence.

The experience that would set him on his destiny as a suicide would combine both a woman and politics. In 1930,

Pavese's mother died. Although their relationship was never close, her death upset him deeply. He became even more cut off from other people, and his thoughts inevitably drifted toward suicide. In 1933, in order to get a position as a teacher, Pavese joined the Fascist Party, a necessity at the time. Soon after, however, he became involved with a woman, another teacher, who was a Communist and anti-Fascist. Pavese believed that his affair with Tina Pizzardo, "the woman with the hoarse voice," would be his great love, and, when she asked him if he would receive letters for her from other anti-fascists, he agreed. Tina, however, was being watched, and the police soon raided Pavese's house and found the letters. Pavese was arrested. If, as Tim Parks points out, he explained that he was in love and was only letting his mistress use his address, he probably would have been released.[88] But this would have meant compromising the source of his happiness, and that was unthinkable. Pavese protected Tina, and the result was that he was first imprisoned, then placed in exile in a remote coastal village in Calabria.

He found the place unbearable. "Study is impossible," he told a friend in a letter. "You can do nothing worth doing in this state of uncertainty, nothing other than to savour utter boredom, misery, spleen and gut-ache."[89] After spending a year under house arrest, he appealed for clemency, and was released. During that time Tina wrote only once, but Pavese rationalized this by saying she was simply protecting herself and other subversives, by avoiding any links to a known anti-fascist. Understandably, on his release Pavese was eager to see her, and he took the first train to Turin. But when he arrived he was told that Tina had married another man the day before. Pavese fainted on the platform. It was bad enough that he had lost his chance at love, which, he believed, would bring with it a home and family – symbols of maturity – but any standing he may have had with the other anti-fascists dissolved when it became known that he had pleaded for clemency. Other arrested subversives stoically endured their fate.

When Pavese asked Tina why she didn't wait and marry him, she told him that "you're good at writing poetry, but you're not good for a woman." It was an answer he probably already knew, but to hear it from the woman he had just spent a year in exile for must have hurt. She also made it clear that it was his dependence on her that turned her away. It's a banal reflection, but Pavese seems to have sought out women that, like his mother, would show him little affection; those that did, didn't interest him. It was a 'no win' situation, and it's little wonder that he could write acid aphorisms like: "A woman, unless she is an idiot, sooner or later meets a piece of human wreckage and tries to rescue him. She sometimes succeeds. But a woman, unless she is an idiot, sooner or later finds a sane, healthy man and makes a wreck of him. She always succeeds."[90] Yet, although this expresses a sentiment shared by many men who have wasted themselves on a woman, another aphorism makes it clear that it is not so much the woman who turns one toward self-destruction, but the dangers of love itself. "One does not kill oneself for the love of *a* woman," Pavese wrote. "One kills oneself because a love, any love, reveals us in our nakedness, our misery, our impotence, our nothingness." If Pavese spent his short life seeking a woman who would love him and whom he could love, he was also seeking that which would make him feel most suicidal.

After Tina, he didn't have much luck. As he told Davide Lajolo, "the woman from Turin . . . ended it between me and women." Much of Pavese's subsequent writing has been combed, predictably, for signs of misogyny; Lajolo even has a chapter entitled, "The Other Women as Revenge," in which he examines Pavese's "contempt for women." Women are raped, murdered, and abandoned in his writings and there are also intimations of his end, prefigured in the fates of some of his women characters. One of his last novels, *Among Women Only*, begins with a failed suicide attempt by one of the central characters. By the end of the novel, she makes another attempt; this time she is successful, and her death is an almost mirror image of Pavese's own, taking barbiturates in a hotel room. "I am afraid nothing matters. We are all whores," one of Pavese's women declares.

Nevertheless, he still tried to find a woman who could

give him the love and stability he needed. Yet Pavese never mastered the knack of making himself attractive. He would use his intelligence and sensitivity to ingratiate himself, but the transition from sympathetic friend to lover was rarely made; his self-consciousness and detachment was unbridgeable, as was his sense of sexual inferiority. He was attracted to and became an intimate friend of one woman, but for five years never tried to kiss her; finally out of the blue he asked her to marry him. She declined. When he met the actress Constance Dowling in Rome, its understandable he would be taken with her: blonde and glamorous, she was also American, and Pavese had a passion for Americana. His university thesis had been on Walt Whitman, and Pavese had translated Melville, Sherwood Anderson, Sinclair Lewis, Dos Passos and Faulker, among others, making modern American literature accessible to Italian readers. But although he enjoyed a brief happiness with Constance – and perhaps the fact that he *was* happy was the most painful thing about the affair, having what he had sought for so long soon snatched from him – it's clear she wasn't Ms Right. When she left Rome for the States, Pavese waited for her to return, but soon he received a letter telling him the affair was over. He was devastated and his final descent had begun. Months later, on hearing that he had won the Strega Prize and soon after had committed suicide, Constance simply remarked, "I didn't know he was so famous," sad indication of how much their fling meant to her.

In his last days, Pavese took to inviting prostitutes to his office at Einaudi. They sat and talked, drank and smoked, but its doubtful he ever availed himself of their services. A few days before he took the room at the Hotel Roma, he met a girl at a dance hall, but more than likely he was tired of trying and wanted to stop. "Suicides are timid murderers. Masochism instead of sadism," he wrote in his journal on 17 August, echoing Otto Weininger. A few months before, the American critic F.O. Mathiessen, whose work Pavese admired, had killed himself, and its probable that Pavese took this as a sign.[91] The night before his last, he made a few phone calls, asking people to dinner, but no one was free. He prepared his journal for publication – he had always written it with this in view – made the necessary arrangements, and, making what he felt was a conscious, rational choice, fulfilled the destiny he had embraced long ago.

Mary Wollstonecraft

Including Mary Wollstonecraft in my "Ten Suicides" is something of a cheat. Although she made two attempts at suicide, both were failures. Yet sadly, less than two years after her second attempt, she died from complications giving birth to her daughter Mary, later Mary Shelley, wife of the poet Percy Shelley, and author, among other works, of *Frankenstein*. That she died so soon after failing to kill herself is a tragedy and an irony; yet in her last years, spent with the writer William Godwin, first as friends, then as cohabiting lovers, and finally as husband and wife, she achieved the kind of happiness that had eluded her throughout most of her life. Novelist, essayist, historian, political philosopher, feminist and teacher, if her personal life was one of trauma and grief, in her creative life, Mary Wollstonecraft produced a body of work that establishes her as one of the most vital and original minds of her age. What makes this especially true is the fact that in the few months in between her two suicide attempts, when she was caught in the turmoil of depression, anger, fear and loneliness, she could produce one of the most influential works of the time, her remarkable *Letters Written During a Short Residence in Sweden, Norway and Denmark*.[92]

Sent on a journey through Scandinavia – ostensibly a business trip on behalf of her one-time lover Gilbert Imlay – that she could travel successfully alone while burdened with suicidal thoughts is itself a considerable achievement. But with its theme of a solitary traveller in a strange and foreign land, encountering her own soul amidst the sublime beauties of nature, Wollstonecraft's book exemplifies and anticipates the Romantic consciousness that would emerge in full force only three years later in Wordsworth and Coleridge's *Lyrical Ballads*.

Yet Wollstonecraft's *A Short Residence* – as the work is commonly known – wasn't the only remarkable work associated with her attempts at suicide. After her death, in an effort to deal with his grief, her husband William Godwin produced the equally groundbreaking *Memoirs of the Author of the Rights of Woman*, perhaps the first work of biography in the modern sense. Godwin's work was highly criticized at the time, not only for his candour in depicting the often difficult moods of his wife, and for making public the details of her unsuccessful infatuation with the artist Henry Fuseli, and her disastrous affair with the American entrepreneur Gilbert Imlay. What many found unforgivable in Godwin's *Memoirs* was the attention he gave to her two attempts at taking her life. What we today would find essential material in 'life-writing' was, for Godwin's late Eighteenth century readership, a serious breach of authorial etiquette, not to say an insulting disregard for the memory of his wife: the poet Southey, on reading the book, remarked that Godwin showed "a want of all feeling in stripping his dead wife naked." Although both authors championed a life free from the constraints and hypocrisy of social conventions and accepted norms, when put into practice – with Mary in her own life, and with William in his account of it – they became targets of censure and indignation, most surprisingly from people who had hitherto applauded their efforts to challenge the status quo.

Mary Wollstonecraft had a difficult childhood, one that produced, as her earliest letters reveal, a basic insecurity. Her father was a sentimental, bullying man, who was as apt to beat his wife as he was to smother Mary and her siblings in drunken affection. And although Mary received little warmth or attention from her mother – as a discipline, her mother often made the talkative Mary sit still for hours without making a sound – she would often sleep on the floor outside her mother's door, in order to protect her from the arbitrary violence meted out by her father. Equally disturbing were the frequent relocations that were a part of Mary's early years. Although he lacked any aptitude for it, her father was obsessed with becoming a farmer, and wasted an inheritance on ventures that soon collapsed, forcing the family to move on. It's understandable that in later life, financial independence and domestic security became her central aims.

Her road to independence started when she was eighteen; she left home, and took a job as a lady's companion. Although it got her away from her family, like Thomas Chatterton, Mary resented being dependent on her employer and being treated like a servant. By this time she had also met and more or less fallen in love – platonically – with Fanny Blood, a young woman, as Godwin describes her, "of extraordinary accomplishments." So important was Mary's introduction to Fanny, that Godwin writes that it "bore a resemblance to the first interview of Werther and Charlotte."[93] This wasn't the only nod to Goethe's tale of failed love and suicide that Godwin makes in reference to Mary; the letters she wrote to her worthless lover Imlay, filled with ecstasy, despair and the obsessive pursuit of an unrequited love, were, he said, worthy of Werther, and in describing Mary as someone whose mind "seems almost of too fine a texture to encounter the vicissitudes of human affairs, to whom pleasure is a transport, and disappointment is agony indescribable," he simply says that "Mary was in this respect a female Werther."[94] Both the early critics of Godwin's *Memoir* and later modern feminists took argument with this association, yet its clear to any unprejudiced reader that Mary had the kind of temperament that we can only call Romantic.

Mary's attachment to Fanny Blood, who was two years older than her, is understandable. She saw her as a kind of model of self-improvement, something that Mary was determined on throughout her life. At this time, Mary's meagre self-esteem was evident. She let her long hair hang limp, and wore dull, coarse clothes. She ate very little, and suffered from headaches, fevers, and feelings of gloom, characteristics that would remain with her throughout her life. ("You talk of the roses which grow profusely in every path of life," she wrote Godwin, "I catch at them, but only encounter thorns."[95]) Fanny, on the other hand, dressed attractively, could sing and play and drew well enough to earn money from it. As one biographer put it, Mary "could not love what she did not also esteem,"[96]

225

and finding little to esteem in her own family, she anchored this need in Fanny. Soon she asked Fanny to instruct her in spelling and composition. Eventually she would live with the Blood family, and so deep was her attachment to her friend that later, when Fanny had married and moved to Portugal, Mary would travel there to assist her in childbirth. Like some presage of Mary's own fate, Fanny would die giving birth, and in memory of her great friend, Mary would name her own first child Fanny. She, too, sadly would have a tragic end.[97]

Although Mary was at first in awe of Fanny, she soon outstripped her. Where Mary had a vigorous, fiery, determined character, Fanny was timid and shy and, as Mary soon discovered, as conventional as other women. Mary was never timid and shy, and she also soon proved herself a capable character. She had tended her ill mother until her death, and when her sister Eliza suffered a nervous breakdown, prompted by a bad marriage and postnatal depression, Mary took charge, taking Eliza away from her failed home in Bermondsey, to set up a school in Newington Green. There Mary met the celebrated Dr. Johnson, who was impressed with her conversation. Mary, however, was more impressed with another doctor, Richard Price, one of the dissenters she met on the green. Unlike the cynical Dr. Johnson, Price believed that men's will and determination could better the world, and that in a just society, our better natures would have an opportunity to emerge, a belief that Mary too held strongly.

Mary's will and determination would have many chances to show their mettle. When she returned from Portugal, she found the school floundering. She arranged teaching positions for her sisters and was forced to accept a job as a governess in Ireland – not, however, before writing her *Thoughts on the Education of Daughters*. Predictably, although the opportunity to travel again was welcome (she was one of the most travelled women of her generation) Mary didn't relish her position as governess, and her outspokenness and dissatisfaction with the trivial concerns of Lady Kingsborough soon led to her dismissal. She was put on the road to destiny by meeting the publisher Joseph Johnson. Johnson recognized her talent, and soon had her reviewing for his new *Analytical Review*. Through Johnson Mary met radical figures like Tom Paine and, more importantly, Godwin. Although there were clearly women writers before, Mary, as a freelance critic and essayist, considered herself "the first of a new genus." Johnson also published her novel *Mary* and her children's book, *Original Stories*. Soon other works appeared. *A Vindication of the Rights of Man*, originally published anonymously, was her response to Edmund Burke's *Reflections on the Revolution in France*. And Tom Paine's *Rights of Man* prompted her most famous work, *Vindication of the Rights of Woman*.

Although in *Vindication of the Rights of Woman* Mary played down the importance of sex in the 'rational' woman's life, her own passions and desires began to make trouble for her. The artist Henry Fuseli, who she met through Johnson, was already married, but this didn't stop Mary from developing a 'rational desire' for him. So rational it was, that she proposed a ménage à trois between herself, Fuseli and his wife. The career-minded Fuseli, however, was shocked, as was his wife, and Mary discovered that the kind of freedom her friends lauded in her writing was not necessarily welcomed in their lives. To avoid humiliation, and to get over Fuseli, she travelled once again, this time to France, where she witnessed the Terror of the Revolution at first hand. On showing horror at the blood-soaked ground below the guillotine, a friend warned that, for her own safety, she had better keep her opinions to herself. She later wrote a history of the revolution.[98]

Yet another danger was in store for her in Paris. Here she met the American adventurer Gilbert Imlay, and all the frustrated passion of her unconsummated attraction to Fuseli found a target. Mary and Imlay became lovers, and soon she was pregnant – an imposition that Imlay quickly regretted. Although she had anticipated a life together based on mutual respect and lofty ideals, which she mistakenly assumed Imlay shared with her, Imlay's interest in Mary soon faded, and, after a brief time in Paris and then Neuilly, they would never live together again. Although on more than one occasion, Imlay declared her as his wife – for her protection in Paris he had registered her as such at the American Embassy, after England declared war on France – they were never technically married. By all accounts, Mary had conceived a love for a man who was unworthy of her, but her idealized picture of Imlay, like that of Fanny, worked against her. If she could not love where she could not esteem, then Imlay *must* be someone worthy of her esteem, even if, as practically everyone around her knew, he wasn't. Readers of the *Letters to Imlay*, published by Godwin, soon recognize the link to Werther. She may have been sexually passionate about Imlay, and the need for little Fanny to have a father was also a concern, but the impression one gets is that Mary refused to recognize that her love was misplaced and that she was the captive of her own ideals.

She made her first suicide attempt in London in 1795, after being apart from Imlay for months, and suffering his repeated indecision about their relationship; although to everyone else it was clear he was through with her, he still showed her sufficient concern to keep her hopes up and more or less told her it was "up to her," a typical male stratagem to avoid responsibility. The laudanum she took, however, only made her wretch, and when Imlay realized that she was serious, he decided to send her on her Scandinavian adventure.[99] He may have known that throwing herself into some purposeful action was the best thing for her, or he may have simply wanted to get her out of his hair. Mary, too, must have seen his request as a means of holding on to him, even if it would be at some distance. A ship Imlay had an interest in with a considerable cargo – £3,500 worth of silver, a fortune at the time – had been lost off the Swedish coast, and it was Mary's task to find out what had happened and recover what she could of his investment. That a woman who had just tried to kill herself would embark on such a voyage is surprising. That she brought along her illegitimate baby daughter and an inexperienced nursemaid smacks of Romantic fiction.

One might think that an account of a business trip would be unpromising reading, yet Mary's reasons for heading to what was more or less *terra incognita* soon become unimportant, and her reflections on the natural scenery, the strange customs, and herself grip the reader from the start; Godwin declared that reading the book made him fall in love with her. Melancholy as she is, feeling herself as "a particle broken off from the grand mass of mankind,"[100] Mary is nevertheless visited by those sudden moments of delight that save Hesse's Steppenwolf from an appointment with the razor. She speaks of feeling "that spontaneous pleasure which gives credibility to one's expectations of happiness,"[101] and recognizes that "the sublime often gave place imperceptibly to the beautiful, dilating the emotions which were painfully concentrated."[102] On approaching the Swedish coast she notes that "the sunbeams that played on the ocean, scarcely ruffled by the lightest breeze, contrasted with the huge dark rocks, that looked like the rude materials of creation forming the barrier of unwrought space . . ."[103]

Although she provides fascinating accounts of the life and people she encounters, it is her response to 'brute creation' and sublime nature that strikes the reader forcefully. As Blake was doing in her own time, and as Wordsworth and Coleridge would after her, Mary was discovering a strange new world within herself. One word that continually comes up is *imagination*. "Without the aid of imagination," she writes, "all the pleasures of the senses must sink into grossness."[104] In a letter to Imlay, who would scarcely understand her, she explained that genius was a product of a fusion of feeling and thought, of desire and imagination, and that she herself had a share in this. Unfortunately, as Mary would painfully discover, Imlay's pleasures were rarely imaginative, and all her entreaties to him to cast off his lower self and become who he 'really' was fell, not on deaf ears, but on gross ones. He already was who he really was, but she couldn't admit this.

When she returned to England, Imlay didn't meet her, as he had promised, yet he felt bound to provide a home for her and his daughter. He had by this time found another lover, one who wasn't careless about contraception, and when Mary eventually found out, she decided again to kill herself. She walked along the river to Battersea, but found the area too busy, so she took a boat further down to Putney. She walked back and forth along the bridge in the pouring rain, thinking that if her clothes were soaked, she would sink faster. Then she climbed the railing and jumped. Her clothes still buoyed her up, so she wrapped them tightly around her. It was harder to drown than she thought, and before becoming unconscious, the pain was unbearable. Some fishermen had seen her and before she was pulled too far by the current, they hauled her out and brought her to a nearby public house. When she recovered, she was indignant and thankless, complaining that even her "fixed determination to die" had failed, although she did later remark that if she ever decided to commit suicide again, she would not do it by drowning. Her 'suicide letter' to Imlay had more or less made it clear what she would do, and soon friends arrived to take her home.

Accepting that she still had to live, and that Imlay had another lover, she again proposed a ménage à trois; Imlay considered this briefly, yet both knew it was impossible, and Mary probably didn't want it anyway. After a time her obsession eased and her one-time lover faded from her consciousness, to be replaced with other, more rewarding concerns.

Notes

1 Bizan Kawamaki, 1908; Takeo Arishima, 1923; Ryunosuke Akutagawa, 1927; Shinichi Makino, 1936; Tamiki Hara, 1951; Michio Kato; 1953; Sakae Kubo; 1958; Ashihei Hino, 1960 are some of the more notable examples.

2 Henry Scott Stokes *The Life and Death of Yukio Mishima* (Penguin: Harmondsworth, 1985) p. 25. I am indebted to Mr. Stokes' book for much of this section.

3 Colin Wilson *The Misfits* (Grafton: London, 1988) p. 242.

4 Malcolm Cowley *Exile's Return* (Penguin: New York, 1994) p. 248.

5 Although Bataille did not commit suicide, murder was something he did contemplate, planning the ritual sacrifice of a victim as part of the activities of a secret society he attempted to organize in Paris in the 1930s. A target was chosen but then unfortunately for Bataille, but fortunately for the intended victim, WWII broke out and the plan was dropped.

6   Geoffrey Wolff *Black Sun* (Hamish Hamilton: London, 1976) p. 21

7   Ibid. p.83.

8   Ibid. p.61.

9   Ibid. p.54.

10 An idea he may have picked up from reading J.K. Huysmans' satanic novel, *Là-Bas*, one of whose characters, the Canon Docre, has crosses tattooed on both feet.

11 Crowley exaggerated the initial A of his signature, fashioning it to look like an erect penis. The sun, of course, is also a phallic symbol.

12 Cowley p.259.

13 It is interesting that another poet, a younger contemporary of Crosby, René Daumal, was, like him, fascinated with death, and in his early work, adopted the black sun as a symbol of "the beyond." See his collection *Counter Heaven*.

14 Wolff p.190.

15 Ibid. pp.239–241. Again, the parallels with Aleister Crowley are striking. See Crowley's infamous *Book of the Law* which contains passages such as, "These are dead, these fellows; they feel not. We are not for the poor and sad: the lords of the earth are our kinsfolk. [. . .] We have nothing with the outcast and unfit: let them die in their misery . . . Compassion is the vice of kings: stamp down the wretched & the weak: this is the law of the strong . . . [. . .] Pity not the fallen! I never knew them. I am not for them. I console not . . ." I've not come across any reference to Crowley in any literature on Crosby, although they were contemporaries and Crowley was known in the Paris and New York of Crosby's day. It's almost a pity Crosby was unaware of him, if he was. Crowley's philosophy of, "Do what thou wilt" would have appealed to him; he had a natural talent for it, as Crowley did for excess, indulging in monumental amounts of drugs, strange sex and other inebriants. On second thoughts, it was perhaps a blessing that the two didn't meet, as Crowley, for whom the sun was also a powerful talisman, would more than likely have manoeuvred large portions of Crosby's fortune into his own pockets.

16 Ibid. p.242.

17 Ibid. p.305

18 Trakl's death is reminiscent of another literary suicide. Like Trakl, the Hungarian doctor, short story writer and music critic

Géza Csáth (pseudonym of Josef Brenner 1887–1919) may have pursued a medical career simply because it would provide close proximity to drugs. Csáth begin smoking opium in 1909; a year later he was injecting large dosages of morphine. After several years working at a clinic, he took up practice as a country doctor in 1913, most likely in order to indulge his habit undetected. By the time he was discharged from service in WWI, he was showing signs of physical and mental decline. He carried knives and had members of his family followed by detectives. Finally, as his infant daughter watched, he shot his wife. Committed to an insane asylum, he made an unsuccessful suicide attempt. He then escaped; en route to Budapest, he was stopped at the Serbian border. Following a brief struggle with the border guards, he swallowed poison and died. For more on Csáth see *The Diary of Géza Csáth* (Atlas Books: London, 2005) and *The Magician's Garden and Other Stories* (Columbia University Press: New York, 1980).

19 Francis Michael Sharp *The Poet's Madness: A Reading of Georg Trakl* (Cornell University Press: London, 1981) p.17.

20 Quoted in Jeremy Reed *Bitter Blue: Tranquillizers, Creativity, Breakdown* (Peter Owen: London, 1995) p.98.

21 Ibid. p.97.

22 Ibid. p.102.

23 Francis Michael Sharp *The Poet's Madness: A Reading of Georg Trakl* (Cornell University Press: London, 1981) p. 24.

24 Ibid. p. 31.

25 Ibid.

26 Some accounts give 22 November as the date of Kleist's suicide, and he himself was unsure of the exact date when writing his last farewells, another example of the uncertainty associated with his life. Oddly, the 22nd is the same date as Harry Crosby and Josephine Bigelow's dual suicide. There is no indication that Crosby was aware of Kleist's earlier pact.

27 Joachim Maass *Kleist: A Biography* (Secker & Warburg: London, 1983) p.35.

28 E.L. Doctorow Foreword to Heinrich Von Kleist *Plays* (Coninuum: New York, 1982) p. x.

29 Thomas Mann "Kleist and his Stories," preface to Heinrich Von Kleist *The Marquise of O and other Stories* (Faber and Faber: London, 1960) p.13.

30 Maass, p. 264.

31 Quoted in David Luke's and Nigel Reeves' Introduction to Heinrich von Kleist *The Marquise of O and other Stories* (Penguin: Harmondsworth, 1978) p. 7.

32 Maass, p. 267.

33 See n. 18 above. Another writer-physician that Beddoes shares obvious similarities with is Georg Büchner, like Beddoes a writer of fragments, as evidenced by his *Woyzeck* (1836). Büchner's father, like Beddoes', performed dissections with his son present. Both travelled and during his years in Germany, it's possible Beddoes and Büchner met, although there is no corroboration of this.

34 Harold Bloom *The Visionary Company* (Cornell University Press: Ithaca, 1971) p. 444.

35 For more on Thomas Beddoes and nitrous oxide, see Mike Jay's *Emperors of Dreams: Drugs in the Nineteenth Century* (Dedalus: Sawtry, 2000).

36 James R. Thompson *Thomas Lovell Beddoes* (Twayne Publishers: Boston, 1985) p.

37 Lytton Strachey "The Last Elizabethan" from *Books and Characters* at http://www.djmcadam.com/last-elizabethan.html

38 They also both shared a title: *The Last Man*. Predictably, Beddoes' tragedy wasn't finished; Shelley's was her second novel.

39 Ibid. p.6. The search for the physical location of the soul has an impressive pedigree. René Descartes, father of modern rational thought, believed it was located in the pineal gland. Before his transformation into a religious thinker, the scientist Emanuel Swedenborg devoted many years of his life to the same pursuit. Today it continues in the work of neuroscientists, and is focused on the cerebral roots of spiritual experience; hence, popular magazine articles about such things as the brain's 'God's spot'.

40 Thompson p. 6

41 Ibid p. 1.

42 One of Paracelsus' aphorisms is, "Decay is the midwife of great things." He believed putrefaction was the key to life and transformation, and once, lecturing a group of learned dons on its virtues, he produced a plate of his own faeces as evidence.

43 Jung called the feminine element in men the *anima*; the masculine element in women he called the *animus*. More recently, another possible literary suicide advocated ideas very similar to Weininger's. In June 1981, police were called to the Highgate, North London home of Charlotte Bach, who in the 1970s had

233

developed a reputation and following as a kind of sexual philosopher and guru. Bach's central idea was, like Weininger's, that human beings contain elements of both sexes in their psyches, and that one's personal evolution and development depends on the way in which one integrates these polarities. Bach developed a complicated system of what we might call 'evolutionary transvestitism' and tried to express it in an enormous work, *Homo Mutans, Homo Luminens* (which might be translated as 'Man the Changer, Man the Light-bringer'), and a later volume *Man and/or Woman*. Her central teaching was that one could either accept or reject one's psychic other (male for women, female for men), and depending on this, one would either develop or remain stagnant. (And it has to be pointed out that rejection is a positive thing in some cases, just as acceptance is a negative one in others.)

Bach found support in some high places, coming under the wing for a time of Colin Wilson, whose book, *The Misfits* (note 3 above) gives a detailed account of her ideas and history. What no one knew, and what the police who came to her flat discovered, was that Charlotte was really a man. When they examined the body, they found that the breasts were false, and that the knickers concealed a penis. Charlotte was really Carl Hadju, a Hungarian con man, hypnotist, novelist, kleptomaniac and, possibly, murderer, who had deceived his followers for years. He had also, it seems, deceived himself, as in his (or her) system, a person with a powerful contrasexual component and who gives in to it – a very masculine woman who goes butch, for example – loses all chance of using the psychic tension for self-development. Charlotte/Carl had evidently done just that, and accounts of her time prior to being found dead indicate she had been depressed and ill. Although there is no evidence that he/she consciously took his/her own life, circumstances suggest a possible suicidal intent. Neighbours called the police after milk bottles had accumulated outside her door. It's quite possible that, depressed at her own deceit, he/she simply ignored whatever symptoms were present, and allowed himself/herself to die. See also my article "The Strange Life of Charlotte Bach" in *Bizarre* winter 2002

44 In defence of Weininger it has to be said that other, somewhat less contentious voices raised similar themes. In his philosophical comedy *Man and Superman* (1904), Bernard Shaw argues that,

contrary to popular belief, men are the dreamers who create civilization while women are down-to-earth pragmatists, who want to secure men's energies for their own ends, which, as Weininger believed, were basically child-bearing. Also contrary to popular belief, in *Back to Methuselah* (1929), Shaw argued that women came first, and created men in order to help with their labours.

45 Although C.G. Jung mentions Weininger briefly in his own *Psychological Types*, it is unclear how much of an influence Weininger's system was on Jung's.

46 Ludwig Wittgenstein *Tractatus Logico-Philosophicus* (Routledge & Kegan Paul: London, 1969) pp. 145–149.

47 One of the more dubious appreciators of Weininger's work was the Italian Dadaist and esoteric philosopher, Julius Evola. Assimilating Weininger's views on women, race and genius, Evola developed his own system of spiritual racism, with which for a brief time he ingratiated himself with Mussolini. He also tried to interest the Nazis in his ideas but had less success. In the 1970s and 80s Evola's ideas formed an ideological justification for several right-wing terrorist acts in Italy, resulting in several deaths, and in recent years his work has seen a resurgence among some New Age and spiritually oriented readers in the United States. For more on Evola see my article "Mussolini's Mystic" in issue 191 (December 2004) of *Fortean Times*.

48 David Abrahamsen *The Mind and Death of a Genius* (Columbia University Press: New York, 1946) p. 15.

49 Ibid. p. 124.

50 Ibid. p. 177.

51 Ibid. p. 88.

52 Ibid. p. 182. It is of course easy to see in this merely the onset of Weininger's madness. Yet it pays to recall that practically all poetry and metaphor is based on precisely the same type of associations, and that while Weininger and other artists (the Strindberg of the *Inferno* period comes to mind) are just as susceptible to madness as the rest of us – more susceptible according to some authorities – they are also privy to insights and perceptions denied the rank and file. Symbolism, the most important aesthetic movement in the nineteenth century, is based on similarly odd correspondences and could be seen by a particular literal mind to be nothing more than evidence of insanity; indeed, Max Nordau's once very influential

Degeneration (1892) did precisely that. Weininger's last works, only published after his death, *On Last Things* and *Aphorisms*, reveal a subtle and poetic mind, often on a par with Nietzsche or Wittgenstein, trying to convey the insights that came to him in his heightened states. It would be a mistake and irresponsible to label him a misogynistic racist and leave it at that, while ignoring the many flashes of genius found in his work.

53 Abrahamsen p. 50.

54 Ellen Mayne "Otto Weininger on the Character of Man" (New Atlantis Foundation: Sussex, 1982).

55 Harold Harris, Introduction to Arthur and Cynthia Koestler *Stranger on the Square* (Hutchinson: London, 1984) p. 11.

56 George Mikes *Arthur Koestler: The Story of a Friendship* (London: 1983).

57 Harris, p. 14.

58 David Cesarani *Arthur Koestler: The Homeless Mind* (William Heineman: London, 1998) p. 555.

59 Arthur Koestler *Bricks to Babel* (Random House: New York, 1980) p. 10.

60 Arthur Koestler *Arrow in the Blue* (Collins: London, 1952) p. 116.

61 Arthur Koestler "Return Trip to Nirvana" in *Drinkers of Infinity* (Hutchison: London, 1968) p. 209.

62 Arthur Koestler *Arrow in the Blue* (Collins: London, 1952) p. 34.

63 Cynthia Koestler *Stranger in the Square* p.160.

64 Arthur Koestler, Ibid. p. 65.

65 Cynthia Koestler, Ibid. pp. 112–113.

66 Cesarani p. 554.

67 Ibid.

68 The comparison with Rimbaud goes beyond mere age. In one of his last poems, the "African Eclogues," Chatterton hits a note reminiscent of the *Le Bateau Ivre* a century away. "On Tiber's banks where scarlet jasmines bloom/And purple aloes shed a rich perfume;/Where, when the sun is melting in his heat/The reeking tygers find a cool retreat/Bask in the sedges, lose the sultry beam/And wanton with their shadows in the stream/ . . ."

69 Quoted in Linda Kelly *The Marvellous Boy: The Life and Myth of Thomas Chatterton* (Weidenfeld and Nicolson: London, 1971) p. xix.

70 Parisian Diarist, quoted in ibid. p. 104.

71 The main story in Croft's book – actually an early version of the non-fiction novel – was that of James Hackman and Martha

Reay. Reay, thirty-three, was a singer, and the mistress of the Earl of Sandwich, who was twenty years her senior; Hackman, twenty, was an officer. Hackman and Reay met and became lovers, but she was prudent enough to realize that Hackman would not be able to support her and the children she had by the Earl. Although sent away for two years, Hackman remained infatuated with her, and on his return, tried to re-ignite their passion. He had been offered a position as a parson and would be able to afford a family. Yet Reay, dubious about starting life again at thirty-five with a much younger man, declined. Hackman persisted and, in an attempt to dissuade him, the Earl had Reay's duenna advise him untruthfully that she had already taken a new lover. Hackman was shattered and determined on suicide, which he proposed to commit at his ex-mistress' feet. Waiting for her outside the Covent Garden opera house, he suddenly changed his mind and shot her instead, then clumsily tried to shoot himself, but only managed to wound himself in the temple. He fell into the gutter, crying to the bystanders, "Kill me, kill me!" He was later executed. On the ground next to the pistol that Hackman used, was found a copy of Werther's last letter to Charlotte.

Croft, who thought of Chatterton as "Apollo reincarnated," and who compared him favourably with Milton, was fascinated with his story and had gathered a great deal of material about it. Loathe to let this go to waste, he inserted it in a long section of his book, which is based on the correspondence between Hackman and Reay during their two-year separation. Constrained to talk only of "matters of general interest," for fear of being discovered by the Earl, Hackman relates to Reay his investigations into Chatterton's story. See Kelly pp. 59–70.

72 Ibid. p. 135.
73 E. H. W. Meyerstein *A Life of Thomas Chatterton* (Inspen and Grant: London, 1930) p. 532.
74 Kelly, p. 29.
75 Richard Holmes *Sidetracks* (Flamingo: London, 2001) p. 12.
76 Ibid pp. 5–50.
77 Constance Dowling started out as a model and chorus girl before moving to Hollywood, where she appeared in a few films in the 1940s, the best known being *Up in Arms* (1944) and *Black Angel* (1946); she also starred in the 50s sci-fi classic, *Gog*. She was involved in a long affair with the screenwriter Elia Kazan,

which ended when Kazan refused to leave his wife. In the late 40s, along with other B list hopefuls, she went to Europe and appeared in a few unmemorable films. She later married the producer Ivan Tors and retired from the screen in 1955.

78 Cesare Pavese *This Business of Living* (Consul Books: London, 1961) p. 24

79 Quoted in Davide Lajolo *An Absurd Vice: A Biography of Cesare Pavese* (New Directions: New York, 1983) p. 242.

80 *The Business of Living* p. 220.

81 Doug Thompson *Cesare Pavese; A Study of The Major Novels and Poems* (Cambridge University Press: Cambridge, 1982) p. 2

82 Ibid. p. 8.

83 Edgar Allan Poe *Complete Stories and Poems* (Doubleday & Co.: New York, 1966) p. 812. "Alone" "From childhood's hour I have not been/ As others were – I have not seen/ As others saw – I could not bring/ My passions from a common spring."

84 *This Business of Living* p. 34.

85 Áine O' Healy *Cesare Pavese* (Twayne Publishers: Boston, 1988) p. 1.

86 Quoted in Lajolo p. 50.

87 Ibid. p. 45.

88 Tim Parks "The Outsider's Art," *The New York Review of Books* vol. 1 no. 17, 6 November 2003.

89 Thompson, p. 7.

90 *This Business of Living* p. 33.

91 On 1 April 1950, F.O. Matthiessen, a Harvard professor of American literature, jumped from the window on the tenth floor of a hotel. A decade earlier Matthiessen had suffered a nervous breakdown, but it's more likely that anxiety about his homosexuality and his left-wing politics in 1950s America – he had been investigated by the House's Un-American Activities Committee – led to his suicide.

92 For the influence *A Short Residence* had on the burgeoning Romantic movement, see Richard Holmes' brilliant essay "The Feminist and the Philosopher" in *Sidetracks*, n. 75 above. See also Claire Tomalin *The Life and Death of Mary Wollstonecraft* (Penguin: London, 1992) p. 228 "The theme of the book – a solitary traveller wandering through wild, rugged and remote places, and suffering from the absence of a lover – helped to set a fashion for questing romantic journeys. Byron, Wordsworth, Shelley, and Mary's as yet unborn daughter Mary, who sends her

Frankenstein north at the end of his story, all read and followed in Mary Wollstonecraft's footsteps."

93 William Godwin *Memoirs of the Author of the Rights of Woman* (Penguin: Harmondsworth, 1987) p. 210.

94 Ibid. p. 242.

95 Quoted in Diane Jacobs *Her Own Woman: The Life of Mary Wollstonecraft* (Abacus: London, 2001) p. 247.

96 Margaret Tims *Mary Wollstonecraft: A Social Pioneer* (Millington Books: London, 1976) p. 11.

97 Fanny Imlay, daughter of Mary and her lover Gilbert Imlay, committed suicide at the age of twenty-two in a Swansea hotel, taking an overdose of laudanum. The exact reasons for her suicide are unclear, although by most accounts she inherited a great part of her mother's tendency to gloom and depression, while Mary's second daughter, Mary Shelley, apparently received the better part of her determination and strength. By the time of her death, her half-sister had eloped with the poet Shelley, who was still married to his first wife Harriet. Godwin, who had become more conservative in his views, abhorred the act, and his second wife – disliked by those who knew Mary – had little love for her step-daughter. Fanny remained at home, out of attachment and respect for her step-father, yet it was clear she was becoming a burden to Godwin, who was facing mounting debts.

   Despite, or perhaps because of Mary Wollstonecraft's efforts, women's prospects had changed very little, and Fanny could look forward to a life very similar to the one her mother fought to avoid. Mary's sisters half-heartedly offered her a position teaching at their school in Ireland, yet Fanny was loath to accept it, dreading a life in provincial Ireland after a childhood amidst progressive circles; the sisters, too, were concerned about the recent scandal of their niece's elopement, and had long since lost any love for their sister or her memory. Fanny's suicide note is, with Crevel's and Beddoes', one of heartbreaking self-loathing: "I have long determined that the best thing I could do was to put an end to the existence of a being whose birth was unfortunate, and whose life has only been a series of pain to those persons who have hurt their health in endeavouring to promote her welfare. Perhaps to hear of my death will give you pain; but you will soon have the blessing of forgetting that such a creature ever existed as . . ." She had torn off her signature, hoping, at the last, to spare her family yet another scandal. Her identity was soon determined, and the undergarments she wore bore the initials "M.W." Her suicide was seen as another argument against the dangerous ideas of her mother. Scandal and bereavement had still not done with Godwin; soon after his step-daughter's suicide, Harriet Shelley drowned herself in the Serpentine.

98   *Historical and Moral View of the Origin and Progress of the French Revolution* (1794).
99   The laudanum attempt turns up in her unfinished novel *The Wrongs of Woman, or Maria.*
100 Mary Wollstonecraft *A Short Residence* (Penguin: Harmonds- worth, 1987) p. 69.
101 Ibid. p. 68.
102 Ibid.
103 Ibid. p. 65.
104 Ibid. p. 73.

Part 2

A Suicidal Miscellany

A Ballade of Suicide

G.K. CHESTERTON

The gallows in my garden, people say,
Is new and neat and adequately tall.
I tie the noose on in a knowing way
As one that knots his necktie for a ball;
But just as all the neighbours — on the wall —
Are drawing a long breathe to shout "Hurray!"
The strangest whim has seized me . . . After all
I think I will not hang myself today.

Tomorrow is the time I get my pay —
My uncle's sword is hanging in the hall —
I see a little cloud all pink and grey —
Perhaps the Rector's mother will *not* call —
I fancy that I heard from Mr. Gall
That mushrooms could be cooked another way —
I never read the works of Juvenal —
I think I will not hang myself today.

The world will have another washing day;
The decadents decay, the pedants pall;
And H.G. Wells has found that children play,
And Bernard Shaw discovered that they squall;
Rationalists are growing rational —
And through the thick woods one finds a stream astray,
So secret that the very sky seemed small —
I think I will not hang myself today.

Envoi

Prince, I can hear the trumpet of Germinal,
The tumbrels toiling up the terrible way;
Even today your royal head may fall —
I think I will not hang myself today.

From *The Notebooks of Samuel Butler*

For Unwritten Articles, Essays and Stories:

A Collection of letters of people who have committed suicide; and also of people who only threaten to do so. The first
may be got abundantly from reports of coroner's inquests, the
second would be harder to come by.

★

In the *fin-de-siècle*, suicide clubs were something of a rage, having sprung up in cosmopolitan centres like London, Paris and St. Petersburg. It was perhaps in Mother Russia that they were most prevalent – the Slavic soul, as exemplified in Dostoyevsky, had a predilection for self-destruction. One famous club, The Black Swan, hosted by Nicolai Riabushinsky, was extremely popular, although how its membership was maintained is unclear. Here, Robert Louis Stevenson shows that London, too, had its own fascination with societies dedicated to a quick escape from the travails of life.

From *The Suicide Club*

ROBERT LOUIS STEVENSON

'Can you muster eighty pounds between you?' he demanded.

Geraldine ostentatiously consulted his pocket-book, and replied in the affirmative.

'Fortunate beings!' cried the young man. 'Forty pounds is the entry money of the Suicide Club.'

'The Suicide Club,' said the Prince, 'why, what the devil is that?'

'Listen,' said the young man; 'this is the age of conveniences, and I have to tell you of the last perfection of the sort. We have affairs in different places; and hence railways were invented. Railways separated us infallibly from our friends; and so telegraphs were made that we might communicate speedily at great distances. Even in hotels we have lifts to spare us a climb of some hundred steps. Now, we know that life is only a stage to play the fool upon as long as the part amuses us. There was one more convenience lacking to modern comfort; a decent easy way to quit that stage; the back stairs to liberty; or, as I said this moment, Death's private door. This, my two fellow-rebels, is supplied by the Suicide Club. Do not suppose that you and I are alone, or even exceptional, in the highly reasonable desire that we profess. A large number of your fellow men, who have grown heartily sick of the performance in which they are expected to join daily and all their lives long, are only kept from flight by one or two considerations. Some have families who would be shocked, or even blamed, if the matter became public; others have a weakness at heart and recoil from the circumstances of death. That is, to some extent, my own experience. I cannot put a pistol to my head and draw the trigger; for something stronger than myself withholds the act; and although I loathe life, I have not the strength enough in my body to take hold of death and be done with it. For such as I and for all who desire to be out of the coil without posthumous scandal, the Suicide Club has been inaugurated. How this has been managed, what is its history, or what may be its ramifications in other lands, I am myself uninformed; and what I know of its constitution, I am not at liberty to communicate to you. To this extent, however, I am at your service. If you are truly tired of life, I will introduce you tonight to a meeting; and if not tonight, at least some time within the next week, you will be easily relieved of your existence. It is now (consulting his watch) eleven; by half past, at latest, we must leave this place; so that you have an hour before you to consider my proposal. It is more serious than a cream tart,' he added, with a smile; 'and I suspect more palatable.'

★

In June 1936, Robert E. Howard, the creator of Conan and author of a host of ripping pulp yarns, mostly published in *Weird Tales*, was told that his mother, on whom he had a morbid fixation, would not recover from a coma. He took the revolver he often carried to protect himself from imaginary pursuers, walked out to the driveway, sat in his car, and blew his brains out. He was only thirty and at the height of his career, earning more income from his writing than any other inhabitant of his home town, Cross Plains, Texas. Unlike the fastidious H.P. Lovecraft, the other giant of *Weird Tales* fame, Howard was resolutely professional, and at the time of his death was about to crack the glossy market. Howard suffered from depression and paranoid delusions, and along with stories of King Kull, Bran Mak Morn, and the gloomy Solomon Kane, he was also the author of over seven hundred poems. The following shows that dark thoughts of death were not solely the domain of existentialists and nineteenth century Romantics.

"Lines Written in the Realization that I Must Die"

ROBERT E. HOWARD

The Back Door gapes and the Black Wall rises;
Twilight gasps in the grip of Night.
Paper and dust are the gems man prizes –
Torches toss in my waning sight.

Drums of glory are lost in the ages,
Bare feet fail on a broken trail –
Let my name fade from the printed pages;
Dreams and visions are growing pale.

Twilight gathers and none can save me.

Well and well, for I would not say:
Let me speak through the stone you gave me:
He never could say what he wished to say.

Why should I shrink from the sign of leaving?
My brain is wrapped in a darkened cloud;
Now in the Night are the sisters weaving
For me a shroud.

Towers shake and the stars reel under,
Skulls are heaped in the Devil's fane;
My feet are wrapped in a rolling thunder,
Jets of agony lance my brain.

What of the world that I leave for ever?
Phantom forms in fading sight —
Carry me out on the ebon river
Into the Night.

★

Like the Austrian novelist and biographer Stefan Zweig, who with his wife Lotte, killed himself with an overdose of veronal in Brazil in 1942, despairing at the collapse of western civilization, Klaus Mann was also a victim of the brutalisation of culture perpetrated by the Nazis. In 1949, Mann died from an intentional overdose of sleeping pills in Cannes. Son of Thomas Mann, Klaus never really escaped from the shadow of his father, with whom he had a difficult relationship. His homosexuality too, caused him much anxiety. Losing his German citizenship in 1933, Mann became a citizen of the world, moving to Amsterdam, gaining Czech nationality, and finally living in the United States, first in Princeton, later New York. His most famous work, *Mephisto*, based on the career of the actor Gustaf Gründgens under the Nazis, first published in 1936, was the subject of a long legal battle in the 1960s, providing Mann with some posthumous fame. Here he calls on his intellectual comrades to shock the world with a wave of mass suicides, rather like Alexander Trocchi's infamous call to his fellow writers in the 1960s, to engage in shooting up heroin en masse.

From *Europe's Search for a New Credo*

KLAUS MANN

A weak, dissonant chorus, the voices of the European intellectuals accompany the prodigious drama. I have heard many voices on my travels, some aggressive and arrogant, others gentle or flippant, passionate or sentimental. I have yet to hear the harmony of coordinated sounds, the concert of reconciled or peacefully competing forces.

"There is no hope. Whether we intellectuals are traitors or whether we are victims, in any case we'd better recognize the utter hopelessness of our situation. Why fool ourselves? We're done for! We're licked!"

These words were uttered by a young student of philosophy and literature I met in the ancient university town of Uppsala, Sweden. What he had to say was certainly characteristic, and 1 believe his words echo the beliefs of your intellectuals in all parts of Europe.

He continued: "we're licked, we're through. Why not admit it at last? The struggle between two great anti-spiritual powers – American money and Russian fanaticism – does not leave any room in the world for intellectual integrity or independence. We are compelled to take sides and, by doing so, to betray everything we should defend and cherish. Koestler is wrong when asserting that one side is a little better than the other – not quite black, just gray. In reality, neither side is good enough – which is to say that both are bad, both are black".

He said a new movement should be launched by European intellectuals, "the movement of despair, the rebellion of the hopeless ones. Instead of trying to appease the powers that be, instead of vindicating the machinations of greedy bankers or the outrages of tyrannical bureaucrats, we ought to go on record with our protest, with an unequivocal expression of our bitterness, our horror. Things have reached a point where only the most dramatic, most radical gesture has a chance to be noticed, to awake the conscience of the blinded hypnotized masses. I'd like to see hundreds, thousands of intellectuals follow the examples of Virginia Woolf, Ernst Toller, Stefan Zweig, Jan Masaryk. A suicide wave among the world's most distinguished minds would shock the peoples out of the lethargy, would make them realize the extreme gravity of the ordeal man has bought upon himself by his folly and selfishness".

In a trembling voice, he said to me, "Let's sign ourselves to absolute despondency. It's the only sincere attitude, and the only one that can be of any help".

While 1 thought of the black future the young men and women of Europe must visualize for themselves, the university student added, very softly, while a faint, timid smile was lightening his pensive young voice: "Do you remember what that great Kierkegaard has told us? *The infinite resignation is the last stage prior to faith . . . Therefore faith hopes also in this life, but . . . by virtue of the absurd, not by virtue of the human understanding*".

From *Religion and the Rebel*

COLIN WILSON

My solipsism I had arrived at by reading of Berkeley and Hume in some textbook of philosophy. I remember explaining to a group of friends in the playground at school why a bar of chocolate existed only in their own minds. Berkeley, added to Einstein and Eliot's *Hollow Men*, made a vertiginous mixture.

Then, quite suddenly, my 'nihilism' received a check. A day came when I seriously contemplated suicide. It was during the long, hot summer of 1947, when I was working as a laboratory assistant. I arrived home one evening in a state of nervous exhaustion, and tried to 'write away' my tension in my journal. I found writing simply an aid to reflection, a crutch for my thoughts. And after about an hour of writing, I found my resistance slowly returning. I thought clearly: This must cease immediately; *I will not go on living like this*. I was all too familiar with these revivals of strength that was sucked away the next day. Then I saw the answer: Kill myself.

It cheered me immensely. I cycled to my evening classes with a feeling of having at last learned to master my destiny. I arrived late, and listened to the professor's sarcasms without interest. It was our evening for analytical chemistry practice. A glass tray contained a mixture of powders which we had to separate. I took some in my watch glass, sniffed it, tested it in a Bunsen flame, and then went into the other room to the reagent shelves. Glass bottles contained cobalt chloride, silver nitrate, potassium iodide and various acids. In the middle there was a bottle of hydrocyanic acid. As I took it down, my mind made a leap, and for an instant I was living in the future, with a burning in my throat and in the pit of my stomach. In that moment I was suddenly supremely aware that what I wanted was not less life, but more. The sensation of drinking the acid was so clear that it was almost as if it had actually taken place. I stood there for a second with the bottle in my hand, but the experience was so vivid that it seemed to last for hours. Then, as someone stood beside me, I put it back, vaguely, as if I had taken it by mistake, and reached down for the methyl red. In one second, I had seen something that I have striven to see all my life since.

David Hume

[. . .] both prudence and courage should engage us to rid ourselves at once of existence when it becomes a burden. It is the only way we can be useful to society, by setting an example, which, if imitated, would present to everyone his chances for happiness in life, and would effectually free him from all danger or misery.

From *Empedocles at Etna*

MATTHEW ARNOLD

ACT II

Evening. The Summit of Etna

Empedocles

Alone! –
On this charr'd, blacken'd, melancholy waste,
Crown'd by the awful peak, Etna's great mouth,
Round which the sullen vapour rolls – alone
Pausanias is far hence, and that is well,
For I must henceforth speak no more with man.
He has his lesson too, and that debt's paid;
And the good, learned, friendly, quiet man,
May bravelier front his life, and in himself
Find henceforth energy and heart; but I,
The weary man, the banish'd citizen –
Whose banishment is not his greatest ill,
Whose weariness no energy can reach,
And for whose hurt courage is not the cure –
What should I do with life and living more?

No, thou art come too late, Empedocles!
And the world hath the day, and must break thee,
Not thou the world. With men thou canst not live,
Their thoughts, their ways, their wishes, are not thine;
And being lonely thou art miserable,
For something has impair'd thy spirit's strength,
And dried its self-sufficing fount of joy.
Thou canst not live with men nor with thyself –
Oh sage! oh sage! – Take then the one way left;
And turn thee to the elements, thy friends,

Thy well-tried friends, thy willing ministers,
And say: — Ye servants, hear Empedocles,
Who asks this final service at your hands!
Before the sophist brood hath overlaid
The last spark of man's consciousness with words —
Ere quite the being of man, ere quite the world
Be disarray'd of their divinity —
Before the soul lose all her solemn joys,
And awe be dead, and hope impossible,
And the soul's deep eternal night come on,
Receive me, hide me, quench me, take me home!

Although the philosopher Ludwig Wittgenstein didn't commit suicide, the idea wasn't foreign to him. Three of his four brothers killed themselves. As a student he had hoped to study under Ludwig Boltzmann, but was prevented from doing this by Boltzmann's suicide in 1906. We've seen that he was on his way to visit the poet Georg Trakl, but on arrival discovered that Trakl had killed himself. We've also seen that Wittgenstein was a great reader of Otto Weininger, who also killed himself. Wittgenstein was a gloomy character, who mortified himself over his homosexuality, and is said to have read Dostoyevsky's *Brothers Karamazov* a dozen times. Like many figures in this book, he set an impossibly high standard for himself, and when he failed to achieve it, thought of killing himself. Although suicide per se does not figure in the works published in his life time, in the number of notebooks and journals to appear since his death from cancer in 1951, it is a frequent theme. Wittgenstein's last words were, "Tell them I've had a wonderful life."

From *Notebooks 1914–1916*

LUDWIG WITTGENSTEIN

If suicide is allowed then everything is allowed.

If anything is not allowed then suicide is not allowed.

This throws a light on the nature of ethics, for suicide is, so to speak, the elementary sin. And when one investigates it, it is like investigating mercury vapour in order to comprehend the nature of vapour.

Or is even suicide in itself neither good nor evil?

George Gordon, Lord Byron, in a letter to Thomas Moore, 1817

I should, many a good day, have blown my brains out, but for the recollection that it would have given pleasure to my mother-in-law; and, even then, if I could have been certain to haunt her — but I won't dwell upon these trifling family matters.

★

On 9 April 1951, the Iranian writer Sadegh Hedayat gassed himself in an apartment in Paris. An earlier attempt at suicide by throwing himself into the Marne was foiled when a couple, making love in a boat, paused to pull him out, perhaps the only time on record when *coitus interuptus* served a life-saving function. Hedayat, whose work since 2006 has been banned in his native country, is best known for his unclassifiable Kafkaesque fantasy, *The Blind Owl*, an eerie nightmarish novel whose closest relative is Alain Resnais' 1961 film *Last Year at Marienbad*. Melancholy, desperation and a sense of doom characterize Hedayat's writing, yet it's unclear how he saw suicide as an escape from these. "The fact of dying," he wrote, "is a fearful thing itself, but the consciousness that one is dead would be far worse." Hedayat was concerned that in the great cosmic economy, the atoms making up his own body would, after his death, go to form the bodies of those he considered "rabble-men." "There were times when I wished I could be endowed after death with large hands, with long sensitive fingers: I would carefully collect together all the atoms of my body and hold them tightly in my hands to prevent them, my property, from passing into the bodies of rabble-men." (*The Blind Owl* [Cannongate: Edinburgh, 2000] p. 82) Nevertheless, Hedayat, like Beddoes and Harry Crosby, had a fascination with death, as this prose poem makes clear.

"Death"

SADEGH HEDAYAT

What a sensational and frightening word "death" is! Even mentioning it rends the heart, rubs smiles off of lips and cuts joy to the quick; it brings on dullness and depression and drives all kinds of troubled thoughts through the mind.

Life and death are inseparable. If not for life, there would be no death. Thus, there must be death in order for life to have meaning. Everything, whether the largest star in the sky or the smallest particle on the earth, will sooner or later die: stones, plants, animals – they all come into existence and will successively be sent back to the world of inexistence. They will all turn into a handful of dust and fall into oblivion. However, the earth keeps spinning recklessly in the endless sky; nature resumes its life on the remains of the dead; the sun shines; the breeze blows; flowers fill the air with their fragrance; birds sing. All living creatures become excited. The sky smiles; the earth nourishes; the angel of death reaps the harvest of life with her old sickle. . . .

Death treats all living creatures equally and determines their fates impartially. It recognizes neither the rich nor the poor; neither the lowly nor the high. It puts human beings, plants and animals next to each other in their dark graves. It is only in the graveyard where executioners and the blood-thirsty stop acting tyrannically and innocents are not tortured. In the graveyard there is neither an oppressor nor an oppressed; young and old rest peacefully. What a peaceful and pleasant sleep! One will never see the next morning and will never hear the bluster and tumult of life. Death is the best haven, a refuge from pains, sorrows, sufferings and cruelties. With death the scintillant fire of lust and capriciousness goes out. All wars, disputes and killings among human beings end and their fierceness, conflicts and self-praise subside in the depth of cold dark soil and the narrow pass of grave.

If death did not exist, everyone would long for it. Cries of despair would rise up to the sky. Everyone would curse nature. How frightening and painful it would be if life were endless. When the hard and arduous test of life extinguishes the beguiling lights of youth, when the wellspring of kindness dries up, when coldness, darkness and ugliness befalls us, it is death which remedies the situation. It is death which puts our bent stature, our wrinkled faces and our afflicted bodies in their resting places.

Oh death, you lessen the sadness and sorrow of life and take its heavy burden off our shoulders. You put an end to the misery of wandering, ill–fated and unhappy men. You are the antidote for grief and despair. You make tearful eyes dry. You are like a compassionate mother who embraces and caresses her child and puts him to sleep after a stormy day. You are not like life – bitter and fierce. You do not drag man to aberration and depravity and throw him to a horrible whirlpool. You laugh at the meanness, lowness, selfishness, stinginess and greediness of human beings and hide their indecent acts. Who has not drunk your poisonous wine? Man has created a terrifying image of you. You, a glorious angel, are regarded as the raging Devil. Why are they afraid of you? Why do they double–cross you and accuse you? You are a shining light, but they take you for darkness. You are the auspicious angel of kindness, but they mourn loudly when you arrive. You are not the messenger of mourning and lamentation. You are a cure for sad hearts. You open the door of hope to the hopeless. You entertain the weary and helpless caravan of life and relieve them from the suffering of their journey. You are praiseworthy. You are everlasting . . .

From *Twilight of the Idols*

FRIEDRICH NIETZSCHE (translator R.J. Hollingdale)

In a certain state it is indecent to go on living. To vegetate on in cowardly dependence on physicians and medicaments after the meaning of life, the *right* to life, has been lost ought to entail the profound contempt of society [. . .] To die proudly when it is no longer possible to live proudly. Death of one's own free choice, death at the proper time, with a clear head and with joyousness, consummated in the midst of children and witnesses: so that an actual leave taking is possible while he who is leaving is still there [. . .] One perishes by no one but oneself. Only 'natural' death is death for the most contemptible reasons, an unfree death, a death at the *wrong* time, a coward's death. From love of *life* one ought to desire to die differently from this: freely, consciously, not accidentally, not suddenly overtaken [. . .] Finally, a piece of advice for *messieurs* the pessimists and other *decadents*. We have no power to prevent ourselves from being born: but we can rectify this error – for it is sometimes an error. When one *does away with* oneself one does the most estimable thing possible: one thereby almost deserves to live [. . .]

*

The German dramatist Frank Wedekind is best known for his "Lulu" plays, *Earth Spirit* and *Pandora's Box*, made into an opera by Alban Berg and a film by G.W. Pabst. Wedekind was a robust character, and before his career as a playwright, he was a well-known cabaret star in Berlin. His familiarity with circus life influenced his Expressionist, aphoristic style, and Lulu, the centre of his best works, is an embodiment of the irrepressible life force. *Spring Awakening*, his first play, about teenage sexuality, caused a scandal, not only for its depiction of suicide, but also because of its masturbation scene. Here 'life', in the guise of a masked man, leads a youth away from the seduction of an early grave and the enticements of a self–destruction.

From *Spring Awakening* (translator Tom Osborn)

FRANK WEDEKIND

MORITZ. We can do anything. Just give me your hand. We can tremble with the timid young girl who thinks she is being idealistic, or with the stubborn old man who is breaking his heart from pride. We can share in the Kaiser's fear when he hears a music hall song in the street, or the poorest labourer's fear at the sound of the judgment day fanfare. We can see the actor's face through his mask, and the poet trying to bury his face in the mask of reality [. . .] We join in when God and the Devil drink each other under the table [. . .] Peace, Melchior, contentment. Just your little finger will do. Your hair will be white before you get another chance like this.

MELCHIOR. If I join you, Moritz – it's because I despise myself. I'm an outlaw. My courage is buried – like her. My feelings I've lost faith in. There's nothing to stop me sinking [. . .]

I revolt myself, more than anything I can think of in the whole world.

MORITZ. So what are you waiting for?

(At this point, Wedekind's symbol of 'life', The Man in the Mask, steps in)

MAN. You can hardly stand up, you're so hungry. D'you think you're fit to decide? (To MORITZ) You clear off.

MELCHIOR. Who are you?

MAN. You'll see in time. (To MORITZ) Well, what are you waiting for? What d'you think you're doing here anyway. Why isn't your head in the right place?

MORITZ. I shot myself.

MAN. So why don't you stay where you belong, in the past? Don't try to unload your smell of the grave on us. Look at those fingers, they're crumbling away already.

MORITZ. Please let me stay.

MELCHIOR. Who are you, sir?

MORITZ. Let me stay a bit longer, I won't be in the way. There's nothing but cold earth down there.

MAN. So what's all this boasting about the sublime? What are you preaching? Deliberate lies from a ghost! You must be desperate [. . .] (To MORITZ) You've been suffering an attack of hopelessness, quite temporary, brought on by circumstances. With a warm dinner inside you, you'll come to your senses.

MELCHIOR. [. . .] A warm dinner won't help after what I've done.

MAN. That depends on the cook [. . .] Come with me and expand your horizon. Come with me and see everything the world has to offer. Give me your trust and I'll give you knowledge.

MELCHIOR. That's what you say.

MAN. It's a fact. D'you think you're still in a position to choose?

MELCHIOR. I can reach to my friend here.

(Here the Masked Man refutes all claims that death is preferable to life.)

MAN. Your friend is trying to sell you something he hasn't got.

Is there anyone who'll sit and smile if he's still got the
breath to laugh – or cry? Sublime smiling – what could be
more hopeless?

MORITZ. He's right, Melchior. I was boasting. Take his offer.
Go with him.

MELCHIOR. Do you believe in God?

MAN. All according to circumstances.

MELCHIOR. So tell me who invented gunpowder.

MAN. Berthold Schwarz – alias Konstantin Anklitzen – a
Franciscan monk about 1300 at Freiburg in Breisgau.

MORITZ. If only he hadn't.

MAN. You'd have used a rope.

★

From *Spleen and Ideal*
"Joyful Death"

CHARLES BAUDELAIRE

In a rich fertile loam where snails recess,
I wish to dig my own deep roomy grave,
There to stretch out my old bones, motionless,
Snug in death's sleep as sharks are in the wave.
Men's testaments and tombs spell queasiness,
The world's laments are not a boon I crave,
Sooner, while yet I live, let the crows press
My carrion blood from out my skull and nave.
O worms, black comrades without eyes or ears,
Behold, a dead man, glad and free, appears!
Lecher philosophers, spawn of decay,
Rummage remorseless through my crumbling head
To tell what torture may remain today
For this my soulless body which is dead.

★

The Stoics had eminently practical ideas about suicide. Given they lived during a particularly dangerous period – the Roman – the thought of an escape hatch must have been a comfort.

From the *Discourses*

EPICTETUS

[. . .] Above all, remember that the door stands open. Do not be more fearful than children. But, just as when they are tired of the game they cry, "I will play no more," so too when you are in a similar situation, cry, "I will play no more" and depart. But if you stay, do not cry.[. . .] Is there smoke in the room? If it is slight, I remain. If it is grievous, I quit it. For you must remember this and hold it fast, that the door stands open.

★

Although unread today, in the early twentieth century, Michael Artzibashev was one of Russia's most popular writers. In pre-WWI England, he, along with other Russian imports like the Ballet Russe, was something of a craze, and no book was more popular than *Sanine*. A Nietzschean celebration of individuality and sensual freedom, its eponymous hero jettisons the Slavic gloom that characterizes most Russian literature, and glories in his own pagan common sense. Several of the characters in *Sanine* kill themselves, and at one point, attending the funeral of a friend who has shot himself, Sanine remarks impatiently "One more fool gone." Like Wedekind, in this early work Artzibashev argued against suicide, and at the end of the novel, his hero, leaving behind the failed lives of his fellows, strides forth to meet the world "facing the jocund, lustrous sun . . . beneath the wide dome of heaven." Unfortunately, Artzibashev didn't maintain this optimism, and in later works, suicide wins out; in his next novel, *The Breaking Point*, practically everyone in it blows his brains out. Here a would-be suicide is saved by a faulty weapon.

From *Sanine* (translator Percy Pinkerton)

MICHAEL ARTZIBASHEV

"No matter what road I choose nor at what goal I aim, show me the pure and perfect ideal for which it were worth while to die! No, it is not that I am weak; it is because life itself is not worthy of sacrifice nor of enthusiasm. Consequently there is no sense in living at all."

Never before had this conclusion seemed so absolutely convincing to him. On his table lay a revolver, and each time he passed it, while walking up and down, its polished steel caught his eye.

He took it up and examined it carefully. It was loaded. He placed the barrel against his temple.

"There! Like that!" he thought. "Bang! and it's all over. Is it a wise or a stupid thing to shoot oneself? Is suicide a cowardly act? Then I suppose that I am a coward!"

The contact of the cold steel on his heated brow was at once pleasant and alarming.

"What about Sina?" he asked himself. "Ah! Well, I shall never get her, and so I leave to some one else this enjoyment." The thought of Sina awoke tender memories, which he strove to repress as sentimental folly.

"Why should I not do it?" His heart seemed to stop beating. Then once more, and deliberately this time, he put the revolver to his brow and pulled the trigger. His blood ran cold; there was a buzzing in his ears and the room seemed to whirl around.

The weapon did not go off; only the click of the trigger could be heard. Half fainting, his hand dropped to his side. Every fibre within him quivered, his head swam, his lips were parched, and his hand trembled so much that when he laid down the revolver it rattled against the table.

"A fine fellow I am!" he thought as, recovering himself, he went to the glass to see what he looked like.

"Then I'm a coward, am I?" "No," he thought proudly, "I am not! I did it right enough. How could I help it if the thing didn't go off?"

★

When George Sterling's poem *A Wine of Wizardry* was published in *Cosmopolitan* magazine in 1907, it was hailed as the greatest poem ever written by an American author. Recognized in San Francisco as the "uncrowned king of Bohemia," Sterling is little read today, and his name is familiar mostly to fans of Jack London; Sterling was the leader of an artist's colony in Carmel, California, with which his friend London was associated. An intimate of the sardonic Ambrose Bierce and mentor to the poet Robinson Jeffers, Sterling was also an important inspiration for the third member of the *Weird Tales* triumvirate, Clark Ashton Smith, who along with Robert E. Howard and H.P. Lovecraft, were the magazine's most popular writers. Sterling's lush, romantic style did not catch on outside the more European environs of San Francisco, and although at the Panama-Pacific International Exposition, his name was carved on the walls along with those of "the immortals," Sterling never became a national poet. By the 1920s he was decidedly passé. Sterling killed himself in 1926, ingesting cyanide in his room at the San Francisco Bohemian Club; he was fifty-six. According to Kevin Starr in *Americans and the Californian Dream 1850–1915* (Oxford Univeristy Press: 1986), "When George Sterling's corpse was discovered in his room at the Bohemian Club, the golden age of San Francisco's bohemia had definitely come to a miserable end."

"Omnia Exeunt in Mysterium"

GEORGE STERLING

I

The stranger in my gates – lo! that am I,
And what my land of birth I do not know,
Nor yet the hidden land to which I go.
One may be lord of many ere he die,

And tell of many sorrows in one sigh,
But know himself he shall not, nor his woe,
Nor to what sea the tears of wisdom flow;
Nor why one star is taken from the sky.

An urging is upon him evermore,
And though he bide, his soul is wanderer,
Scanning the shadows with a sense of haste
Where fade the tracks of all who went before –
A dim and solitary traveller
On ways that end in evening and the waste.

II

How dumb the vanished billions who have died!
With backward gaze conjectural we wait,
And ere the invading Shadow penetrate,
The echo from a mighty heart that cried
Is made a sole memorial to pride.
From out that night's inscrutable estate
A few cold voices wander, desolate
With all that love has lost or grief has sighed.

Slaves, seamen, captains, councillors and kings,
Gone utterly, save for those echoes far!
As they before, I tread a forfeit land
Till the supreme and ancient silence flings
Its pall between the dreamer and the star.
O desert wide! O little grain of sand!

III

As one that knew not of the sea might come
From slender sources of a mountain stream,
And, wending where the sandy shallows gleam
And boulder-strewn the stumbling waters hum
And white with haste the falling torrents drum,
Might stand in darkness at the land's extreme,
And stare in doubt, where, ghostly and supreme,
Muffled in mist and night, the sea lay dumb, –

So shalt thou follow life, a downward rill
A-babble as with question and surmise,
To wait at last where no star beaconeth,
And find the midnight desolate and chill,
And face below its indecisive skies
The Consummation, mystery and death.

★

Leo Tolstoy did not kill himself, although his adulterous heroine Anna Karenina famously did, throwing herself in front of a
train, to avoid the complications of an affair. Although most
readers today find her actions somewhat extreme, Anna's
death ranks with that of Emma Bovary (see below) as one of
the great literary suicides. Tolstoy did face suicidal urges,
though, and in his existential work *A Confession*, he examines
the moral vacuum that led him to the brink of madness.
Curiously, it is precisely the emptiness of literary success that
planted the idea of suicide in Tolstoy's troubled psyche.

From *A Confession* (translator Aylmer Maude)

LEO TOLSTOY

Some day I will narrate the touching and instructive history
of my life during those ten years of my youth[. . .]

I cannot think of those years without horror, loathing,
and heartache. I killed men in war, and challenged men to
duels in order to kill them; I lost at cards, consumed the labour
of peasants, sentenced then to punishments, lived loosely
and deceived people. Lying, robbery, adultery of all kinds,
drunkenness, violence, murder – there was no crime I did not
commit, and for all that people praised my conduct, and my
contemporaries considered and consider me to be a compara-
tively moral man.

So I lived for ten years.

During that time I began to write from vanity, covetous-
ness, and pride. In my writings I did the same as in my life. To
get fame and money, for the sake of which I wrote, it was
necessary to hide the good and display the evil. And I did so.
How often in my writings I contrived to hide under the guise
of indifference, or even of banter, those strivings of mine
towards goodness, which gave meaning to my life!

To remember that time, and my own state of mind and that of those men (though there are thousands like them today) [Tolstoy means writers], is sad and terrible and ludicrous, and arouses exactly the feeling one experiences in a lunatic asylum.

In spite of the fact that I now regarded authorship as of no importance, I yet [. . .]continued to write. I had already tasted the temptation of authorship: the temptation of immense monetary rewards and applause for my insignificant work; and I devoted myself to it as a means of improving my material position, and of stifling in my soul all questions as to the meaning of my own life, or of life in general [. . .]

. . . but five years ago something very strange began to happen to me. At first I experienced moments of perplexity and arrest of life, as though I did not know what to do or how to live; and I felt lost and became dejected. But this passed, and I went on living as before. Then these moments of perplexity began to recur oftener and oftener, and always in the same form. They were always expressed by the questions: What's it for? What does it lead to?

At first it seemed to me that these were aimless and irrelevant questions. I thought that it was all well known, and that if I should ever wish to deal with the solution, it would not cost me much effort [. . .]The questions, however, began to repeat themselves frequently, and more and more insistently to demand replies [. . .]

That occurred which happens to every one sickening with a mortal internal disease. At first trivial signs of indisposition appear, to which the sick man pays no attention; then these signs reappear more and more often and merge into one uninterrupted period of suffering. The suffering increases, and before the sick man can look round, what he took for a mere indisposition has already become more important to him than anything else in the world – it is death!

That is what happened to me [. . .] The questions seemed such stupid, simple childish questions, but as soon as I touched them and tried to solve them, I at once became convinced,

273

(1) that they are not childish and stupid but the most important and profound of life's questions; and (2) that, try as I would, I could not solve them. Before occupying myself with my estate, the education of my son, or the writing of a book, I had to know *why* I was doing it. As long as I did not know why, I could do nothing, and could not live . . . when thinking of the fame my works would bring me, I said to myself, "Very well; you will be more famous than Gogol or Pushkin or Shakespeare or Molière, or that all the writers in the world – and what of it?" [. . .]

I felt that what I had been standing on had collapsed, and that I had nothing left under my feet [. . .]

The truth was that life is meaningless. I had, as it were, [. . .]come to a precipice and saw clearly that there was nothing ahead of me but destruction [. . .] there was nothing ahead but suffering and real death – complete annihilation.

It had come to this, that I, a healthy, fortunate man, felt that I could no longer live: some irresistible power impelled me to rid myself one way or other of life. I cannot say I *wished* to kill myself. The power which drew me away from life was stronger, fuller, and more widespread that any mere wish [. . .] All my strength drew me away from life. The thought of self-destruction now came to me as naturally as thoughts of how to improve my life had come formerly. And it was seductive that I had to be wily with myself lest I should carry it out too hastily [. . .] it was then that I, a man favoured by fortune, hid a cord from myself, lest I should hang myself from the cross-piece of the partition in my room; and I ceased to go out shooting with a gun, lest I should be tempted by so easy a way of ending my life [. . .]

My mental condition presented itself to me in this way: my life is a stupid and spiteful joke someone has played on me [. . .] I was only surprised that I could have avoided understanding this from the very beginning – Today or tomorrow sickness and death will come (they had come already) to those I love or to me; nothing will remain but stench and worms. Sooner or later my affairs, whatever they may be, will be forgotten, and I shall not exist. Then why go on making any effort? [. . .] One can only live while one is intoxicated with life; as soon as one is sober it is impossible not to see that it is all a mere fraud and a stupid fraud!

[. . .] I was like one lost in a wood who, horrified at having lost his way, rushes about, wishing to find the road. He knows that each step he takes confuses him more and more; but still he cannot help rushing about.

It was terrible indeed. And to rid myself of the terror I wished to kill myself [. . .] The horror of darkness was too great, and I wished to free myself from it as quickly as possible by noose or bullet. That was the feeling which drew me most strongly to suicide.

I found that for people of my circle there were four ways out of the terrible position in which we are all placed.

The first was that of ignorance. In consists in not knowing, not understanding, that life is an evil and an absurdity [. . .]

The second way out is Epicureanism. It consists, while knowing the hopelessness of life, in making use meanwhile of the advantages one has [. . .]

The third escape is that of strength and energy. It consists, when one has understood that life is an evil and an absurdity, in destroying life. A few exceptionally strong and consistent people act so. Having understood the stupidity of the joke that has been played on them, and having understood that it is better to be dead that to be alive, and that it is best of all not to exist, they act accordingly and promptly end this stupid joke, since there are means: a rope around one's neck, water, a knife to stick into one's heart, or the trains on the railways; and the number of those of our circle who act in this way becomes greater and greater, and for the most part they act so at the best time of their life, when the strength of their mind is in full bloom, and few habits degrading man's mind have as yet been acquired.

The fourth way out is that of weakness. It consists in seeing the truth of the situation, and yet clinging to life, knowing in advance that nothing can come of it. People of this kind know that death is better than life, but, not having the strength to act rationally [. . .] they seem to wait for something [. . .]I found

myself in that category [. . .]This was repulsive to me and
tormenting, but I remained in that position . . .

★

The Irish-Greek-American-and naturalized Japanese writer
Lafcadio Hearn is one of the great eccentrics of literature.
Starting out as a tabloid journalist specializing in the sensational and macabre in cities like Cincinnati and New Orleans,
Hearn later went to Japan on assignment, and wound up staying, becoming the nation's official spokesman to the West. In
this excerpt, Hearn shows that the kind of *Liebstodt* we associate with Wagnerian excess is not foreign to the psyche of the
Far East.

From "The Red Bridal"

LAFCADIO HEARN

Falling in love at first sight is less common in Japan than in the
West; partly because of the peculiar constitution of Eastern
society, and partly because much sorrow is prevented by early
marriages which parents arrange. Love suicides, on the other
hand, are not infrequent; but they have the particularity of
being nearly always double. Moreover, they must be considered, in the majority of instances, the results of improper
relationships. Still, there are honest and brave exceptions; and
these occur usually in country districts. The love in such a
tragedy may have evolved suddenly out of the most innocent
and natural boy-and-girl friendship, and may have a history
dating back to the childhood of the victims. But even then
there remains a very curious difference between a Western
double suicide for love and a Japanese *jōshi*. The Oriental
suicide is not the result of a blind, quick frenzy of pain. It is

not only cool and methodical: it is sacramental. It involves a marriage of which the certificate is death. The twain pledge themselves to each other in the presence of the gods, write their farewell letters, and die. No pledge can be more profound and sacred that this. And therefore, if it should happen that, by sudden outside interference and by medical skill, one of the pair is snatched from death, that one is bound by the most solemn obligation of love and honour to cast away life at the first possible opportunity. Of course, if both are saved, all may go well. But it were better to commit any crime of violence punishable with half a hundred years of state prison than to become known as a man who, after pledging his faith to die with a girl, had left her to travel to the Meido alone. The woman who should fail in her vow might be partially forgiven; but the man who survived a *jōshi* through interference, and allowed himself to live on because his purpose was once frustrated, would be regarded all his mortal days as a perjurer, a murderer, a bestial coward, a disgrace to human nature.

★

Werthermania understandably provoked a backlash. Thackeray's spoof takes a very common sense view of superheated Romanticism.

"Sorrows Of Werther"

WILLIAM MAKEPEACE THACKERAY

Werther had a love for Charlotte,
Such as words could never utter,
Would you know how he first met her?
She was cutting bread and butter.
Charlotte was a married lady,
And a mortal man was Werther,
And for all the wealth of Indies
Would do nothing that might hurt her.
So he sighed and pined and ogled,
And his passion boiled and bubbled;
Till he blew his silly brains out,
And no more was by them troubled.
Charlotte, having seen his body
Borne before her on a shutter,
Like a well conducted person
Went on cutting bread and butter.

★

Dostoyevsky's *The Possessed* (or, as it is sometimes translated, *The Devils*) remains, I think, with Hesse's *Steppenwolf*, *the* novel of suicide. Not only because the two main characters, Kirilov and Stavrogin, both kill themselves, but because their suicides are embedded in a profound meditation on the dangers and responsibility of human freedom. In these excerpts, Kirilov tries to elucidate how his suicide is an expression of his free will, and Stavrogin's 'Confession' shows how the abyss of freedom can lead a man to the saintly or the demonic.

From *The Possessed* (translator Constance Garnett)

FYODOR DOSTOYEVSKY

"You still have the same intentions?" Stavrogin asked after a moment's silence, and with a certain wariness.

"Yes," answered Kirilov shortly, guessing at once from his voice what he was asking about, and he began taking the weapons from the table.

"When?" Nikolay Vsyevolodovitch inquired still more cautiously, after a pause.

In the meantime Kirilov had put both boxes back in the trunk, and sat down at his place again.

"That doesn't depend on me, as you know – when they tell me," he muttered, as though disliking; but at the same time with evident readiness to answer any other question. He kept his black, lustreless eyes fixed continually on Stavrogin with a calm but warm and kindly expression in them.

"I understand shooting oneself, of course," Nikolay Vsyev-olodovitch began suddenly, frowning a little, after a dreamy silence lasted three minutes. "I sometimes have the thought of it myself, and then there always came a new idea: if one did something wicked, or worse still, something shameful, that is, disgraceful, only very shameful and . . . ridiculous, such as people would remember for a thousand years and hold in scorn for a thousand years, and suddenly the thought comes: 'One blow in the temple and there would be nothing more.' One wouldn't care then for men and that they would hold one in scorn for a thousand years, would one?"

"You call that a new idea?" said Kirilov, after a moment's thought.

"I . . . didn't call it so, but when I thought it I felt it was a new idea."

"You 'felt the idea'?" observed Kirilov. "That's good. There are lots of ideas that are always there and yet suddenly become new. That's true. I see a great deal now as though it were for the first time."

"Supposed you had lived in the moon," Stavrogin interrupted, not listening, but pursuing his own thought, "and suppose there you had done all these nasty and ridiculous things [. . .] You know from here for certain they will laugh at you and hold you in scorn for a thousand years as long as the moon lasts. But now you are here, looking at the moon from here. You don't care here for anything you've done there, and that the people there will hold you in scorn for a thousand years, do you?"

"I don't know," answered Kirilov. "I've not been in the moon," he added, without irony, simply to state the fact.

"Whose baby was that just now?"

"The old woman's mother-in-law is here – no, daughter-in-law, it's all the same. Three days. She's lying ill with the baby, it cries a lot at night, it's the stomach. The mother sleeps, but the old woman picks it up; I play ball with it. The ball's from Hamburg. I bought it in Hamburg to throw and catch, it strengthens the spine. It's a girl."

"Are you fond of children?"

"I am," answered Kirilov, though rather indifferently.

"Then, you're fond of life?"

"Yes, I'm fond of life! What of it?"

"Though you've made up your mind to shoot yourself!"

"What of it? Why connect it? Life's one thing and that's another. Life exists, but death doesn't at all."

"You've begun to believe in a future eternal life?"

"No, not in a future eternal life, but in eternal life here. There are moments, you reach moments, and time suddenly stands still, and it will become eternal."

"You hope to reach such a moment?"

"Yes."

"That'll scarcely be possible in our time," Nikolay Vsyevolodovitch responded slowly and, as it were, dreamily; the two spoke without the slightest irony. "In the Apocalypse the angel swears that there will be no more time."

"I know. That's very true; distinct and exact. When all mankind attains happiness then there will be no more time, for there'll be no need of it — a very true thought."

"Where will they put it?"

"Nowhere. Time's not an object but an idea. It will be extinguished in the mind."

"The old commonplaces of philosophy, the same from the beginning of time," Stavrogin muttered with a kind of disdainful compassion.

"Always the same, always the same, from the beginning of time, and never any other," Kirilov said with sparkling eyes, as though there were almost a triumph in that idea.

"You seem to be very happy, Kirilov."

"Yes, very happy," he answered, as though making the most ordinary reply.

"But you were so distressed lately, angry with Liputin."

"H'm . . . I'm not scolding now. I didn't know then that I was happy. Have you seen a leaf, a leaf from a tree?"

"Yes."

"I saw a yellow one lately, a little green. It was decayed at the edges. It was blown by the wind. When I was ten years old I used to shut my eyes in the winter on purpose and fancy a green leaf, bright, with veins on it, and the sun shining. I used to open my eyes and not believe them, because it was very nice, and I used to shut them again."

"What's that? An allegory?"

"N-no . . . why? I'm not speaking of an allegory, but of a leaf, only a leaf. The leaf is good. Everything's good."

"Everything?"

"Everything. Man is unhappy because he doesn't know he's happy. It's only that. That's all, that's all! If anyone finds out he'll become happy at once, that minute. The mother-in-law will die, but the baby will remain. It's all good. I discovered it all of a sudden."

"And if anyone dies of hunger, and if anyone insults and outrages the little girl, is that good?"

"Yes! And if anyone blows his brains out for the baby, that's good too. And if anyone doesn't, that's good too. It's all good, all. It's good for all those who know that its all good. If they knew that it was good for them, it would be good for them, but as long as they don't know it's good for them, it will be bad for them. That's the whole idea, the whole if it."

"When did you find out you were so happy?"

"Last week, on Tuesday — no, Wednesday, for it was Wednesday by that time, in the night."

"By what reasoning?"

"I don't remember; I was walking about the room; never mind. I stopped my clock. It was thirty-seven minutes past two."

★

"Kirilov, I've never been able to understand why you mean to kill yourself. I only know it's from conviction . . . strong conviction. But if you feel a yearning to express yourself, so to say, I am at your service [. . .] Only you must think of the time."

"What time is it?"

"Oh oh, just two." Pyotr Stepanovitch looked at his watch and lighted a cigarette.

"It seems we can come to terms after all," he reflected.

"I've nothing to say to you," muttered Kirilov.

"I remember that something about God comes into it [. . .]

you explained it to me once – twice, in fact. If you shoot yourself, you become God; that's it, isn't it?"

"Yes, I become God."

Pyotr Stepanovitch did not even smile; he waited. Kirilov looked at him subtly.

"You are a political impostor and intriguer. You want to lead me on into philosophy and enthusiasm and to bring about a reconciliation so as to disperse my anger, and then, when I am reconciled with you, beg from me a note to say I killed Shatov."

Pyotr Stepanovitch answered with almost natural frankness.

"Well, supposing I am such a scoundrel. But at the last moments, does that matter to you, Kirilov? What are we quarrelling about? Tell me, please. You are one sort of man and I am another – what of it? And what's more, we are both of us . . ."

"Scoundrels."

"Yes, scoundrels if you like. But you know that that's only words."

"All my life I wanted it not to be only words. I lived because I did not want it to be. Even now every day I want it to be not words."

"Well, everyone seeks to be where he is best off. The fish . . . that is, everyone seeks his own comfort, that's all. That's been a commonplace for ages and ages."

"Comfort, do you say?"

"Oh, it's not worth while quarrelling over words."

"No, you were right in what you said; let it be comfort. God is necessary and so must exist."

"Well, that's all right, then."

"But I know He doesn't and can't."

"That's more likely."

"Surely you must understand that a man with two such ideas can't go on living?"

"Must shoot himself, you mean?"

"Surely you must understand that one might shoot oneself for that alone? You don't understand that there may be one man, one man out of your thousands of millions, one man who won't bear it and does not want to."

"All I understand is that you seem to be hesitating [. . .]That's very bad."

★

"If there is no God, then I am God."

"There, I could never understand that point of yours: why are you God?"

"If God exists, all is His will and from His will I cannot escape. If not, it's all my will and I am bound to show my self-will."

"Self-will? But why are you bound?"

"Because all will has become mine. Can it be that no one in the whole planet, after making an end of God and believing in his own will, will dare to express his self-will on the most vital point? It's like a beggar inheriting a fortune and being afraid of it and not daring to approach the bag of gold, thinking himself too weak to own it. I want to manifest my self-will. I may be the only one, but I'll do it."

"Do it by all means."

"I am bound to shoot myself because the highest point of my self-will is to kill myself with my own hands."

"But you won't be the only one to kill yourself; there are lots of suicides."

"With good cause. But to do it without any cause at all, simply for self-will, I am the only one."

"He won't shoot himself," flashed across Pyotr Stepanovitch's mind again.

"Do you know," he observed irritably, "if I were in your place I should kill someone else to show my self-will, not myself. You might be of use. I'll tell you whom, if you are not afraid. Then you needn't shoot yourself today, perhaps. We may come to terms."

"To kill someone would be the lowest point of self-will, and you show your whole soul in that. I am not you: I want the highest point and I'll kill myself."

★

From "Stavrogin's Confession"

I've tried my strength everywhere. You advised me to do this "that I might learn to know myself." As long as I was experiencing for myself and for others it seemed infinite, as it has all my life. Before your eyes I endured a blow from your brother; I acknowledged my marriage in public. But to what to apply my strength, that is what I've never seen, and do not see now in spite of all your praises [. . .] I am still capable, as I always was, of desiring to do something good, and of feeling pleasure from it; at the same time I desire evil and feel pleasure from that too. But both feelings are always too petty, and are never very strong. My desires are too weak; they are not enough to guide me. On a log one may cross a river but not on a chip [. . .]

As always I blame no one. I've tried the depths of debauchery and wasted my strength over it. But I don't like vice and I didn't want it [. . .]. One may argue about everything endlessly, but from me nothing has come but negation, with no greatness of soul, no force. Even negation has not come from me. Everything has always been petty and spiritless. Kirilov, in the greatness of his soul, could not compromise with an idea, and shot himself; but I see, of course, that he was great-souled because he had lost his reason. I can never lose my reason, and I can never believe in an idea to such a degree as he did. I cannot even be interested in an idea to such a degree [. . .]

I know I ought to kill myself, to brush myself off the earth like a nasty insect; but I am afraid of suicide, for I am afraid of showing greatness of soul. I know that it will be another sham again – the last deception in an endless series of deceptions. What good is there in deceiving oneself? Simply to play at greatness of soul? Indignation and shame I can never feel, therefore not despair [. . .]

In Nikolay Vsyevolodovitch's wing of the house all the doors were open and he was nowhere to be seen.

"Wouldn't he be upstairs?"

It was remarkable that several servants followed Varvara Petrovna while the others all stood waiting in the drawing room. They would never have dared to commit such a breach of etiquette before. Varara Petrovna saw it and said nothing.

They went upstairs. There, there were three rooms; but they found no one there.

"Wouldn't his honour have gone up there?" someone suggested, pointing to the door of the loft. And in fact, the door of the loft which was always closed had been opened and was standing ajar. The loft was right under the roof and was reached by a long, very steep and narrow wooden ladder. There was a sort of little room up there too.

"I am not going up there. Why should he go up there?" said Varvara Petrovna, turning terribly pale as she looked at the servants. They gazed back at her and said nothing. Dasha was trembling.

Varvara Petrovna rushed up the ladder; Dasha followed, but she had hardly entered the loft when she uttered a scream and fell senseless.

Stavrogin was hanging there behind the door. On the table lay a piece of paper with the words in pencil: "No one is to blame, I did it myself." Beside it on the table lay a hammer, a piece of soap, and a large nail – obviously an extra one in case of need. The strong silk cord upon which Nikolay Vsyevolodovitch had hanged himself had evidently been chosen and prepared beforehand and was thickly smeared with soap. Everything proved that there had been premeditation and consciousness up to the last moment.

At the inquest our doctors absolutely and emphatically rejected all idea of insanity."

★

Although Schopenhauer argued that life was a tremendous mistake, he did not promote suicide, and he himself enjoyed a rather comfortable existence. Here he takes argument with the idea that suicide should be considered a crime. It is, he feels, although inadvisable in most instances, rather an understandable blunder.

On Suicide

ARTHUR SCHOPENHAUER

As far as I know, none but the votaries of the monotheistic, that is, Jewish, religions look upon suicide as a crime. This is all the more striking, inasmuch as neither in the Old nor in the New Testament is there to be found any prohibition or positive disapproval of it; so the religious teachers are forced to base their condemnations of suicide on philosophical grounds of their own invention. These are so very bad that writers of this kind endeavour to make up for the weakness of their arguments by the strong terms in which they express their abhorrence of the practice; in other words, the declaim against it. They tell us that suicide is the greatest piece of cowardice; that only a madman could be guilty of it; and other insipidities of the same kind; or else they make the nonsensical remark that suicide is *wrong*; when it is quite obvious that there is nothing in the world which every man has a more unassailable title to than his own life and person.

Suicide is actually accounted a crime; and a crime which, especially under the vulgar bigotry that prevails in England, is followed by an ignominious burial and the seizure of the man's property; and for that reason, in a case of suicide, the jury almost always brings in a verdict of insanity. Now let the reader's own moral feeling decide as to whether or not suicide is a criminal act. Think of the impression that would be made upon you by the news that someone you know has committed the crime, say, of murder or theft, or been guilty of some act of cruelty or deception; and compare it with your feelings when you hear that he has met a voluntary death. While in the one case a lively sense of indignation and extreme resentment will be aroused, and you will call loudly for punishment or revenge, in the other you will be moved to grief and sympathy; and mingled with your thoughts will be admiration for his courage, rather than the moral disapproval which follows upon a wicked action. Who has not had acquaintances, friends, relations, who of their own free will have left this world; and are these to be thought of with horror as criminals?

I am of the opinion that the clergy should be challenged to explain what right they have to go into the pulpit, or take up their pens, and stamp as a crime an action which many men whom we hold in affection and honour have committed; and to refuse an honourable burial to those who relinquish this world voluntarily. They have no Biblical authority to boast of, justifying their condemnation of suicide; nay, not even any philosophical arguments that will hold water; and it must be understood that it is arguments we want, and that we will not be put off with mere phrases or words of abuse. If the criminal law forbids suicide, that is not an argument valid in the Church; and besides, the prohibition is ridiculous, for what penalty can frighten a man who is not afraid of death itself? If the law punishes people for trying to commit suicide, it is punishing the want of skill that makes the attempt a failure [. . .]

[. . .] The only valid moral argument against suicide is that it thwarts the attainment of the highest moral aim by substituting an apparent release from this world of misery for a real one. But from a *mistake* to a *crime* is a far cry; and it is as a crime that the clergy of Christendom wish us to regard suicide.

The kernel of Christianity is the truth that suffering – *the Cross* – is the true end and object of life. Hence Christianity condemns suicide as thwarting this end; whilst the ancient world, taking a lower point of view, held it in approval, in honour. But if that is to be accounted a valid reason against suicide, it involves the recognition of asceticism; that is to say, it is valid only from a much higher ethical standpoint than has ever been adopted by moral philosophers of Europe. If we abandon that high standpoint, there is no tenable moral reason left for condemning suicide. The extraordinary energy and zeal with which the clergy attack suicide is not supported by either any passages in the Bible or by any considerations of weight; so it looks as though they must have some secret reason for their contention. May it not be that the voluntary surrender of life is a bad compliment for him who said that *all things were good*? If so, this offers another instance of the crass optimism of these religions, denouncing suicide to escape being denounced by it.

It will generally be found that as soon as the terrors of life outweigh those of death, a man will put an end to his life. But the terrors of death offer considerable resistance; they stand like a sentinel at the gate leading out of this world. Perhaps no man alive would not have already put an end to his, if this end was of a purely negative character, a sudden halt to existence. There is something positive to it; it is the destruction of the body; and a man shrinks from this, because his body is the manifestation of the will to live.

Yet the struggle with that sentinel is, as a rule, not as hard as it may seem from a long way off, mainly because of the antagonism between the ills of the body and the ills of the mind. If we are in great bodily pain, or the pain lasts a long time, we become indifferent to other troubles; all we think about is getting well. In the same way great mental suffering makes us insensible to bodily pain; we despise it; if it should outweigh the other, it distracts our thoughts, and we welcome it as a pause in our mental suffering. It is this feeling that makes suicide easy; for the bodily pain accompanying it loses all significance in the eyes of one who is tortured by an excess of mental suffering. This is especially evident in the case of those who are driven to suicide by some morbid and exaggerated ill-humour [. . .].

Suicide may also be regarded as an experiment, a question which man puts to Nature [. . .] What change will death produce in a man's existence and in his insight into the nature of things? It is a clumsy experiment, for it requires the destruction of the very consciousness which asks the question and awaits the answer.

★

L. H. Myers is best known, and that by only a few, for his masterpiece *The Root and the Flower*, a trilogy of novels set in an imaginary Medieval India, but which is really a philosophical and ethical indictment of early twentieth century England, specifically of the Bloomsbury set, through which he moved briefly and with much disdain. Myers was born in 1881 into a distinguished family. His father, the poet and scholar F.W. Myers, was one of the founding members of the Society for Psychical Research; the author of the monumental *Human Personality and its Survival of Bodily Death*, he is also responsible for the word 'telepathy'. As a boy L.H. Myers attended some of the séances conducted at the Myers household, and, along with a financial bequest, Myers inherited his father's passion for the spiritual and metaphysical. F.W. Myers' own interest in the afterlife may have been prompted by his love for his cousin's wife, who committed suicide; there is some suspicion that Myers senior's own death was in some way 'willed', in order for him to unite with his lost love. L.H. Myers was a contradictory personality. Although his novels are characterized by an extreme ethical fastidiousness and ascetic sensibility (one of his few literary friends was the novelist David Lindsay, whose fantastic *A Voyage to Arcturus* displays a similar outlook) Myers himself was an incorrigible womaniser; and although in his last years he committed himself to Communism, he maintained a substantial interest in a successful expensive French restaurant, Boulestins. Myers had a belief in the transcendental, but also a taste for racing. These contradictions took their toll, and Myers' view of society, depicted in a sociological analysis which he destroyed before his death, along with an autobiographical work, was as unforgiving as his insight into himself. "Why should anyone want to go on living once they know what the world is like?" he asked. Myers answered that query on 7 April 1944 when, like Witkacy, fearing the coming collapse of western civilization, he took an overdose of sleeping pills. This extract from his early eccentric novel *The Orissers*, although not directly about suicide, displays the kind of unblinking self-analysis that eventually led Myers' to his destruction.

From *The Orissers*

L. H. MYERS

Each one of us has a fixed, unconscious notion of what constitutes his character, and is prevented from carrying into effect the behests of his imagination, by an irrational, but compelling instinct to conform with that accepted idea of himself. This compulsion is strongest when intimates are present. The unfortunate ego, partly in deference to the suggestion of others, and partly in self-protection against them, has encrusted itself in a hard shell. It has made public profession of a certain 'character', which its manner and behaviour are constrained to illustrate. This is its response to a need to exhibit a definite outline, by which its fellow creatures shall recognize it; but it is also – and, alas, more urgently still! – a response to its own need to possess a form by which it shall recognize itself.

In the conduct of everyday life each one of us like to refer to some fairly well-defined conception of his own character in order to decide without trouble what to do, what to say, and even what to think. We require some rule of thumb in our current self-manifestations; for a perpetual effort of choice would be an intolerable burden. Do we not all habitually repose with a sense of satisfaction upon what we take to be our fixed characteristics – upon the supposedly fatal element within us? And of those *given* characteristics are not even the most trifling our pride? "Yes," we reflect with complacency, "I'm like that. It is strange; but that's what I always am." What pride in discovering in the malleable substance of ourselves some streak supposedly resistant – something irresponsible, something demonic, something which the reason cannot coerce, nor the consciousness incorporate, something genuine, in fact – in the sense of being spontaneous, self-existent, and inevitable – when all the rest of the poor little personality is a make-up, in which the only inevitabilities are those imposed by helplessness.

Man, then, assumes a character, and, having done so, can let the character-part play itself. But this sacrifice of variability has its disadvantages. The character develops at the expense of the perceptions and the imagination. The young man is apt to feel at times that he is investing himself in habiliments which cramp him. He would fain throw them off; but almost irresistible is the force of precedent; that is, the force of interior and exterior expectation. Besides it is only in moments of unusual excitation that the ego gathers the energy to rebel. For the most part it prefers to take its ease in an inert illustration of the public personality, which has, indeed, become "a second nature."

★

As noted, the Portuguese poet and novelist Mário De Sá-Carneiro killed himself at the age of 26, taking a massive dose of strychnine in a small room in Paris. It was a painful and ignominious end, a far cry from the kind of fulfilment Sá-Carneiro envisions death to be in much of his fiction. It was also something the ill-fated poet had been moving toward almost inexorably. For most of his short life, suicide was not far from Sá-Carneiro's mind. This is understandable; while still at school, Sá-Carneiro's best friend blew his brains out in front of the class. Both boys shared the loss of their mother at an early age, and the absence of an emotional ballast – hardly compensated for by an over-anxious nanny and an absent affluent father – led Sá-Carneiro to see himself as a perpetual outsider, forever waiting for life to "turn up." Sadly, it never did, and even leaving Lisbon for Paris, the cultural capital of the world, did little to relieve Sá-Carneiro's sense of crushing ennui. When his father married an ex-prostitute and, because of his extravagant life-style, was forced to cut off the allowance that allowed his world-weary son to remain in Paris, the thought of returning to provincial Lisbon proved too much. Sá-Carneiro had invited a friend to witness his last moments, but the poet's screams sent him out in search of a doctor. As it was for his friend, Fernando Pessoa, madness was a constant preoccupation for Sá-Carneiro, and his work almost overwhelms with a feverish, delirious intensity. Paradoxes abound. Pessoa described him as a "sane madman," and Sá-Carneiro himself spoke of his "healthy morbidity" and once complained that he was "dying of starvation, of excess." Wedding over-ripe *fin-de-siècle* decadence with Futurist speed and brutality, Sá-Carneiro created an idiosyncratic prose, that rushes headlong into what he called "the Great Shadow."

From *The Great Shadow* (translator Margaret Jull Costa)

MÁRIO DE SÁ-CARNEIRO

The artist often considered suicide, as a cure for his anxiety. And then he would be torn apart by an infinite tenderness, a limitless pity for himself. Did he really have to destroy himself? Yes, it was perhaps his only salvation. How sad! And he imagined himself as someone crossing a bridge carrying a precious bundle which, when he was already close to his destination, he had to throw into the river in a final gesture of despair, since he lacked the strength to carry it any further.

He had more than once decided, positively decided, to put a bullet through his heart. He had even got as far as buying a gun. In the end, though, at least up until now, he had always given up the idea with a feeling of great joy, a joy that soon dissipated: even if he didn't commit suicide, he would have to die one day. *If only not committing suicide could save him from death . . .*

★

As mentioned earlier, Emma Bovary's death so impressed the translator Eleanor Marx that she committed suicide in the same way. Yet the idea may not have been her own. When she discovered that her lover Edward Aveling had secretly married a young actress, in response to her distress, he proposed a suicide pact, which, however, he had no intention of honouring. Yet the idea appealed to the romantic Eleanor, and Aveling even went so far as to procure the prussic acid she used for her. Aveling was rightly castigated for his actions, yet no legal charges were made against him, although it seems clear that this was some form of manslaughter, if not murder. What is surprising is that a reader of Flaubert's wrenching account of Emma Bovary's last minutes should be prompted to follow suit. Perhaps no other depiction of suicide presents its results in such meticulous and off-putting detail.

From *Madame Bovary*

GUSTAVE FLAUBERT

"Ah, now it is beginning!" she murmured.

"What do you say?"

She rolled her head with a gentle movement full of anguish, at the same time continually opening her jaws as though there had been something very heavy pressing down upon her tongue. At eight o'clock the vomiting recommenced.

Charles noticed that there was at the bottom of the basin a sort of white grit, attached to the sides of the porcelain.

"It is extraordinary! It is most peculiar!" he repeated.

But she said in a loud voice:

"No, you are mistaken!"

Thereupon, softly and almost like a caress, he passed his hand over her body. She uttered a piercing scream. He started back, terrified.

Then she began to groan, feebly at first. A deep shudder shook her shoulders, and she became paler than the sheet in which her nervous fingers were burying themselves. Her irregular pulse was now almost imperceptible.

Drops of sweat oozed over her bluish face, which seemed as it were congealed in the exhalation of a metallic vapour. Her teeth chattered, her eyes, grown larger, gazed vaguely around her, and to every question she only replied by nodding her head; two or three times he even smiled. Little by little her groans became louder. A hollow shriek escaped her; she maintained that she was better, and that she would get up very soon. But convulsions seized her; she cried out:

"Ah! It is cruel, my God!"

He threw himself upon his knees by the bedside.

"Speak! What have you eaten? Answer, in Heaven's name!"

And he looked at her with eyes of tenderness such as she had never seen.

"Ah, well, there . . . there!" she said, in a failing voice.

He sprang to the writing desk, broke the seal, and read aloud: "Let no one be accused . . ." He stopped, passed his hand over his eyes, and read over again.

"What! . . . Help! Help!"

And he could only repeat the one word: "Poisoned! Poisoned!" . . .

★ ★ ★ ★ ★ ★ ★ ★ ★

"Do not weep!" she said to him. "Soon I shall no longer torment you!"

"Why? What has driven you to it?"

She answered:

"It had to be, my dear."

"Were you not happy? Is it my fault? I have done all I could . . .!"

"Yes . . . that is true . . . you are kind, you!"

And she passed her fingers through his hair slowly. The sweetness of this sensation placed an additional burden on his grief; he felt his whole existence crumbling with despair at the thought that he must lose her at the moment when, on the contrary, she was confessing for him more love than ever before; and he could think of nothing to do; he did not know, did not dare, the urgency of an immediate decision completing his confusion.

She had done, she reflected, with all the betrayals, the meannesses and the numberless longings that had been wont to torture her. She hated no one now; a twilit chaos fell over her mind, and of all the sounds of earth Emma heard no longer any save the intermittent lamentation of that poor soul, gentle and indistinct like the last echo of a symphony that is dying away.

★ ★ ★ ★ ★ ★ ★ ★ ★ ★

It was not long before she began to vomit blood. Her lips became more tightly compressed. Her limbs fidgeted restlessly, her body was covered with brown spots, and her pulse slipped under the fingers like a tightly stretched thread, like a harp-string about the snap.

Next she began to scream horribly; she cursed the poison, abused it, besought it to make haste, and with her stiffened arms pushed away everything that Charles, in an agony greater than her own, strove to make her drink [. . .]

Her chest began immediately to heave rapidly. The whole tongue protruded from her mouth; her eyes, as they rolled about, grew pale like two globes of a dying lamp, till she might have been thought already dead had it not been for the frightful acceleration in the movement of her ribs, which were shaken by a furious breathing, as if the soul were making leaps to set itself free. Félicité knelt before the crucifix, and the chemist himself wavered a little on his legs, while M. Canivet looked vaguely out of the window into the square. Bouornisien had again fallen to praying, his face bowed over the edge of the bed, and his long, black cassock dragging behind him on the floor of the room. Charles was at the other side, on his knees, with his arms stretched out towards Emma. He had taken her hands and was pressing them, as at each beat of heart they gave a jump like the rebound of a falling ruin. As the death-rattle grew louder, the priest quickened his prayers; they mingled with Bovary's stifled sobs, and sometimes everything seemed to be lost in the dull murmur of the Latin words, which sounded like the tolling of a death-knell.

Suddenly there was heard on the pavement outside a noise of heavy wooden shoes, together with the scraping sound of a stick; and a voice came up, a hoarse voice, that was singing:

"Souvent la chaleur d'un beau jour
Fait rêver fillette à l'amour."

Emma raised herself like a corpse that is galvanized, her hair in disorder, the pupils of her eyes fixed, and dilated wide.

"Pour amasser dilieimment
Les épis que la faux moissone,
Ma Nanette va s'inclinant
Vers le sillion qui nous les donne."

"The blind man!" she cried.

And Emma burst into laughter, cruel, frantic, despairing laughter, fancying that she could see the hideous face of the poor wretch standing out in the eternal darkness like a crowning terror.

"Il soufflé bien fort ce-jour-là
Et le jupon courts'envola!"

A convulsion flung her back on the mattress. All around her drew near. She had ceased to exist.

★

Like Schopenhauer, the Romanian philosopher Emile Cioran held a highly pessimistic view of human life, something that can be gleaned from the titles of his lucid, aphoristic works, for instance *On the Heights of Despair, A Short History of Decay* and *The Trouble with Being Born*. Although suicide preoccupies his reflections, Cioran himself did not indulge in it; his reasons for abstaining may be detected in the brief selection below. A resident of Paris from the late 1940s, Cioran moved among its literary and artistic figures, becoming friends with many of them, including the poet Paul Celan. A fellow Romanian, Celan lost his parents to the Nazi death camps and was himself sent to a labour camp for eighteen months. His most famous poem, "Death Fugue," depicts in cryptic brevity the horrors inflicted on those of his and his parents generation. Celan came to prominence in the 1950s, his poetry providing an unflinching insight into the dark side of history. Celan's own psyche was understandably shaken by his experiences, and when he was accused of plagiarism by the wife of the German poet Yvan Goll, he suffered a nervous breakdown. In the 1960s his depression and paranoia increased, and after attacks on his wife, Celan spent a month in a psychiatric hospital. A great reader of the philosopher Martin Heidegger, who never apologized for his own involvement with Nazism, after the two met Heidegger is reported to have said "Celan is sick – hopelessly." He became suicidal and threw himself into the Seine on 7 April 1970. Cioran claims that he ran into Celan just before he killed himself, and tried to cheer him up. If true, there is an irony here of mythic proportions: not only is Cioran an unlikely candidate to cheer *anyone* up, in his early, Romanian years, he briefly espoused an admiration for the Nazi 'experiment', although, unlike Heidegger, he later renounced his naïve enthusiasm.

E. M. CIORAN

It is not worth the bother of killing yourself, since you always kill yourself too late.

*

On the suicide: "[. . .] the fact consecrates him forever. Inferior to ourselves in this way or that, if yet we cling to life, and he is able to 'fling it away like a flower', as caring nothing for it, we account him in the deepest way our born superior."

WILLIAM COWPER

One evening in November, 1763, as soon as it was dark, affecting as cheerful and unconcerned an air as possible, I went into an apothecary's shop, and asked for an half ounce phial of laudanum. The man seemed to observe me narrowly; but if he did, I managed my voice and countenance, so as to deceive him. The day that required my attendance at the bar of the House, being not yet come, and about a week distant, I kept my bottle close in my side-pocket, resolved to use it when I should be convinced there was no other way of escaping. This, indeed, seemed evident already; but I was willing to allow myself every possible chance of that sort, and to protract the horrid execution of my purpose, till the last moment; but Satan was impatient of delay.

The day before the period above mentioned arrived, being at Richard's coffee-house at breakfast, I read the newspaper, and in it a letter, which the further I perused it, the more closely engaged my attention [. . .] The author appeared to be acquainted with my purpose of self-destruction, and to have written the letter on purpose to secure and hasten the execution of it. My mind, probably, at this time, began to be disordered; however it was, I was certainly given up to a strong delusion. I said within myself, 'your cruelty shall be gratified; you shall have your revenge!' and, flinging down the paper, in a fit of strong passion, I rushed hastily out of the room; directing my way to the fields, where I intended to find some house to die in; or, if not, determined to poison myself in a ditch [. . .]

Before I had walked a mile [. . .] a thought struck me that I might yet spare my life; that I had nothing to do, but to sell what I had [. . .] go on board a ship, and transport myself to France [. . .] Not a little pleased with this expedient, I returned to my chambers to pack up all that I could at so short a notice; but while I was looking over my portmanteau, my mind changed again; and self-murder was recommended to me once more in all its advantages.

Not knowing where to poison myself, for I was liable to continual interruption in my chambers from my laundress and her husband, I laid aside that intention, and resolved upon drowning. For that purpose I immediately took a coach, and ordered the man to drive to Tower wharf; intending to throw myself into the river from the Custom House quay [. . .] I left the coach upon the Tower wharf, intending never to return to it; but upon coming to the quay, I found the water low, and a porter seated upon some goods there, as if on purpose to prevent me. This passage to the bottomless pit being mercifully shut against me, I returned back to the coach, and ordered it to the Temple. I drew up the shutters, once more had recourse to the laudanum, and determined to drink it off directly; but God ordained otherwise. A conflict, that shook me to pieces, suddenly took place; not properly a trembling, but a convulsive agitation, which deprived me in a manner of the use of my limbs; and my mind was as much shaken as my body.

Distracted by the desire for death, and the dread of it, twenty times I had the phial to my mouth, and as often received an irresistible check; and even at the time it seemed to me that an invisible hand swayed the bottle downwards, as often as I set it against my lips [. . .] Panting for breath, and in a horrible agony, I flung myself back into the corner of the coach. A few drops of laudanum which touched my lips [. . .] began to have a stupefying effect upon me. Regretting the loss of so fair an opportunity, yet utterly unable to avail myself of it, I determined not to live; and already half dead with anguish, I once more returned to the Temple. Instantly I repaired to my room, and having shut both the outer and the inner door, prepared myself for the last scene of the tragedy. I poured the laudanum into a small basin, set it on a chair by the bedside, half undressed myself, and laid down between the blankets, shuddering with horror at what I was about to perpetrate [. . .]

At length [. . .] with the most confirmed resolution, I reached forth my hand towards the basin, when the fingers of both hands were as closely contracted, as if bound with a cord, and became entirely useless. Still, indeed, I could have made shift with both hands, dead and lifeless as they were, to have raised the basin to my mouth, for my arms were not at all affected: but this new difficulty struck me with wonder; it had the air of a divine interposition [. . .] The horror of the crime was immediately exhibited to me in so strong a light, that, being seized with a kind of furious indignation, I snatched up the basin, poured away the laudanum into a phial of foul water, and, not content with that, flung the phial out of the window [. . .]

I spent the rest of the day in a kind of stupid insensibility; undetermined as to the manner of dying, but still bent on self–murder [. . .] I went to bed to take, as I thought, my last sleep in this world. The next morning was to place me at the bar of the House, and I was determined not to see it. I slept as usual, and awoke about three o'clock. Immediately I arose, and by the help of a rushlight, found my penknife, took it into bed with me, and lay with it for some hours directly pointed against my heart. Twice or thrice I placed it upright under my left breast, leaning all my weight upon it; but the point was broken off square, and it would not penetrate [. . .]

Not one hesitating thought now remained, but I fell greed–ily to the execution of my purpose. My garter was made of a broad piece of scarlet binding, with a sliding buckle, being sown together at the ends: by the help of the buckle, I formed a noose, and fixed it about my neck, straining it so tight that I hardly left a passage for my breath, or for the blood to circulate [. . .] At each corner of the bed was placed a wreath of carved work, fastened by an iron pin, which passed through the midst of it: the other part of the garter, which made a loop, I slipped over one of these, and hung by it some seconds, drawing my feet under me, that they might not touch the floor; but the iron bent, and the carved work slipped off, and the garter with it. I then fastened it to the frame of the tester, winding it round, and tying it in a strong knot. The frame broke short, and let me down again.

The third effort was more likely to succeed. I set the door open, which reached within a foot of the ceiling; by the help of a chair I could command the top of it, and the loop being large enough to admit a large angle of the door, was easily fixed so as not to slip off again. I pushed away the chair with my feet, and hung at whole length. While I hung there, I distinctly heard a voice say three times '*Tis over!*' [. . .] I hung so long that I lost all sense, all consciousness of existence.

When I came to myself again, I thought myself in hell; the sound of my own dreadful groans was all that I heard, and a feeling, like that produced by a flash of lightning, just beginning to seize upon me, passed over my whole body. In a few seconds I found myself fallen on my face on the floor. In about half a minute I recovered my feet; and reeling, staggering, stumbled into bed again [. . .]

★

From *Foundations of a Metaphysics of Morals*

IMMANUEL KANT

Firstly, under the head of necessary duty to oneself: He who contemplates suicide should ask himself whether his action can be consistent with the idea of humanity as an end in itself. If he destroys himself in order to escape from painful circumstances, he uses a person merely as a mean to maintain a tolerable condition up to the end of life. But a man is not a thing, that is to say, something which can be used merely as means, but must in all his actions be always considered as an end in himself. I cannot, therefore, dispose in any way of a man in my own person so as to mutilate him, to damage or kill him. (It belongs to ethics proper to define this principle more precisely, so as to avoid all misunderstanding, e.g., as to the amputation of the limbs in order to preserve myself, as to exposing my life to danger with a view to preserve it, etc. This question is therefore omitted here.)

From the *Phaedo* (translator Benjamin Jowett)

PLATO

Then tell me, Socrates, why is suicide held not to be right? as I have certainly heard Philolaus affirm when he was staying with us at Thebes: and there are others who say the same, although none of them has ever made me understand him.

But do your best, replied Socrates, and the day may come when you will understand. I suppose that you wonder why, as most things which are evil may be accidentally good, this is to be the only exception (for may not death, too, be better than life in some cases?), and why, when a man is better dead, he is not permitted to be his own benefactor, but must wait for the hand of another.

By Jupiter! yes, indeed, said Cebes, laughing, and speaking in his native Doric.

I admit the appearance of inconsistency, replied Socrates, but there may not be any real inconsistency after all in this. There is a doctrine uttered in secret that man is a prisoner who has no right to open the door of his prison and run away; this is a great mystery which I do not quite understand. Yet I, too, believe that the gods are our guardians, and that we are a possession of theirs. Do you not agree?

Yes, I agree to that, said Cebes.

And if one of your own possessions, an ox or an ass, for example took the liberty of putting himself out of the way when you had given no intimation of your wish that he should die, would you not be angry with him, and would you not punish him if you could?

Certainly, replied Cebes.

Then there may be reason in saying that a man should wait, and not take his own life until God summons him, as he is now summoning me.

Yes, Socrates, said Cebes, there is surely reason in that. And yet how can you reconcile this seemingly true belief that God is our guardian and we his possessions, with that willingness to die which we were attributing to the philosopher? That the wisest of men should be willing to leave this service in which they are ruled by the gods who are the best of rulers is not reasonable, for surely no wise man thinks that when set at liberty he can take better care of himself than the gods take of him. A fool may perhaps think this – he may argue that he had better run away from his master, not considering that his duty is to remain to the end, and not to run away from the good, and that there is no sense in his running away. But the wise man will want to be ever with him who is better than himself. Now this, Socrates, is the reverse of what was just now said; for upon this view the wise man should sorrow and the fool rejoice at passing out of life.

The earnestness of Cebes seemed to please Socrates. Here, said he, turning to us, is a man who is always inquiring, and is not to be convinced all in a moment, nor by every argument.

And in this case, added Simmias, his objection does appear to me to have some force. For what can be the meaning of a truly wise man wanting to fly away and lightly leave a master who is better than himself? And I rather imagine that Cebes is referring to you; he thinks that you are too ready to leave us, and too ready to leave the gods who, as you acknowledge, are our good rulers.

Yes, replied Socrates; there is reason in that. And this indictment you think that I ought to answer as if I were in court?

That is what we should like, said Simmias.

Then I must try to make a better impression upon you than I did when defending myself before the judges. For I am quite ready to acknowledge, Simmias and Cebes, that I ought to be grieved at death, if I were not persuaded that I am going to other gods who are wise and good (of this I am as certain as I can be of anything of the sort) and to men departed (though I am not so certain of this), who are better than those whom I leave behind; and therefore I do not grieve as I might have

307

done, for I have good hope that there is yet something remaining for the dead, and, as has been said of old, some far better thing for the good than for the evil.

But do you mean to take away your thoughts with you, Socrates? said Simmias. Will you not communicate them to us? — the benefit is one in which we too may hope to share. Moreover, if you succeed in convincing us, that will be an answer to the charge against yourself.

I will do my best, replied Socrates. But you must first let me hear what Crito wants; he was going to say something to me.

Only this, Socrates, replied Crito: the attendant who is to give you the poison has been telling me that you are not to talk much, and he wants me to let you know this; for that by talking heat is increased, and this interferes with the action of the poison; those who excite themselves are sometimes obliged to drink the poison two or three times.

Then, said Socrates, let him mind his business and be prepared to give the poison two or three times, if necessary; that is all.

I was almost certain that you would say that, replied Crito; but I was obliged to satisfy him.

From the *Laws* (translator Benjamin Jowett)

PLATO

And what shall he suffer who slays him who of all men, as they say, is his own best friend? I mean the suicide, who deprives himself by violence of his appointed share of life, not because the law of the state requires him, nor yet under the compulsion of some painful and inevitable misfortune which has come upon him, nor because he has had to suffer from irremediable and intolerable shame, but who from sloth or want of manliness imposes upon himself an unjust penalty. For him, what ceremonies there are to be of purification and burial God knows, and about these the next of kin should enquire of the interpreters and of the laws thereto relating, and do according to their injunctions. They who meet their death in this way shall be buried alone, and none shall be laid by their side; they shall be buried ingloriously in the borders of the twelve portions of the land, in such places as are uncultivated and nameless, and no column or inscription shall mark the place of their interment.

*

Ode on Melancholy

JOHN KEATS

NO, no! go not to Lethe, neither twist
Wolf's-bane, tight-rooted, for its poisonous wine;
Nor suffer thy pale forehead to be kist
By nightshade, ruby grape of Proserpine;
Make not your rosary of yew-berries,
Nor let the beetle, nor the death-moth be
Your mournful Psyche, nor the downy owl
A partner in your sorrow's mysteries;
For shade to shade will come too drowsily,
And drown the wakeful anguish of the soul.

But when the melancholy fit shall fall
Sudden from heaven like a weeping cloud,
That fosters the droop-headed flowers all,
And hides the green hill in an April shroud;
Then glut thy sorrow on a morning rose,
Or on the rainbow of the salt sand-wave,
;Or on the wealth of globed peonies;
Or if thy mistress some rich anger shows,
Emprison her soft hand, and let her rave,
And feed deep, deep upon her peerless eyes.

She dwells with Beauty – Beauty that must die;
And Joy, whose hand is ever at his lips
Bidding adieu; and aching Pleasure nigh,
Turning to poison while the bee-mouth sips:
Ay, in the very temple of Delight
Veil'd Melancholy has her sovran shrine,
Though seen of none save him whose strenuous tongue
Can burst Joy's grape against his palate fine;
His soul shall taste the sadness of her might,
And be among her cloudy trophies hung.

Dorothy Parker attempted suicide three times, hence her familiarity with the repertoire.

Resume

DOROTHY PARKER

Razors pain you;
Rivers are damp;
Acids stain you;
And drugs cause cramp.
Guns aren't lawful;
Nooses give;
Gas smells awful;
You might as well live.

★

WOODY ALLEN: That's quite a lovely Jackson Pollock, isn't it?

GIRL IN MUSEUM: Yes it is.

WOODY ALLEN: What does it say to you?

GIRL IN MUSEUM: It restates the negativeness of the universe, the hideous lonely emptiness of existence, nothingness, the predicament of man forced to live in a barren, godless eternity, like a tiny flame flickering in an immense void, with nothing but waste, horror, and degradation, forming a useless bleak straightjacket in a black absurd cosmos.

WOODY ALLEN: What are you doing Saturday night?

GIRL IN MUSEUM: Committing suicide.

WOODY ALLEN: What about Friday night?

★

EDNA ST. VINCENT MILLAY

I know a hundred ways to die:
I've often thought I'd try one:
Lie down beneath a motor truck
Some day when standing by one.
Or throw myself from off a bridge —
Except such things must be
So hard upon the scavengers
And men that clean the sea.
I know some poison I could drink.
I've often thought I'd taste it.
But mother bought it for the sink,
And drinking it would waste it.

INDEX OF NAMES

Books by Gary Lachman

In addition to the books Gary Lachman has written and edited for Dedalus he is the author of the following books:

1. **Rudolf Steiner: An Introduction to His Life and Work**
   Floris Books, 2007 UK; Penguin, 2007 US

2. **Into the Interior: Discovering Swedenborg**
   Swedenborg Society, 2006

3. **In Search of P.D. Ouspensky**
   Quest Books, Second Edition, 2006

4. **A Secret History of Consciousness**
   Lindisfarne, 2003

5. **Turn Off Your Mind: The Mystic Sixties and the Dark Side of the Age of Aquarius**
   Disinformation Co. 2004, US
   An updated and revised version of this book will be published by Dedalus in 2008 under the title of *The Dedalus Book of the 1960s: Turn Off Your Mind*

As Gary Valentine

6. **New York Rocker: My Life in the Blank Generation**
   Macmillan, 2002 UK; Thunder's Mouth Press, 2006 US

Forthcoming

7. **Politics and the Occult: The Left, The Right and The Radically Unseen**
   Quest Books, 2008

Recommended Reading

If you enjoyed reading *The Dedalus Book of Literary Suicides: Dead Letters* there are other books on our list, which should appeal to you. If you like books about writers and social history we recommend:

The Dedalus Book of the Occult – *Lachman*
The Dedalus Book of Absinthe – *Baker*
Emperors of Dreams: Drugs in the 19th C – *Mike Jay*

We have also published books by writers discussed *in The Dedalus Book of Literary Suicides*:

Lucio's Confession – *Sa-Carneiro*
The Great Shadow – *Sa-Carneiro*
The German Refugees – *Goethe*
Tales from the Saragossa Manuscript – *Potocki*

Other books which deal with death and the darker side of life in our list you might enjoy are:

The Red Laugh – *Andreyev*
The Late Mattia Pascal – *Pirandello*
Bruges-la-Morte – *Rodenbach*
The Double Life of Daniel Glick – *Caldera*
Exquisite Corpse – *Irwin*
Satan Wants Me – *Irwin*
Paris Noir – *Yonnet*
The Maimed – *Ungar*

These can be bought from your local bookshop or online from amazon.co.uk or direct from Dedalus, either online or by post. Please write to **Cash Sales, Dedalus Limited, 24–26, St Judith's Lane, Sawtry, Cambs, PE28 5XE**. For further details of the Dedalus list please go to our website www.dedalusbooks.com or write to us for a catalogue

The Dedalus Book of the Occult – *Gary Lachman*

"From the Enlightenment to Modernism, ideas of the occult have shadowed literary culture, and Lachman's generous primer introduces the main exponents of diverse traditions alongside their more respectable contemporaries."

SB Kelly in *Scotland on Sunday*

"It's a sure thing that anyone with a taste for literary esoterica and magical history will learn something from *A Dark Muse*. It's a cavernous grotto full of dark glittering jewels, but one haunted by the shades of so many intriguing characters that keeping to the true path is difficult, and you lose your way forever. Verdict – Fine encyclopaedia of occult lives and thought. 9/10"

Mark Pilkington in *Fortean Times*

"Brisk, workmanlike and lucid, this is a survey of 'adventurous souls' whose output was the reverse: 'often crazy, sometimes hilarious and, on occasion, clearly insane'. Lachman's gallery of occultists ranges from the hypnotist Mesmer (1734–1815), whose salon had 'an orgy-like atmosphere', through Goethe and Balzac (who achieved enlightenment by drinking an estimated 50,000 cups of coffee), to Algernon Blackwood, an early TV celebrity who wrote the original *Starlight Express*, and Aleister Crowley – aka the Great Beast 666."

Christopher Hirst in *The Independent*

£9.99   ISBN 978 1 903517 20 8   378p   B. Format

The Dedalus Book of Absinthe – *Phil Baker*

"This is the sort of book it would be very easy to do badly. Phil Baker has, instead, done a magnificent job; it is formidably researched, beautifully written, and abundant with telling detail and pitch-black humour."

Sam Leith, *The Daily Telegraph*

"As to whether absinthe is harmful or this book irresponsible – I don't give a damn. All I know is that the former is very pleasant and the book is informative, amusingly written and perceptive."

Nicholas Lezard, *Guardian Pick of the Week*

"James Joyce in *Finnegan's Wake* described a character as 'absintheminded', while lesser punsters spoke of absinthe making 'the tart grow fonder'. It reaches across time, this 'potent concoction of eccentricity and beauty'. Alluring, then informative and witty."

Brian Case, *Time Out*

"One of the most fascinating themes in this witty, erudite and desperately poignant study is that of the cultural war waged between England and France at the end of the 19th century. English moralists would wax not very eloquent on the sapping effects of absinthe on the susceptible French soul, always uncomfortably aware that the French were producing writers and artists of a calibre unmatched in England."

Murrough O'Brien in *The Independent on Sunday*

£6.99   ISBN 978 1 903517 40 6   296p   B. Format

Emperors of Dreams: Drugs in the 19th C – *Mike Jay*

"An excellent book . . . it states with precision as well as poetry the nature of the drug experience."
    Pick of the Week by Nicholas Lezard in *The Guardian*

Coleridge and de Quincey swilling bitter draughts of laudanum, Sigmund Freud and Sherlock Holmes dallying with cocaine, Baudelaire and Gautier rapt in hashish fantasies behind velvet curtains, even Queen Victoria swallowing her prescription dose of cannabis – these snapshot images are familiar, but what is the story which lies behind them? How did cannabis and cocaine, opium and ether, mushrooms and mescaline enter the worlds of nineteenth century Britain, Europe and America, and what was their impact on the century's dreams and nightmares?

Emperors of Dreams paints a fresh and startling picture both of today's illicit drugs and of the nineteenth century in general. It shows that the age of Empire and Victorian values was awash with drugs, and traces their course through the rapidly evolving arenas of science and colonial expansion and the demimondes of popular subculture and literary fashion, putting into context the drug habits and references of writers as diverse as Coleridge, de Quincey, Baudelaire, Dumas, Conan Doyle, Robert Louis Stevenson, William James and Sigmund Freud.

"Mike Jay's sensible yet stylish book is the first attempt to survey the nineteenth-century drug scene at large . . . one of the pleasures of Jay's approach lies in showing that drugs did not have the histories we might, from a present-day perspective, expect. . . . a fine book."
    Dr Roy Porter in *The Times Higher Education Supplement*

£9.99   ISBN 978 1 873982 48 8   277p   B. Format

Paris Noir: The Secret History of a City – *Jacques Yonnet*

"Yonnet evokes a wonderful and frightening world that lurks in the dark interstices of the City of Light: beggars, whores and poets, people who are quick to draw a knife or cast a spell, and are completely foreign to notions of 'responsible' drinking and sexual behaviour. The Old Man Who Appears After Midnight, Tricksy-Pierrot, the Watchmaker of Backward-Running Time and many others haunt a warren of streets and stews where supernatural events are frequent: a vicious one-eyed ginger tom is reincarnated as a murderous lover; a gypsy curse putrefies a hostile hostelry.

What makes Yonnet's memoir so special is the way the real and fantastic meet. After all, it is set during the Occupation, and the author was a Resistance hero. The secrets of Paris play a role in the struggle against the Germans and their collaborators. Thus, the occultist spiv Keep-on-Dancin' initiates Yonnet to a "psychic circuit" that enables him to unmask a Gestapo informer in "the room where only the truth can be told".

Yonnet portrays Paris as a character in her own right: the city is "edgy", the Seine "sulks". The geography determines the behaviour of its inhabitants, and will live on after their deaths. Certain *névralgique* points in the city incite Parisians to raise barricades, be it during revolutions or the Liberation of 1944. But, like François Villon and Charles Baudelaire, Yonnet conveys the fragility of things. The yarns drunkenly spun in dive bars strive to conjure away a fundamental loneliness: "men are so isolated, prisoners of their own wretched selves, that they can be unbelievably sociable".
Gavin Bond in *Scotland on Sunday*

£9.99   ISBN 978 1 903517 48 2   280p   B. Format

Exquisite Corpse – *Robert Irwin*

"*Exquisite Corpse* is one of the best novels I have read by an English person in my reading time. When I first read it I was completely bowled over."

A.S. Byatt on Radio 4's *Saturday Review*

"A surrealist painter named Casper documents the romantic obsession that removes him from his bohemian life in London, Paris and Munich. As Casper searches for his beloved Caroline in Nazi Germany, Robert Irwin cleverly entwines historical detail with a critique of the Surrealist movement. Eccentric characters – both fictional and non-fictional – appear in Casper's admittedly inaccurate recollection of events. Irwin accomplishes his ambitious task to complete an intense but humorous novel."

Tom Ireland in *The Big Issue*

"The final chapter of the novel reads like a realistic epilogue to the book, but may instead be a hypnogogic illusion, which in turn casts doubt on many other events in the novel. Is Caroline merely a typist from Putney or the very vampire of Surrealism? It's for the reader to decide."

Steven Moore in *The Washington Post*

". . . little clues alerting us to the fact that someone is toying with us are dotted about the place, and there's a final chapter which obliges us to read the damn thing all over again. Well-controlled, intelligent."

The Guardian

£6.99   ISBN 978 1 903517 38 3   235p   B. Format

Satan Wants Me – *Robert Irwin*

". . . the Lodge requires him to find a new partner, and they make him fill in the dating agency form that leads to Maud, one of the more memorable characters in recent fiction. Peter's initial contempt for Maud as a straight and boring hairdresser soon gives way to a kinky *menage à trois*, in which Sally eagerly dons a dog collar and frilly apron and has herself tattooed with the words 'I am Sally, the slave of Maud and Peter'. So extraordinary is Maud, in fact, that she has more than a little to do with the title of the book. . . . No doubt this contributes to the feel of *Satan Wants Me* as something to relish and curl up with, capable of inducing sensations rarely felt by people who have to read novels as work."

Phil Baker in *The Times Literary Supplement*

"Irwin is a writer of immense subtlety and craftmanship, and offers us a vivid and utterly convincing portrait of life on the loopier fringes of the Sixties. *Satan Wants Me* is black, compulsive and very, very funny."

Christopher Hart in *The Daily Telegraph*

"Irwin's writing is witty and scabrous but it is also subtle in a way that keeps catching the reader out. The blend of the fantastical with the philosophical has been the defining characteristic of Irwin's fiction and in Peter's drug-drenched, satan-haunted diary, it has found its perfect expression."

Tom Holland in *The New Statesman & Society*

"Part of the book's fertile comedy stems from the ironic interweaving of the jargons of sociology, hippiedom and magick. It is hard to resist a pot-head mystic who hopes the Apocalypse will come on Wednesday because it will break up the week."

Tom Deveson in *The Sunday Times*

£7.99   ISBN 978 1 903517 58 1   320p   B. Format

The Late Mattia Pascal – *Luigi Pirandello*

"This is Pirandello's third novel, published in 1904, and marks the start of a major theme in his work – the nature of identity."
     The Sunday Times

"Pascal, a landowner fallen on hard times and trapped in a miserable marriage, runs away from home and wins a lot of money at the gaming tables in Monte Carlo. Meanwhile a body has been found in the millrace of his village and it is assumed that Pascal has killed himself. Seizing what looks like a chance to create a new life, he travels to Rome under an assumed name and struggles to invent a different identity which he can inhabit. He fails, returns home, finds his wife has remarried and has to act out the role of being as it were a living ghost. All these tragic events are recounted with verve and wit and comes across clearly in Simborowski's spirited translation from the Italian."
     Robert Nye in *The Guardian*

"The novel is a *tour de force* of cynicism about the human condition."
     Nicoletta Simborowski

£7.99   ISBN 978 094626 18 2   251p   B. Format